A

DAILY EXPRESS
LIBRARY

THE
GOLDEN TREASURY

1936.

FIRST SET

THE PASSIONATE ELOPEMENT
By Compton Mackenzie

THE GRAND BABYLON HOTEL
By Arnold Bennett

THE GOLDEN TREASURY
By Francis Turner Palgrave

THE
GOLDEN TREASURY

OF THE MOST BEAUTIFUL SONGS & LYRICAL POEMS IN THE ENGLISH LANGUAGE

Selected and Arranged by

FRANCIS TURNER PALGRAVE

A DAILY EXPRESS PUBLICATION
LONDON

Made and Printed in Great Britain by
Key and Whiting Ltd., London

CONTENTS

A*

PREFACE

THIS little Collection differs, it is believed, from others
in the attempt made to include in it all the best original
Lyrical pieces and Songs in our language, by writers
not living,—and none beside the best. Many familiar
verses will hence be met with; many also which should
be familiar:—the Editor will regard as his fittest readers
those who love Poetry so well, that he can offer them
nothing not already known and valued.

The Editor is acquainted with no strict and exhaustive
definition of Lyrical Poetry; but he has found the task
of practical decision increase in clearness and in facility
as he advanced with the work, whilst keeping in view
a few simple principles. Lyrical has been here held
essentially to imply that each Poem shall turn on some
single thought, feeling, or situation. In accordance with
this, narrative, descriptive, and didactic poems,—unless
accompanied by rapidity of movement, brevity, and
the colouring of human passion,—have been excluded.
Humorous poetry, except in the very unfrequent instances where a truly poetical tone pervades the whole,
with what is strictly personal, occasional, and religious,
has been considered foreign to the idea of the book.
Blank verse and the ten-syllable couplet, with all pieces
markedly dramatic, have been rejected as alien from
what is commonly understood by Song, and rarely
conforming to Lyrical conditions in treatment. But it
is not anticipated, nor is it possible, that all readers
shall think the line accurately drawn. Some poems,
as Gray's 'Elegy,' the 'Allegro' and 'Penseroso,' Wordsworth's 'Ruth' or Campbell's 'Lord Ullin,' might be
claimed with perhaps equal justice for a narrative or
descriptive selection: whilst with reference especially
to Ballads and Sonnets, the Editor can only state that
he has taken his utmost pains to decide without caprice
or partiality.

This also is all he can plead in regard to a point even
more liable to question;—what degree of merit should

give rank among the Best.   That a Poem shall be worthy
of the writer's genius,—that it shall reach a perfection
commensurate with its aim,—that we should require
finish in proportion to brevity,—that passion, colour,
and originality cannot atone for serious imperfections in
clearness, unity, or truth,—that a few good lines do not
make a good poem,—that popular estimate is serviceable
as a guidepost more than as a compass,—above all, that
Excellence should be looked for rather in the Whole
than in the Parts,—such and other such canons have
been always steadily regarded.   He may however add
that the pieces chosen, and a far larger number rejected,
have been carefully and repeatedly considered; and
that he has been aided throughout by two friends of
independent and exercised judgement, besides the
distinguished person addressed in the Dedication.   It
is hoped that by this procedure the volume has been
freed from that onesidedness which must beset individual
decisions:—but for the final choice the Editor is alone
responsible.

It would obviously have been invidious to apply the
standard aimed at in this Collection to the Living.
Nor, even in the cases where this might be done without
offence, does it appear wise to attempt to anticipate the
verdict of the Future on our contemporaries.   Should
the book last, poems by Tennyson, Bryant, Clare, Lowell,
and others, will no doubt claim and obtain their place
among the best.   But the Editor trusts that this will be
effected by other hands, and in days far distant.

Chalmers' vast collection, with the whole works of all
accessible poets not contained in it, and the best
Anthologies of different periods, have been twice
systematically read through: and it is hence improbable
that any omissions which may be regretted are due to
oversight.   The poems are printed entire, except in a
very few instances (specified in the notes) where a stanza
has been omitted.   The omissions have been risked only
when the piece could be thus brought to a closer lyrical
unity: and, as essentially opposed to this unity, extracts,
obviously such, are excluded.   In regard to the text,
the purpose of the book has appeared to justify the choice

of the most poetical version, wherever more than one exists: and much labour has been given to present each poem, in disposition, spelling, and punctuation, to the greatest advantage.

For the permission under which the copyright pieces are inserted, thanks are due to the respective Proprietors, without whose liberal concurrence the scheme of the collection would have been defeated.

In the arrangement, the most poetically-effective order has been attempted. The English mind has passed through phases of thought and cultivation so various and so opposed during these three centuries of Poetry, that a rapid passage between Old and New, like rapid alteration of the eye's focus in looking at the landscape, will always be wearisome and hurtful to the sense of Beauty. The poems have been therefore distributed into Books corresponding, I to the ninety years closing about 1616, II thence to 1700, III to 1800, IV to the half-century just ended. Or, looking at the Poets who more or less give each portion its distinctive character, they might be called the Books of Shakespeare, Milton, Gray, and Wordsworth. The volume, in this respect, so far as the limitations of its range allow, accurately reflects the natural growth and evolution of our Poetry. A rigidly chronological sequence, however, rather fits a collection aiming at instruction than at pleasure, and the Wisdom which comes through Pleasure:—within each book the pieces have therefore been arranged in gradations of feeling or subject. The development of the symphonies of Mozart and Beethoven has been here thought of as a model, and nothing placed without careful consideration. And it is hoped that the contents of this Anthology will thus be found to present a certain unity, 'as episodes,' in the noble language of Shelley, 'to that great Poem which all poets, like the co-operating thoughts of one great mind, have built up since the beginning of the world.'

As he closes his long survey, the Editor trusts he may add without egotism, that he has found the vague general verdict of popular Fame more just than those

have thought who, with too severe a criticism, would
confine judgements on Poetry to 'the selected few of
many generations.' Not many appear to have gained
reputation without some gift or performance that, in
due degree, deserved it: and if no verses by certain
writers who show less strength than sweetness, or more
thought than mastery in expression, are printed in this
volume, it should not be imagined that they have been
excluded without much hesitation and regret,—far less
that they have been slighted. Throughout this vast and
pathetic array of Singers now silent, few have been
honoured with the name Poet, and have not possessed
a skill in words, a sympathy with beauty, a tenderness
of feeling, or seriousness in reflection, which render their
works, although never perhaps attaining that loftier and
finer excellence here required,—better worth reading than
much of what fills the scanty hours that most men spare
for self-improvement, or for pleasure in any of its more
elevated and permanent forms.—And if this be true of
even mediocre poetry, for how much more are we
indebted to the best! Like the fabled fountain of the
Azores, but with a more various power, the magic of
this Art can confer on each period of life its appropriate
blessing: on early years Experience, on maturity Calm,
on age Youthfulness. Poetry gives treasures 'more
golden than gold,' leading us in higher and healthier
ways than those of the world, and interpreting to us the
lessons of Nature. But she speaks best for herself. Her
true accents, if the plan has been executed with success,
may be heard throughout the following pages:—wherever the Poets of England are honoured, wherever the
dominant language of the world is spoken, it is hoped
that they will find fit audience.

                                                    F. T. P.

Εἰς τὸν λειμῶνα καθίσας,
ἔδρεπεν ἕτερον ἐφ᾿ ἑτέρῳ
αἱρόμενος ἄγρευμ᾿ ἀνθέων
ἁδομένᾳ ψυχᾷ.

[Eurip, *frag.* 754.]

['He sat in the meadow and plucked
with glad heart the spoil of the
flowers, gathering them one by one.']

THE
GOLDEN TREASURY

BOOK FIRST

1

SPRING

Spring, the sweet Spring, is the year's pleasant king;
Then blooms each thing, then maids dance in a ring,
Cold doth not sting, the pretty birds do sing,
    Cuckoo, jug-jug, pu-we, to-witta-woo!

The palm and may make country houses gay,   5
Lambs frisk and play, the shepherds pipe all day,
And we hear ay birds tune this merry lay,
    Cuckoo, jug-jug, pu-we, to-witta-woo!

The fields breathe sweet, the daisies kiss our feet,
Young lovers meet, old wives a-sunning sit,   10
In every street these tunes our ears do greet,
    Cuckoo, jug-jug, pu-we, to-witta-woo!
      Spring! the sweet Spring!

                    T. Nash

2

SUMMONS TO LOVE

      Phoebus, arise!
     And paint the sable skies
     With azure, white, and red:
Rouse Memnon's mother from her Tithon's bed
That she thy càreer may with roses spread: 5
The nightingales thy coming each-where sing:

          Make an eternal spring,
Give life to this dark world which lieth dead;
          Spread forth thy golden hair
In larger locks than thou wast wont before,   10
          And emperor-like decore
With diadem of pearl thy temples fair:
          Chase hence the ugly night
Which serves but to make dear thy glorious light.

          —This is that happy morn,   15
          That day, long-wishéd day
          Of all my life so dark,
(If cruel stars have not my ruin sworn
          And fates my hopes betray),
          Which, purely white, deserves   20
An everlasting diamond should it mark.
This is the morn should bring unto this grove
My Love, to hear and recompense my love.
          Fair King, who all preserves,
          But show thy blushing beams,   25
          And thou two sweeter eyes
Shalt see than those which by Peneüs' streams
          Did once thy heart surprise.
Now, Flora, deck thyself in fairest guise:
          If that ye, winds, would hear   30
A voice surpassing far Amphion's lyre,
          Your furious chiding stay;
          Let Zephyr only breathe,
          And with her tresses play.
          —The winds all silent are,   35
          And Phoebus in his chair
          Ensaffroning sea and air
          Makes vanish every star:
          Night like a drunkard reels
Beyond the hills, to shun his flaming wheels: 40
The fields with flowers are deck'd in every hue,
The clouds with orient gold spangle their blue;
          Here is the pleasant place—
And nothing wanting is, save She, alas!

                              W. Drummond of Hawthornden

3
TIME AND LOVE

I

When I have seen by Time's fell hand defaced
    The rich proud cost of out-worn buried age;
When sometime lofty towers I see down-razed,
    And brass eternal slave to mortal rage;

When I have seen the hungry ocean gain   5
    Advantage on the kingdom of the shore,
And the firm soil win of the watery main,
    Increasing store with loss, and loss with store;

When I have seen such interchange of state,
    Or state itself confounded to decay,   10
Ruin hath taught me thus to ruminate—
    That Time will come and take my Love away:

—This thought is as a death, which cannot choose
But weep to have that which it fears to lose.

W. Shakespeare

4
II

Since brass, nor stone, nor earth, nor boundless sea,
    But sad mortality o'ersways their power,
How with this rage shall beauty hold a plea,
    Whose action is no stronger than a flower?

O how shall summer's honey breath hold out   5
    Against the wreckful siege of battering days,
When rocks impregnable are not so stout
    Nor gates of steel so strong, but time decays?

O fearful meditation! where, alack!   9
    Shall Time's best jewel from Time's chest lie hid?
Or what strong hand can hold his swift foot back,
    Or who his spoil of beauty can forbid?

O! none, unless this miracle have might,
That in black ink my love may still shine bright.

W. Shakespeare

5

THE PASSIONATE SHEPHERD TO
HIS LOVE

Come live with me and be my Love,
And we will all the pleasures prove
That hills and valleys, dale and field,
And all the craggy mountains yield.

There will we sit upon the rocks   5
And see the shepherds feed their flocks,
By shallow rivers, to whose falls
Melodious birds sing madrigals.

There will I make thee beds of roses
And a thousand fragrant posies,   10
A cap of flowers, and a kirtle
Embroider'd all with leaves of myrtle.

A gown made of the finest wool,
Which from our pretty lambs we pull,
Fair linéd slippers for the cold,   15
With buckles of the purest gold.

A belt of straw and ivy buds
With coral clasps and amber studs:
And if these pleasures may thee move,
Come live with me and be my Love.   20

Thy silver dishes for thy meat
As precious as the gods do eat,
Shall on an ivory table be
Prepared each day for thee and me.

The shepherd swains shall dance and sing   25
For thy delight each May-morning:
If these delights thy mind may move,
Then live with me and be my Love.

                                                   C. Marlowe

6

A MADRIGAL

Crabbéd Age and Youth
Cannot live together:
  Youth is full of pleasance,
Age is full of care;
  Youth like summer morn,   5
Age like winter weather,
  Youth like summer brave,
Age like winter bare:
  Youth is full of sport,
  Age's breath is short,   10
Youth is nimble, Age is lame:
  Youth is hot and bold,
  Age is weak and cold,
Youth is wild, and Age is tame:—
  Age, I do abhor thee,   15
  Youth, I do adore thee;
O! my Love, my Love is young!
  Age, I do defy thee—
  O sweet shepherd, hie thee,
For methinks thou stay'st too long.   20

W. Shakespeare

7

Under the greenwood tree
Who loves to lie with me,
And turn his merry note
Unto the sweet bird's throat—
Come hither, come hither, come hither!   5
    Here shall he see
    No enemy
But winter and rough weather.

Who doth ambition shun
And loves to live i' the sun,   10

Seeking the food he eats
And pleased with what he gets—
Come hither, come hither, come hither!
Here shall he see
No enemy   15
But winter and rough weather.

W. Shakespeare

8

It was a lover and his lass
With a hey and a ho, and a hey-nonino!
That o'er the green cornfield did pass
In the spring time, the only pretty ring time,
When birds do sing hey ding a ding ding: 5
Sweet lovers love the Spring.

Between the acres of the rye
These pretty country folks would lie:

This carol they began that hour,
How that a life was but a flower: 10

And therefore take the present time
With a hey and a ho, and a hey-nonino!
For love is crownéd with the prime
In spring time, the only pretty ring time,
When birds do sing hey ding a ding ding: 15
Sweet lovers love the Spring.

W. Shakespeare

9

PRESENT IN ABSENCE

Absence, hear thou my protestation
Against thy strength,
Distance, and length;
Do what thou canst for alteration:

For hearts of truest mettle   5
Absence doth join, and Time doth settle.

Who loves a mistress of such quality,
      He soon hath found
      Affection's ground
Beyond time, place, and all mortality.   10
      To hearts that cannot vary
      Absence is Present, Time doth tarry.

By absence this good means I gain,
      That I can catch her,
      Where none can watch her,   15
In some close corner of my brain:
      There I embrace and kiss her;
      And so I both enjoy and miss her.

Anon.

10

ABSENCE

Being your slave, what should I do but tend
   Upon the hours and times of your desire?
I have no precious time at all to spend
   Nor services to do, till you require:

Nor dare I chide the world-without-end hour   5
   Whilst I, my sovereign, watch the clock for you,
Nor think the bitterness of absence sour
   When you have bid your servant once adieu:

Nor dare I question with my jealous thought
   Where you may be, or your affairs suppose,   10
But like a sad slave, stay and think of nought
   Save, where you are, how happy you make those;—

So true a fool is love, that in your will,
Though you do anything, he thinks no ill.

W. Shakespeare

11

How like a winter hath my absence been
    From Thee, the pleasure of the fleeting year!
What freezings have I left, what dark days seen,
    What old December's bareness everywhere!

And yet this time removed was summer's time;   5
    The teeming autumn, big with rich increase,
Bearing the wanton burden of the prime
    Like widow'd wombs after their lords' decease:

Yet this abundant issue seem'd to me
    But hope of orphans, and unfather'd fruit;   10
For summer and his pleasures wait on thee,
    And, thou away, the very birds are mute;

Or if they sing, 'tis with so dull a cheer,
That leaves look pale, dreading the winter 's near.
                                                    W. Shakespeare

12

A CONSOLATION

When in disgrace with fortune and men's eyes
    I all alone beweep my outcast state,
And trouble deaf heaven with my bootless cries,
    And look upon myself, and curse my fate;

Wishing me like to one more rich in hope,   5
    Featured like him, like him with friends possest,
Desiring this man's art, and that man's scope,
    With what I most enjoy contented least;

Yet in these thoughts myself almost despising,
    Haply I think on Thee—and then my state,   10
Like to the lark at break of day arising
    From sullen earth, sings hymns at heaven's gate;

For thy sweet love remember'd such wealth brings,
That then I scorn to change my state with kings.
                                                    W. Shakespeare

13

THE UNCHANGEABLE

O never say that I was false of heart,
  Though absence seem'd my flame to qualify:
As easy might I from myself depart
  As from my soul, which in thy breast doth lie;

That is my home of love; if I have ranged,   5
  Like him that travels, I return again,
Just to the time, not with the time exchanged,
  So that myself bring water for my stain.

Never believe, though in my nature reign'd
  All frailties that besiege all kinds of blood,   10
That it could so preposterously be stain'd
  To leave for nothing all thy sum of good:

For nothing this wide universe I call,
Save thou, my rose: in it thou art my all.
                                    W. Shakespeare

14

To me, fair Friend, you never can be old,
  For as you were when first your eye I eyed
Such seems your beauty still.   Three winters cold
  Have from the forests shook three summers' pride;

Three beauteous springs to yellow autumn turn'd   5
  In process of the seasons have I seen,
Three April perfumes in three hot Junes burn'd,
  Since first I saw you fresh, which yet are green.

Ah! yet doth beauty, like a dial-hand,
  Steal from his figure, and no pace perceived;   10
So your sweet hue, which methinks still doth stand,
  Hath motion, and mine eye may be deceived:

For fear of which, hear this, thou age unbred,—
Ere you were born, was beauty's summer dead.
                                    W. Shakespeare

15

DIAPHENIA

Diaphenia like the daffadowndilly,
  White as the sun, fair as the lily,
Heigh ho, how I do love thee!
  I do love thee as my lambs
  Are belovéd of their dams;   5
How blest were I if thou would'st prove me.

Diaphenia like the spreading roses,
  That in thy sweets all sweets encloses,
Fair sweet, how I do love thee!
  I do love thee as each flower   10
  Loves the sun's life-giving power;
For dead, thy breath to life might move me.

Diaphenia like to all things blesséd
  When all thy praises are expresséd,
Dear joy, how I do love thee!   15
  As the birds do love the spring,
  Or the bees their careful king:
Then in requite, sweet virgin, love me!
                                        H. Constable

16

ROSALYNDE

Like to the clear in highest sphere
  Where all imperial glory shines,
Of selfsame colour is her hair
  Whether unfolded, or in twines:
    Heigh ho, fair Rosalynde!   5
Her eyes are sapphires set in snow,
  Resembling heaven by every wink;
The Gods do fear whenas they glow,
  And I do tremble when I think
    Heigh ho, would she were mine!   10

Her cheeks are like the blushing cloud
   That beautifies Aurora's face,
Or like the silver crimson shroud
   That Phoebus' smiling looks doth grace;
      Heigh ho, fair Rosalynde!   15
Her lips are like two budded roses
   Whom ranks of lilies neighbour nigh,
Within which bounds she balm encloses
   Apt to entice a deity:
      Heigh ho, would she were mine!   20

Her neck is like a stately tower
   Where Love himself imprison'd lies,
To watch for glances every hour
   From her divine and sacred eyes:
      Heigh ho, for Rosalynde!   25
Her paps are centres of delight,
   Her breasts are orbs of heavenly frame,
Where Nature moulds the dew of light
   To feed perfection with the same:
      Heigh ho, would she were mine!   30

With orient pearl, with ruby red,
   With marble white, with sapphire blue
Her body every way is fed,
   Yet soft in touch and sweet in view:
      Heigh ho, fair Rosalynde!   35
Nature herself her shape admires;
   The Gods are wounded in her sight;
And Love forsakes his heavenly fires
   And at her eyes his brand doth light:
      Heigh ho, would she were mine!   40

Then muse not, Nymphs, though I bemoan
   The absence of fair Rosalynde,
Since for a fair there's fairer none,
   Nor for her virtues so divine:
      Heigh ho, fair Rosalynde;   45
Heigh ho, my heart! would God that she were mine!

                                T. Lodge

17

COLIN

Beauty sat bathing by a spring
  Where fairest shades did hide her;
The winds blew calm, the birds did sing,
  The cool streams ran beside her.
My wanton thoughts enticed mine eye   5
  To see what was forbidden:
But better memory said, fie!
  So vain desire was chidden:—
      Hey nonny nonny O!
      Hey nonny nonny!   10

Into a slumber then I fell,
  When fond imagination
Seem'd to see, but could not tell
  Her feature or her fashion.
But ev'n as babes in dreams do smile,   15
  And sometimes fall a-weeping,
So I awaked, as wise this while
  As when I fell a-sleeping:—
      Hey nonny nonny O!
      Hey nonny nonny!   20
                          The Shepherd Tony

18

TO HIS LOVE

Shall I compare thee to a summer's day?
  Thou art more lovely and more temperate:
Rough winds do shake the darling buds of May,
  And summer's lease hath all too short a date:

Sometime too hot the eye of heaven shines,   5
  And often is his gold complexion dimm'd:
And every fair from fair sometime declines,
  By chance, or nature's changing course, untrimm'd.

But thy eternal summer shall not fade
  Nor lose possession of that fair thou owest;   10
Nor shall death brag thou wanderest in his shade,
  When in eternal lines to time thou growest:

So long as men can breathe, or eyes can see,
So long lives this, and this gives life to thee.

                              W. Shakespeare

19

TO HIS LOVE

When in the chronicle of wasted time
  I see descriptions of the fairest wights,
And beauty making beautiful old rhyme
  In praise of ladies dead, and lovely knights;

Then in the blazon of sweet beauty's best   5
  Of hand, of foot, of lip, of eye, of brow,
I see their antique pen would have exprest
  Ev'n such a beauty as you master now.

So all their praises are but prophecies
  Of this our time, all you prefiguring;   10
And, for they look'd but with divining eyes,
  They had not skill enough your worth to sing:

For we, which now behold these present days,
Have eyes to wonder but lack tongues to praise.

                              W. Shakespeare

20

LOVE'S PERJURIES

On a day, alack the day!
Love, whose month is ever May,
Spied a blossom passing fair
Playing in the wanton air:
Through the velvet leaves the wind,   5
All unseen, 'gan passage find;

That the lover, sick to death,
Wish'd himself the heaven's breath.
Air, quoth he, thy cheeks may blow;
Air, would I might triumph so!   10
But, alack, my hand is sworn
Ne'er to pluck thee from thy thorn:
Vow, alack, for youth unmeet;
Youth so apt to pluck a sweet.
Do not call it sin in me   15
That I am forsworn for thee:
Thou for whom Jove would swear
Juno but an Ethiope were,
And deny himself for Jove,
Turning mortal for thy love.   20

                                         W. Shakespeare

21

A SUPPLICATION

Forget not yet the tried intent
Of such a truth as I have meant;
My great travail so gladly spent,
                    Forget not yet!

Forget not yet when first began   5
The weary life ye know, since whan
The suit, the service none tell can;
                    Forget not yet!

Forget not yet the great assays,
The cruel wrong, the scornful ways,   10
The painful patience in delays,
                    Forget not yet!

Forget not! O, forget not this,
How long ago hath been, and is
The mind that never meant amiss—   15
                    Forget not yet!

> Forget not then thine own approved
> The which so long hath thee so loved,
> Whose steadfast faith yet never moved—
>   Forget not this!   20
>   *Sir T. Wyatt*

22

TO AURORA

O if thou knew'st how thou thyself dost harm,
    And dost prejudge thy bliss, and spoil my rest;
    Then thou would'st melt the ice out of thy breast
And thy relenting heart would kindly warm.

O if thy pride did not our joys controul,   5
    What world of loving wonders should'st thou see!
    For if I saw thee once transform'd in me,
Then in thy bosom I would pour my soul;

Then all my thoughts should in thy visage shine,
    And if that aught mischanced thou should'st not
        moan   10
    Nor bear the burthen of thy griefs alone;
No, I would have my share in what were thine:

And whilst we thus should make our sorrows one,
This happy harmony would make them none.
                    W. Alexander, Earl of Sterline

23

TRUE LOVE

Let me not to the marriage of true minds
    Admit impediments.   Love is not love
Which alters when it alteration finds,
    Or bends with the remover to remove:—

O no! it is an ever-fixéd mark   5
    That looks on tempests, and is never shaken;
It is the star to every wandering bark,
    Whose worth's unknown, although his height be
        taken.

Love's not Time's fool, though rosy lips and cheeks
   Within his bending sickle's compass come;   10
Love alters not with his brief hours and weeks,
   But bears it out ev'n to the edge of doom:—

If this be error, and upon me proved,
I never writ, nor no man ever loved.
                            W. Shakespeare

24

A DITTY

My true-love hath my heart, and I have his,
   By just exchange one for another given:
I hold his dear, and mine he cannot miss,
   There never was a better bargain driven:
      My true-love hath my heart, and I have his.   5

His heart in me keeps him and me in one,
   My heart in him his thoughts and senses guides:
He loves my heart, for once it was his own,
   I cherish his because in me it bides:
      My true-love hath my heart, and I have his. 10
                            Sir P. Sidney

25

LOVE'S OMNIPRESENCE

Were I as base as is the lowly plain,
   And you, my Love, as high as heaven above,
Yet should the thoughts of me your humble swain
   Ascend to heaven, in honour of my Love.

Were I as high as heaven above the plain,   5
   And you, my Love, as humble and as low
As are the deepest bottoms of the main,
   Whereso'er you were, with you my love should go.

Were you the earth, dear Love, and I the skies,
  My love should shine on you like to the sun,   10
And look upon you with ten thousand eyes
  Till heaven wax'd blind, and till the world were done.

Whereso'er I am, below, or else above you,
Whereso'er you are, my heart shall truly love you.

J. Sylvester

26

CARPE DIEM

O Mistress mine, where are you roaming?
O stay and hear! your true-love's coming
    That can sing both high and low;
Trip no further, pretty sweeting,
Journeys end in lovers' meeting—   5
    Every wise man's son doth know.

What is love? 'tis not hereafter;
Present mirth hath present laughter;
    What's to come is still unsure:
In delay there lies no plenty,—   10
Then come kiss me, Sweet-and-twenty,
    Youth's a stuff will not endure.

W. Shakespeare

27

WINTER

When icicles hang by the wall
  And Dick the shepherd blows his nail,
And Tom bears logs into the hall,
  And milk comes frozen home in pail;
When blood is nipt, and ways be foul,   5
Then nightly sings the staring owl
    Tuwhoo!
Tuwhit! tuwhoo! A merry note!
While greasy Joan doth keel the pot.

B

When all aloud the wind doth blow,   10
    And coughing drowns the parson's saw,
And birds sit brooding in the snow,
    And Marian's nose looks red and raw;
When roasted crabs hiss in the bowl—
Then nightly sings the staring owl   .15
                    Tuwhoo!
Tuwhit! tuwhoo! A merry note!
While greasy Joan doth keel the pot.

                                        W. Shakespeare

28

That time of year thou may'st in me behold
    When yellow leaves, or none, or few, do hang
Upon those boughs which shake against the cold,
    Bare ruin'd choirs, where late the sweet birds sang.

In me thou see'st the twilight of such day   5
    As after sunset fadeth in the west,
Which by and by black night doth take away,
    Death's second self, that seals up all in rest.

In me thou see'st the glowing of such fire,
    That on the ashes of his youth doth lie   10
As the death-bed whereon it must expire,
    Consumed with that which it was nourish'd by:

—This thou perceiv'st, which makes thy love more strong,
To love that well which thou must leave ere long.

                                        W. Shakespeare

29

REMEMBRANCE

When to the sessions of sweet silent thought
    I summon up remembrance of things past,
I sigh the lack of many a thing I sought,
    And with old woes new wail my dear time's waste;

Then can I drown an eye, unused to flow,   5
  For precious friends hid in death's dateless night,
And weep afresh love's long-since-cancell'd woe,
  And moan the expense of many a vanish'd sight.

Then can I grieve at grievances foregone,
  And heavily from woe to woe tell o'er   10
The sad account of fore-bemoanéd moan,
  Which I new pay as if not paid before:

—But if the while I think on thee, dear friend,
All losses are restored, and sorrows end.
                                        W. Shakespeare

30

REVOLUTIONS

Like as the waves make towards the pebbled shore,
  So do our minutes hasten to their end;
Each changing place with that which goes before,
  In sequent toil all forwards do contend.

Nativity, once in the main of light,   5
  Crawls to maturity, wherewith being crown'd,
Crooked eclipses 'gainst his glory fight,
  And Time that gave doth now his gift confound.

Time doth transfix the flourish set on youth,
  And delves the parallels in beauty's brow;   10
Feeds on the rarities of nature's truth,
  And nothing stands but for his scythe to mow:

And yet, to times in hope, my verse shall stand
Praising thy worth, despite his cruel hand.
                                        W. Shakespeare

31

Farewell! thou art too dear for my possessing,
  And like enough thou know'st thy estimate:
The charter of thy worth gives thee releasing;
  My bonds in thee are all determinate.

For how do I hold thee but by thy granting?   5
   And for that riches where is my deserving?
The cause of this fair gift in me is wanting,
   And so my patent back again is swerving.

Thyself thou gav'st, thy own worth then not knowing,
   Or me, to whom thou gav'st it, else mistaking;   10
So thy great gift, upon misprision growing,
   Comes home again, on better judgement making.

Thus have I had thee as a dream doth flatter;
In sleep, a king ; but waking, no such matter.
                        W. Shakespeare

32

THE LIFE WITHOUT PASSION

They that have power to hurt, and will do none,
   That do not do the thing they most do show,
Who, moving others, are themselves as stone,
   Unmovéd, cold, and to temptation slow,—

They rightly do inherit Heaven's graces,   5
   And husband nature's riches from expense;
They are the lords and owners of their faces,
   Others, but stewards of their excellence.

The summer's flower is to the summer sweet,
   Though to itself it only live and die;   10
But if that flower with base infection meet,
   The basest weed outbraves his dignity:

For sweetest things turn sourest by their deeds;
Lilies that fester smell far worse than weeds.
                        W. Shakespeare

33

THE LOVER'S APPEAL

And wilt thou leave me thus?
  Say nay! say nay! for shame!
  To save thee from the blame
  Of all my grief and grame.
And wilt thou leave me thus?   5
  Say nay! say nay!

And wilt thou leave me thus,
  That hath loved thee so long
  In wealth and woe among?
  And is thy heart so strong   10
As for to leave me thus?
  Say nay! say nay!

And wilt thou leave me thus,
  That hath given thee my heart
  Never for to depart   15
  Neither for pain nor smart?
And wilt thou leave me thus?
  Say nay! say nay!

And wilt thou leave me thus,
  And have no more pity   20
  Of him that loveth thee?
  Alas! thy cruelty!
And wilt thou leave me thus?
  Say nay! say nay!

Sir T. Wyatt

34

THE NIGHTINGALE

As it fell upon a day
In the merry month of May,
Sitting in a pleasant shade
Which a grove of myrtles made,

Beasts did leap and birds did sing,   5
Trees did grow and plants did spring,
Every thing did banish moan
Save the Nightingale alone.
She, poor bird, as all forlorn,
Lean'd her breast up-till a thorn,   10
And there sung the dolefull'st ditty
That to hear it was great pity.
Fie, fie, fie, now would she cry;
Tereu, tereu, by and by:
That to hear her so complain   15
Scarce I could from tears refrain;
For her griefs so lively shown
Made me think upon mine own.
—Ah, thought I, thou mourn'st in vain,
None takes pity on thy pain: 20
Senseless trees, they cannot hear thee,
Ruthless beasts, they will not cheer thee;
King Pandion, he is dead,
All thy friends are lapp'd in lead:
All thy fellow birds do sing   25
Careless of thy sorrowing:
Even so, poor bird, like thee
None alive will pity me.

                                        R. Barnfield

35

Care-charmer Sleep, son of the sable Night,
    Brother to Death, in silent darkness born,
Relieve my languish, and restore the light;
    With dark forgetting of my care return.

And let the day be time enough to mourn   5
The shipwreck of my ill-adventured youth:
    Let waking eyes suffice to wail their scorn,
Without the torment of the night's untruth.

Cease, dreams, the images of day-desires,
    To model forth the passions of the morrow;   10

Never let rising Sun approve you liars
   To add more grief to aggravate my sorrow:

Still let me sleep, embracing clouds in vain,
And never wake to feel the day's disdain.

S. Daniel

36

MADRIGAL

Take, O take those lips away
   That so sweetly were forsworn,
And those eyes, the break of day,
   Lights that do mislead the morn:
But my kisses bring again,   5
       Bring again—
Seals of love, but seal'd in vain,
       Seal'd in vain!

W. Shakespeare

37

LOVE'S FAREWELL

Since there's no help, come let us kiss and part,—
   Nay I have done, you get no more of me;
And I am glad, yea, glad with all my heart,
   That thus so cleanly I myself can free;

Shake hands for ever, cancel all our vows,   5
   And when we meet at any time again,
Be it not seen in either of our brows
   That we one jot of former love retain.

Now at the last gasp of love's latest breath,
   When, his pulse failing, passion speechless lies,   10
When faith is kneeling by his bed of death,
   And innocence is closing up his eyes,

—Now if thou would'st, when all have given him over,
From death to life thou might'st him yet recover!

M. Drayton

38

TO HIS LUTE

My lute, be as thou wert when thou didst grow
  With thy green mother in some shady grove,
  When immelodious winds but made thee move,
And birds their ramage did on thee bestow.

Since that dear Voice which did thy sounds approve, 5
Which wont in such harmonious strains to flow,
  Is reft from Earth to tune those spheres above,
What art thou but a harbinger of woe?

Thy pleasing notes be pleasing notes no more,
  But orphans' wailings to the fainting ear; 10
  Each stroke a sigh, each sound draws forth a tear;
For which be silent as in woods before:

Or if that any hand to touch thee deign,
Like widow'd turtle still her loss complain.

W. Drummond

39

BLIND LOVE

O me! what eyes hath love put in my head
  Which have no correspondence with true sight:
Or if they have, where is my judgement fled
  That censures falsely what they see aright?

If that be fair whereon my false eyes dote, 5
  What means the world to say it is not so?
If it be not, then love doth well denote
  Love's eye is not so true as all men's: No,

How can it? O how can love's eye be true,
  That is so vex'd with watching and with tears? 10
No marvel then though I mistake my view:
  The sun itself sees not till heaven clears.

O cunning Love! with tears thou keep'st me blind,
Lest eyes well-seeing thy foul faults should find!

W. Shakespeare

40

THE UNFAITHFUL SHEPHERDESS

While that the sun with his beams hot
  Scorchéd the fruits in vale and mountain,
Philon the shepherd, late forgot,
  Sitting beside a crystal fountain,
    In shadow of a green oak tree   5
    Upon his pipe this song play'd he:
Adieu Love, adieu Love, untrue Love,
Untrue Love, untrue Love, adieu Love;
Your mind is light, soon lost for new love.

So long as I was in your sight   10
  I was your heart, your soul, and treasure;
And evermore you sobb'd and sigh'd
  Burning the flames beyond all measure:
    —Three days endured your love to me,
    And it was lost in other three!   15
Adieu Love, adieu Love, untrue Love,
Untrue Love, untrue Love, adieu Love;
Your mind is light, soon lost for new love.

Another Shepherd you did see
  To whom your heart was soon enchainéd; 20
Full soon your love was leapt from me,
  Full soon my place he had obtainéd.
    Soon came a third, your love to win,
    And we were out and he was in.
Adieu Love, adieu Love, untrue Love,   25
Untrue Love, untrue Love, adieu Love;
Your mind is light, soon lost for new love.

Sure you have made me passing glad
  That you your mind so soon removéd,
Before that I the leisure had   30
  To choose you for my best belovéd:

B*

For all your love was past and done
Two days before it was begun:—
Adieu Love, adieu Love, untrue Love,
Untrue Love, untrue Love, adieu Love;   35
Your mind is light, soon lost for new love.

Anon.

41

A RENUNCIATION

If women could be fair, and yet not fond,
  Or that their love were firm, not fickle still,
I would not marvel that they make men bond
  By service long to purchase their good will;
But when I see how frail those creatures are,   5
I muse that men forget themselves so far.

To mark the choice they make, and how they change,
  How oft from Phoebus they do flee to Pan;
Unsettled still, like haggards wild they range,
  These gentle birds that fly from man to man;   10
Who would not scorn and shake them from the fist,
And let them fly, fair fools, which way they list?

Yet for disport we fawn and flatter both,
  To pass the time when nothing else can please,
And train them to our lure with subtle oath,   15
  Till, weary of their wiles, ourselves we ease;
And then we say when we their fancy try,
To play with fools, O what a fool was I!

E. Vere, Earl of Oxford

42

Blow, blow, thou winter wind,
Thou art not so unkind
  As man's ingratitude;
Thy tooth is not so keen
Because thou art not seen,   5
  Although thy breath be rude.

Heigh ho! sing heigh ho! unto the green holly:
Most friendship is feigning, most loving mere folly:
    Then, heigh ho! the holly!
    This life is most jolly.   10

    Freeze, freeze, thou bitter sky,
    That dost not bite so nigh
      As benefits forgot:
    Though thou the waters warp,
    Thy sting is not so sharp   15
      As friend remember'd not.
Heigh ho! sing heigh ho! unto the green holly:
Most friendship is feigning, most loving mere folly:
    Then, heigh ho! the holly!
    This life is most jolly.   20
                    W. Shakespeare

43

MADRIGAL

My thoughts hold mortal strife
I do detest my life,
And with lamenting cries,
Peace to my soul to bring,
Oft call that prince which here doth monarchize: 5
   —But he, grim grinning King,
Who caitiffs scorns, and doth the blest surprise,
Late having deck'd with beauty's rose his tomb,
Disdains to crop a weed, and will not come.
                    W. Drummond

44

DIRGE OF LOVE

  Come away, come away, Death,
And in sad cypres let me be laid;
  Fly away, fly away, breath;
I am slain by a fair cruel maid.

My shroud of white, stuck all with yew,   5
    O prepare it!
My part of death, no one so true
    Did share it.

Not a flower, not a flower sweet
On my black coffin let there be strown;   10
    Not a friend, not a friend greet
My poor corpse, where my bones shall be thrown:
A thousand thousand sighs to save,
    Lay me, O where
Sad true lover never find my grave,   15
    To weep there.

                     W. Shakespeare

45

FIDELE

Fear no more the heat o' the sun
    Nor the furious winter's rages;
Thou thy worldly task hast done,
    Home art gone and ta'en thy wages:
Golden lads and girls all must,   5
As chimney-sweepers, come to dust.

Fear no more the frown o' the great,
    Thou art past the tyrant's stroke;
Care no more to clothe and eat;
    To thee the reed is as the oak: 10
The sceptre, learning, physic, must
All follow this, and come to dust.

Fear no more the lightning-flash
    Nor the all-dreaded thunder-stone;
Fear not slander, censure rash;   15
    Thou hast finish'd joy and moan:
All lovers young, all lovers must
Consign to thee, and come to dust.

                     W. Shakespeare

46

A SEA DIRGE

Full fathom five thy father lies:
 Of his bones are coral made;
Those are pearls that were his eyes:
 Nothing of him that doth fade
But doth suffer a sea-change   5
Into something rich and strange.
Sea-nymphs hourly ring his knell:
Hark! now I hear them,—
 Ding, dong, bell.

        W. Shakespeare

47

A LAND DIRGE

Call for the robin-redbreast and the wren,
 Since o'er shady groves they hover
 And with leaves and flowers do cover
The friendless bodies of unburied men.
 Call unto his funeral dole   5
 The ant, the field-mouse, and the mole,
To rear him hillocks that shall keep him warm
And (when gay tombs are robb'd) sustain no harm;
But keep the wolf far thence, that's foe to men,
For with his nails he'll dig them up again. 10

        J. Webster

48

POST MORTEM

If thou survive my well-contented day
 When that churl Death my bones with dust shall cover,
And shalt by fortune once more re-survey
 These poor rude lines of thy deceaséd lover;

Compare them with the bettering of the time,   5
   And though they be outstripp'd by every pen,
Reserve them for my love, not for their rhyme
   Exceeded by the height of happier men.

O then vouchsafe me but this loving thought—
   'Had my friend's muse grown with this growing age, 10
A dearer birth than this his love had brought,
   To march in ranks of better equipage:

But since he died, and poets better prove,
Theirs for their style I'll read, his for his love.'

                                      W. Shakespeare

49

THE TRIUMPH OF DEATH

No longer mourn for me when I am dead
   Than you shall hear the surly sullen bell
Give warning to the world, that I am fled
   From this vile world, with vilest worms to dwell;

Nay, if you read this line, remember not   5
   The hand that writ it; for I love you so,
That I in your sweet thoughts would be forgot
   If thinking on me then should make you woe.

O if, I say, you look upon this verse
   When I perhaps compounded am with clay,   10
Do not so much as my poor name rehearse,
   But let your love even with my life decay;

Lest the wise world should look into your moan,
And mock you with me after I am gone.

                                      W. Shakespeare

50

MADRIGAL

Tell me where is Fancy bred,
Or in the heart, or in the head?
How begot, how nourishéd?
      Reply, reply.

It is engender'd in the eyes,   5
With gazing fed; and Fancy dies
In the cradle where it lies:
   Let us all ring Fancy's knell;
   I'll begin it,—Ding, dong, bell.
      —Ding, dong, bell.   10
                  W. Shakespeare

51

CUPID AND CAMPASPE

Cupid and my Campaspe play'd
At cards for kisses; Cupid paid:
He stakes his quiver, bow, and arrows,
His mother's doves, and team of sparrows;
Loses them too; then down he throws   5
The coral of his lip, the rose
Growing on 's cheek (but none knows how);
With these, the crystal of his brow,
And then the dimple of his chin;
All these did my Campaspe win: 10
At last he set her both his eyes—
She won, and Cupid blind did rise.
   O Love! has she done this to thee?
   What shall, alas! become of me?
                     J. Lyly

52

Pack, clouds, away, and welcome day,
   With night we banish sorrow;
Sweet air blow soft, mount lark aloft
   To give my Love good-morrow!
Wings from the wind to please her mind   5
   Notes from the lark I'll borrow;
Bird prune thy wing, nightingale sing,
   To give my Love good-morrow;
     To give my Love good-morrow
     Notes from them all I'll borrow.   10

Wake from thy nest, Robin-red-breast,
  Sing birds in every furrow;
And from each bill, let music shrill
  Give my fair Love good-morrow!
Blackbird and thrush in every bush,   15
  Stare, linnet, and cock-sparrow,
You pretty elves, amongst yourselves
  Sing my fair Love good-morrow!
    To give my Love good-morrow
    Sing birds in every furrow!   20

                                        T. Heywood

                        53

                  PROTHALAMION

Calm was the day, and through the trembling air
  Sweet-breathing Zephyrus did softly play—
  A gentle spirit, that lightly did delay
Hot Titan's beams, which then did glister fair;
    When I (whom sullen care,   5
Through discontent of my long fruitless stay
  In princes' court, and expectation vain
Of idle hopes, which still do fly away
  Like empty shadows, did afflict my brain)
    Walk'd forth to ease my pain   10
Along the shore of silver-streaming Thames;
  Whose rutty bank, the which his river hems,
  Was painted all with variable flowers,
And all the meads adorn'd with dainty gems
    Fit to deck maidens' bowers,   15
    And crown their paramours
Against the bridal day, which is not long:
Sweet Thames! run softly, till I end my song.

There in a meadow by the river's side
  A flock of nymphs I chancéd to espy,   20
  All lovely daughters of the flood thereby,
With goodly greenish locks all loose untied
    As each had been a bride;

And each one had a little wicker basket
   Made of fine twigs, entailéd curiously,   25
In which they gather'd flowers to fill their flasket,
   And with fine fingers cropt full feateously
      The tender stalks on high.
Of every sort which in that meadow grew
They gather'd some; the violet, pallid blue,   30
   The little daisy that at evening closes,
The virgin lily and the primrose true,
     With store of vermeil roses,
     To deck their bridegrooms' posies
Against the bridal day, which was not long: 35
Sweet Thames! run softly, till I end my song.

With that I saw two swans of goodly hue
   Come softly swimming down along the lee;
   Two fairer birds I yet did never see;
The snow which doth the top of Pindus strow   40
   Did never whiter show,
Nor Jove himself, when he a swan would be
   For love of Leda, whiter did appear;
Yet Leda was (they say) as white as he,
   Yet not so white as these, nor nothing near;   45
     So purely white they were,
That even the gentle stream, the which them bare,
Seem'd foul to them, and bade his billows spare
   To wet their silken feathers, lest thy might
Soil their fair plumes with water not so fair,   50
     And mar their beauties bright,
     That shone as Heaven's light
Against their bridal day, which was not long:
Sweet Thames! run softly, till I end my song.

Eftsoons the nymphs, which now had flowers their fill,
   Ran all in haste to see that silver brood   56
   As they came floating on the crystal flood;
Whom when they saw, they stood amazéd still
     Their wondering eyes to fill;
Them seem'd they never saw a sight so fair   60
   Of fowls, so lovely, that they sure did deem
Them heavenly born, or to be that same pair

Which through the sky draw Venus' silver team;
   For sure they did not seem
To be begot of any earthly seed,   65
But rather angels, or of angels' breed;
   Yet were they bred of summer's heat, they say,
In sweetest season, when each flower and weed
     The earth did fresh array;
     So fresh they seem'd as day,   70
Even as their bridal day, which was not long:
Sweet Thames! run softly, till I end my song.

Then forth they all out of their baskets drew
   Great store of flowers, the honour of the field,
   That to the sense did fragrant odours yield,   75
All which upon those goodly birds they threw
     And all the waves did strew,
That like old Peneus' waters they did seem
   When down along by pleasant Tempe's shore
Scatter'd with flowers, through Thessaly they stream, 80
   That they appear, through lilies' plenteous store,
     Like a bride's chamber-floor.
Two of those nymphs meanwhile two garlands bound
Of freshest flowers which in that mead they found,
   The which presenting all in trim array,   85
Their snowy foreheads therewithal they crown'd;
     Whilst one did sing this lay
     Prepared against that day,
Against their bridal day, which was not long:
Sweet Thames! run softly, till I end my song.   90

'Ye gentle birds! the world's fair ornament,
   And Heaven's glory, whom this happy hour
   Doth lead unto your lovers' blissful bower,
Joy may you have, and gentle heart's content
     Of your love's couplement;   95
And let fair Venus, that is queen of love,
   With her heart-quelling son upon you smile,
Whose smile, they say, hath virtue to remove
   All love's dislike, and friendship's faulty guile
     For ever to assoil.   100

Let endless peace your steadfast hearts accord,
And blessed plenty wait upon your board;
  And let your bed with pleasures chaste abound,
That fruitful issue may to you afford
    Which may your foes confound,   105
    And make your joys redound
Upon your bridal day, which is not long:
Sweet Thames! run softly, till I end my song.'

So ended she; and all the rest around
  To her redoubled that her undersong,   110
  Which said their bridal day should not be long:
And gentle Echo from the neighbour ground
    Their accents did resound.
So forth those joyous birds did pass along
  Adown the lee that to them murmur'd low,   115
As he would speak but that he lack'd a tongue,
  Yet did by signs his glad affection show,
    Making his stream run slow.
And all the fowl which in his flood did dwell
'Gan flock about these twain, that did excel   120
  The rest, so far as Cynthia doth shend
The lesser stars. So they, enrangéd well,
    Did on those two attend,
    And their best service lend
Against their wedding day, which was not long: 125
Sweet Thames! run softly, till I end my song.

At length they all to merry London came,
  To merry London, my most kindly nurse,
  That to me gave this life's first native source,
Though from another place I take my name,   130
    An house of ancient fame:
There when they came whereas those bricky towers
  The which on Thames' broad aged back do ride,
Where now the studious lawyers have their bowers,
  There whilome wont the Templar-knights to bide, 135
    Till they decay'd through pride;
Next whereunto there stands a stately place,
Where oft I gainéd gifts and goodly grace

Of that great lord, which therein wont to dwell,
Whose want too well now feels my friendless case;   140
      But ah! here fits not well
      Old woes, but joys, to tell
Against the bridal day, which is not long:
Sweet Thames! run softly, till I end my song.

Yet therein now doth lodge a noble peer,   145
   Great England's glory and the world's wide wonder,
   Whose dreadful name late through all Spain did
      thunder,
And Hercules' two pillars standing near
      Did make to quake and fear:
Fair branch of honour, flower of chivalry!   150
   That fillest England with thy triumphs' fame,
Joy have thou of thy noble victory,
   And endless happiness of thine own name
      That promiseth the same;
That through thy prowess and victorious arms   155
Thy country may be freed from foreign harms,
   And great Eliza's glorious name may ring
Through all the world, fill'd with thy wide alarms,
      Which some brave Muse may sing
      To ages following,   160
Upon the bridal day, which is not long:
Sweet Thames! run softly, till I end my song.

From those high towers this noble lord issúing
   Like radiant Hesper, when his golden hair
   In th' ocean billows he hath bathéd fair,   165
Descended to the river's open viewing
      With a great train ensuing.
Above the rest were goodly to be seen
   Two gentle knights of lovely face and feature,
Beseeming well the bower of any queen,   170
   With gifts of wit and ornaments of nature,
      Fit for so goodly stature,
That like the twins of Jove they seem'd in sight
Which deck the baldric of the Heavens bright;

They two, forth pacing to the river's side,   175
Received those two fair brides, their love's delight;
    Which, at th' appointed tide,
    Each one did make his bride
Against their bridal day, which is not long:
Sweet Thames! run softly, till I end my song.   180

E. Spenser

54

THE HAPPY HEART

Art thou poor, yet hast thou golden slumbers?
    O sweet content!
Art thou rich, yet is thy mind perplexed?
    O punishment!
Dost thou laugh to see how fools are vexed   5
To add to golden numbers, golden numbers?
O sweet content! O sweet, O sweet content!
  Work apace, apace, apace, apace;
  Honest labour bears a lovely face;
Then hey nonny nonny, hey nonny nonny!   10

Canst drink the waters of the crispéd spring?
    O sweet content!
Swimm'st thou in wealth, yet sink'st in thine own tears?
    O punishment!
Then he that patiently want's burden bears   15
No burden bears, but is a king, a king!
O sweet content! O sweet, O sweet content!
  Work apace, apace, apace, apace;
  Honest labour bears a lovely face;
Then hey nonny nonny, hey nonny nonny!   20

T. Dekker

55

This Life, which seems so fair,
Is like a bubble blown up in the air
    By sporting children's breath,
    Who chase it everywhere
And strive who can most motion it bequeath.   5
And though it sometime seem of its own might,

    Like to an eye of gold, to be fix'd there,
And firm to hover in that empty height,
That only is because it is so light.
    —But in that pomp it doth not long appear;   10
For, when 'tis most admired, in a thought,
Because it erst was nought, it turns to nought.

                                        W. Drummond

56

SOUL AND BODY

Poor Soul, the centre of my sinful earth,
    [Fool'd by] those rebel powers that thee array,
Why dost thou pine within, and suffer dearth,
    Painting thy outward walls so costly gay?

Why so large cost, having so short a lease,   5
    Dost thou upon thy fading mansion spend?
Shall worms, inheritors of this excess,
    Eat up thy charge? is this thy body's end?

Then, Soul, live thou upon thy servant's loss,
    And let that pine to aggravate thy store;   10
Buy terms divine in selling hours of dross;
    Within be fed, without be rich no more:—

So shalt thou feed on death, that feeds on men,
And death once dead, there's no more dying then.

                                        W. Shakespeare

57

LIFE

The World's a bubble, and the Life of Man
        Less than a span:
In his conception wretched, from the womb
        So to the tomb;
Curst from the cradle, and brought up to years   5
        With cares and fears.
Who then to frail mortality shall trust,
But limns the water, or but writes in dust.

Yet since with sorrow here we live opprest,
        What life is best?   10
Courts are but only superficial schools
        To dandle fools:
The rural parts are turn'd into a den
        Of savage men:
And where's a city from all vice so free,   15
But may be term'd the worst of all the three?

Domestic cares afflict the husband's bed,
        Or pains his head:
Those that live single, take it for a curse,
        Or do things worse: 20
Some would have children: those that have them moan
        Or wish them gone:
What is it, then, to have, or have no wife,
But single thraldom, or a double strife?

Our own affections still at home to please   25
        Is a disease:
To cross the sea to any foreign soil,
        Perils and toil:
Wars with their noise affright us; when they cease,
        We are worse in peace;—   30
What then remains, but that we still should cry
Not to be born, or, being born, to die?

                    Lord Bacon

58

THE LESSONS OF NATURE

Of this fair volume which we World do name
    If we the sheets and leaves could turn with care,
Of Him who it corrects, and did it frame,
    We clear might read the art and wisdom rare:

Find out His power which wildest powers doth tame,   5
    His providence extending everywhere,
    His justice which proud rebels doth not spare,
In every page, no period of the same.

But silly we, like foolish children, rest
    Well pleased with colour'd vellum, leaves of gold,   10
Fair dangling ribbands, leaving what is best,
    On the great Writer's sense ne'er taking hold;

Or if by chance we stay our minds on aught,
It is some picture on the margin wrought.

                                                    W. Drummond

59

Doth then the world go thus, doth all thus move?
    Is this the justice which on Earth we find?
    Is this that firm decree which all both bind?
Are these your influences, Powers above?

    Those souls which vice's moody mists most blind,   5
Blind Fortune, blindly, most their friend doth prove;
And they who thee, poor idol, Virtue! love,
    Ply like a feather toss'd by storm and wind.

Ah! if a Providence doth sway this all,
    Why should best minds groan under most distress?   10
Or why should pride humility make thrall,
    And injuries the innocent oppress?

Heavens! hinder, stop this fate; or grant a time
When good may have, as well as bad, their prime.

                                                    W. Drummond

60

THE WORLD'S WAY

Tired with all these, for restful death I cry—
  As, to behold desert a beggar born,
And needy nothing trimm'd in jollity,
  And purest faith unhappily forsworn,

And gilded honour shamefully misplaced,   5
  And maiden virtue rudely strumpeted,
And right perfection wrongfully disgraced,
  And strength by limping sway disabled,

And art made tongue-tied by authority,
  And folly, doctor-like, controlling skill,   10
And simple truth miscall'd simplicity,
  And captive Good attending captain Ill:—

—Tired with all these, from these would I be gone,
Save that, to die, I leave my Love alone.
                                    W. Shakespeare

61

SAINT JOHN BAPTIST

The last and greatest Herald of Heaven's King
  Girt with rough skins, hies to the deserts wild,
Among that savage brood the woods forth bring,
  Which he more harmless found than man, and mild.

His food was locusts, and what there doth spring,   5
  With honey that from virgin hives distill'd;
Parch'd body, hollow eyes, some uncouth thing
  Made him appear, long since from earth exiled.

There burst he forth: 'All ye whose hopes rely
  On God, with me amidst these deserts mourn,   10
Repent, repent, and from old errors turn!'
  —Who listen'd to his voice, obey'd his cry?

Only the echoes, which he made relent,
Rung from their flinty caves, Repent! Repent!
                                    W. Drummond

THE GOLDEN TREASURY

BOOK SECOND

62

ODE ON THE
MORNING OF CHRIST'S NATIVITY

This is the month, and this the happy morn
    Wherein the Son of Heaven's Eternal King
Of wedded maid and virgin mother born,
    Our great redemption from above did bring;
    For so the holy sages once did sing   5
That He our deadly forfeit should release,
And with His Father work us a perpetual peace.

That glorious Form, that Light unsufferable,
    And that far-beaming blaze of Majesty
Wherewith He wont at Heaven's high council-table 10
    To sit the midst of Trinal Unity,
    He laid aside; and, here with us to be,
Forsook the courts of everlasting day,
And chose with us a darksome house of mortal clay.

Say, heavenly Muse, shall not thy sacred vein   15
    Afford a present to the Infant God?
Hast thou no verse, no hymn, or solemn strain
    To welcome Him to this His new abode,
    Now while the heaven, by the sun's team untrod,
Hath took no print of the approaching light,   20
And all the spangled host keep watch in squadrons
    bright?

See how from far, upon the eastern road,
    The star-led wizards haste with odours sweet:
O run, prevent them with thy humble ode
    And lay it lowly at His blessed feet;   25

Have thou the honour first thy Lord to greet,
And join thy voice unto the angel quire
From out His secret altar touch'd with hallow'd fire.

THE HYMN

    It was the winter wild
    While the heaven-born Child   30
All meanly wrapt in the rude manger lies;
    Nature in awe to Him
    Had doff'd her gaudy trim,
With her great Master so to sympathize:
    It was no season then for her   35
To wanton with the sun, her lusty paramour.

    Only with speeches fair
    She woos the gentle air
To hide her guilty front with innocent snow;
    And on her naked shame,   40
    Pollute with sinful blame,
The saintly veil of maiden white to throw;
    Confounded, that her Maker's eyes
Should look so near upon her foul deformities.

    But He, her fears to cease,   45
    Sent down the meek-eyed Peace;
She, crown'd with olive green, came softly sliding
    Down through the turning sphere,
    His ready harbinger,
With turtle wing the amorous clouds dividing;   50
    And waving wide her myrtle wand,
She strikes a universal peace through sea and land.

    No war, or battle's sound
    Was heard the world around:
The idle spear and shield were high unhung;   55
    The hookéd chariot stood
    Unstain'd with hostile blood;
The trumpet spake not to the arméd throng;
    And kings sat still with awful eye,
As if they surely knew their sovran Lord was by. 60

But peaceful was the night
    Wherein the Prince of Light
His reign of peace upon the earth began:
    The winds, with wonder whist,
    Smoothly the waters kist,   65
Whispering new joys to the mild oceân—
    Who now hath quite forgot to rave,
While birds of calm sit brooding on the charméd wave.

    The stars, with deep amaze,
    Stand fix'd in steadfast gaze,   70
Bending one way their precious influence;
    And will not take their flight
    For all the morning light,
Or Lucifer that often warn'd them thence;
    But in their glimmering orbs did glow   75
Until their Lord Himself bespake, and bid them go.

    And though the shady gloom
    Had given day her room,
The sun himself withheld his wonted speed,
    And hid his head for shame,   80
    As his inferior flame
The new-enlighten'd world no more should need:
    He saw a greater Sun appear
Than his bright throne or burning axletree could bear.

    The shepherds on the lawn   85
    Or ere the point of dawn
Sate simply chatting in a rustic row;
    Full little thought they than
    That the mighty Pan
Was kindly come to live with them below;   90
    Perhaps their loves, or else their sheep
Was all that did their silly thoughts so busy keep.

    When such music sweet
    Their hearts and ears did greet
As never was by mortal finger strook—   95
    Divinely-warbled voice

Answering the stringéd noise,
As all their souls in blissful rapture took:
The air, such pleasure loth to lose,
With thousand echoes still prolongs each heavenly
        close.   100

Nature that heard such sound
Beneath the hollow round
Of Cynthia's seat the airy region thrilling,
Now was almost won
To think her part was done,   105
And that her reign had here its last fulfilling;
She knew such harmony alone
Could hold all heaven and earth in happier union.

At last surrounds their sight
A globe of circular light,   110
That with long beams the shamefaced night array'd;
The helméd Cherubim
And sworded Seraphim
Are seen in glittering ranks with wings display'd,
Harping in loud and solemn quire   115
With unexpressive notes, to Heaven's new-born Heir.

Such music (as 'tis said)
Before was never made
But when of old the sons of morning sung,
While the Creator great   120
His constellations set
And the well-balanced world on hinges hung;
And cast the dark foundations deep,
And bid the weltering waves their oozy channel keep.

Ring out, ye crystal spheres!   125
Once bless our human ears,
If ye have power to touch our senses so;
And let your silver chime
Move in melodious time;
And let the bass of heaven's deep organ blow;   130

    And with your ninefold harmony
Make up full consort to the angelic symphony.

      For if such holy song,
      Enwrap our fancy long,
  Time will run back, and fetch the age of gold;   135
      And speckled vanity
      Will sicken soon and die,
  And leprous sin will melt from earthly mould;
    And Hell itself will pass away,
And leave her dolorous mansions to the peering day.

      Yea, Truth and Justice then   141
      Will down return to men,
  Orb'd in a rainbow; and, like glories wearing,
      Mercy will sit between
      Throned in celestial sheen,   145
  With radiant feet the tissued clouds down steering;
    And Heaven, as at some festival,
Will open wide the gates of her high palace hall.

      But wisest Fate says No;
      This must not yet be so;   150
  The Babe yet lies in smiling infancy
      That on the bitter cross
      Must redeem our loss;
  So both Himself and us to glorify:
    Yet first, to those ychain'd in sleep   155
The wakeful trump of doom must thunder through the
      deep,

      With such a horrid clang
      As on mount Sinai rang
  While the red fire and smouldering clouds outbrake:
      The aged Earth aghast   160
      With terror of that blast
  Shall from the surface to the centre shake,
    When, at the world's last sessión,
The dreadful Judge in middle air shall spread His throne.

And then at last our bliss   165
Full and perfect is,
But now begins; for from this happy day
The old Dragon under ground,
In straiter limits bound,
Nor half so far casts his usurpéd sway;   170
And, wroth to see his kingdom fail,
Swinges the scaly horror of his folded tail.

The oracles are dumb;
No voice or hideous hum
Runs through the archéd roof in words deceiving: 175
Apollo from his shrine
Can no more divine,
With hollow shriek the steep of Delphos leaving:
No nightly trance or breathéd spell
Inspires the pale-eyed priest from the prophetic cell.

The lonely mountains o'er   181
And the resounding shore
A voice of weeping heard, and loud lament;
From haunted spring and dale
Edged with poplar pale   185
The parting Genius is with sighing sent;
With flower-inwoven tresses torn
The nymphs in twilight shade of tangled thickets mourn.

In consecrated earth
And on the holy hearth   190
The Lars and Lemures moan with midnight plaint;
In urns, and altars round
A drear and dying sound
Affrights the Flamens at their service quaint;
And the chill marble seems to sweat,   195
While each peculiar Power forgoes his wonted seat.

Peor and Baalim
Forsake their temples dim,
With that twice-batter'd god of Palestine;
And moonéd Ashtaroth   200
Heaven's queen and mother both,

Now sits not girt with tapers' holy shine;
  The Lybic Hammon shrinks his horn,
In vain the Tyrian maids their wounded Thammuz
      mourn.

  And sullen Moloch, fled,   205
    Hath left in shadows dread
His burning idol all of blackest hue;
    In vain with cymbals' ring
    They call the grisly king,
In dismal dance about the furnace blue;   210
  The brutish gods of Nile as fast,
Isis, and Orus, and the dog Anubis, haste.

    Nor is Osiris seen
    In Memphian grove, or green,
Trampling the unshower'd grass with lowings loud:
    Nor can he be at rest   216
    Within his sacred chest;
Nought but profoundest hell can be his shroud;
    In vain with timbrell'd anthems dark
The sable-stoléd sorcerers bear his worshipt ark.   220

    He feels from Juda's land
    The dreaded infant's hand;
The rays of Bethlehem blind his dusky eyn;
    Nor all the gods beside
    Longer dare abide,   225
Not Typhon huge ending in snaky twine:
    Our Babe, to show his Godhead true,
Can in His swaddling bands control the damnéd crew.

    So, when the sun in bed
    Curtain'd with cloudy red   230
Pillows his chin upon an orient wave,
    The flocking shadows pale
    Troop to the infernal jail,
Each fetter'd ghost slips to his several grave;
    And the yellow-skirted fays   235
Fly after the night-steeds, leaving their moon-loved
      maze.

    But see, the Virgin blest
    Hath laid her Babe to rest;
Time is, our tedious song should here have ending:
    Heaven's youngest-teeméd star   240
    Hath fix'd her polish'd car,
Her sleeping Lord with hand-maid lamp attending:
    And all about the courtly stable
Bright-harness'd angels sit in order serviceable.

                                        J. Milton

63

SONG FOR SAINT CECILIA'S DAY, 1687

From Harmony, from heavenly Harmony
    This universal frame began:
    When Nature underneath a heap
    Of jarring atoms lay
And could not heave her head,   5
The tuneful voice was heard from high
    Arise, ye more than dead!
Then cold, and hot, and moist, and dry
In order to their stations leap,
    And Music's power obey.   10
From harmony, from heavenly harmony
    This universal frame began:
    From harmony to harmony
Through all the compass of the notes it ran,
The diapason closing full in Man.   15

What passion cannot Music raise and quell?
    When Jubal struck the chorded shell
    His listening brethren stood around,
    And, wondering, on their faces fell
    To worship that celestial sound.   20
Less than a god they thought there could not dwell
    Within the hollow of that shell
    That spoke so sweetly and so well.
What passion cannot Music raise and quell?

                                        c

The trumpet's loud clangor   25
  Excites us to arms,
With shrill notes of anger
  And mortal alarms.
The double double double beat
  Of the thundering drum   30
  Cries 'Hark! the foes come;
Charge, charge, 'tis too late to retreat!'

The soft complaining flute
  In dying notes discovers
  The woes of hopeless lovers,   35
Whose dirge is whisper'd by the warbling lute.

  Sharp violins proclaim
Their jealous pangs and desperation,
Fury, frantic indignation,
Depth of pains, and height of passion   40
  For the fair disdainful dame.

But oh! what art can teach,
What human voice can reach
  The sacred organ's praise?
Notes inspiring holy love,   45
  Notes that wing their heavenly ways
To mend the choirs above.

Orpheus could lead the savage race,
And trees unrooted left their place
  Sequacious of the lyre: 50
But bright Cecilia raised the wonder higher:
When to her Organ vocal breath was given,
An Angel heard, and straight appear'd—
  Mistaking Earth for Heaven!

Grand Chorus

  As from the power of sacred lays   55
    The spheres began to move,
  And sung the great Creator's praise
    To all the blest above;

So when the last and dreadful hour
This crumbling pageant shall devour   60
The trumpet shall be heard on high,
The dead shall live, the living die,
And Music shall untune the sky.

J. Dryden

64

ON THE LATE MASSACRE IN PIEDMONT

Avenge, O Lord! Thy slaughter'd Saints, whose bones
  Lie scatter'd on the Alpine mountains cold;
   Even them who kept Thy truth so pure of old,
When all our fathers worship stocks and stones,

Forget not: in Thy book record their groans   5
  Who were Thy sheep, and in their ancient fold
   Slain by the bloody Piemontese, that roll'd
Mother with infant down the rocks. Their moans

The vales redoubled to the hills, and they
  To Heaven. Their martyr'd blood and ashes sow   10
O'er all the Italian fields, where still doth sway

  The triple tyrant: that from these may grow
A hundred-fold, who, having learnt Thy way,
  Early may fly the Babylonian woe.

J. Milton

65

HORATIAN ODE UPON CROMWELL'S
RETURN FROM IRELAND

The forward youth that would appear,
Must now forsake his Muses dear,
    Nor in the shadows sing
    His numbers languishing.

'Tis time to leave the books in dust,   5
And oil th' unuséd armour's rust,
    Removing from the wall
    The corslet of the hall.

So restless Cromwell could not cease
In the inglorious arts of peace,   10
    But through adventurous war
    Urgéd his active star:

And like the three-fork'd lightning, first
Breaking the clouds where it was nurst,
    Did thorough his own side   15
    His fiery way divide:

(For 'tis all one to courage high
The emulous, or enemy;
    And with such, to enclose
    Is more than to oppose;)   20

Then burning through the air he went
And palaces and temples rent;
    And Caesar's head at last
    Did through his laurels blast.

'Tis madness to resist or blame   25
The face of angry heaven's flame;
    And if we would speak true,
    Much to the man is due

Who, from his private gardens, where
He lived reservéd and austere   30
    (As if his highest plot
    To plant the bergamot),

Could by industrious valour climb
To ruin the great work of Time,
    And cast the Kingdoms old   35
    Into another mould;

Though Justice against Fate complain,
And plead the ancient Rights in vain—
    But those do hold or break
    As men are strong or weak.   40

Nature, that hateth emptiness,
Allows of penetration less,
    And therefore must make room
    Where greater spirits come.

What field of all the Civil War   45
Where his were not the deepest scar?
    And Hampton shows what part
    He had of wiser art;

Where, twining subtle fears with hope,
He wove a net of such a scope   50
    That Charles himself might chase
    To Carisbrook's narrow case;

That thence the Royal actor borne
The tragic scaffold might adorn:
    While round the arméd bands   55
    Did clap their bloody hands;

He nothing common did or mean
Upon that memorable scene,
    But with his keener eye
    The axe's edge did try;   60

Nor call'd the Gods, with vulgar spite,
To vindicate his helpless right;
    But bow'd his comely head
    Down, as upon a bed.

—This was that memorable hour   65
Which first assured the forcéd power
    So when they did design
    The Capitol's first line,

A Bleeding Head, where they begun,
Did fright the architects to run;   70
    And yet in that the State
    Foresaw its happy fate!

And now the Irish are ashamed
To see themselves in one year tamed:
    So much one man can do   75
    That does both act and know.

They can affirm his praises best,
And have, though overcome, confest
    How good he is, how just
    And fit for highest trust;   80

Nor yet grown stiffer with command,
But still in the Republic's hand—
    How fit he is to sway
    That can so well obey!—

He to the Commons' feet presents   85
A Kingdom for his first year's rents,
    And (what he may) forbears
    His fame, to make it theirs:

And has his sword and spoils ungirt
To lay them at the Public's skirt.   90
    So when the falcon high
    Falls heavy from the sky,

She, having kill'd, no more does search
But on the next green bough to perch,
    Where, when he first does lure,   95
    The falconer has her sure.

—What may not then our Isle presume
While victory his crest does plume?
    What may not others fear
    If thus he crowns each year?   100

As Caesar he, ere long, to Gaul,
To Italy an Hannibal,
    And to all states not free
    Shall climacteric be.

The Pict no shelter now shall find   105
Within his parti-colour'd mind,
    But from this valour sad,
    Shrink underneath the plaid—

Happy, if in the tufted brake
The English hunter him mistake,   110
    Nor lay his hounds in near
    The Caledonian deer.

But thou, the War's and Fortune's son,
March indefatigably on;
    And for the last effect   115
    Still keep the sword erect:

Besides the force it has to fright
The spirits of the shady night,
  The same arts that did gain
  A power, must it maintain.   120

A. Marvell

66

LYCIDAS

Elegy on a Friend drowned in the Irish Channel

Yet once more, O ye laurels, and once more
Ye myrtles brown, with ivy never sere,
I come to pluck your berries harsh and crude,
And with forced fingers rude
Shatter your leaves before the mellowing year.   5
Bitter constraint, and sad occasion dear
Compels me to disturb your season due:
For Lycidas is dead, dead ere his prime,
Young Lycidas, and hath not left his peer:
Who would not sing for Lycidas? he knew   10
Himself to sing, and build the lofty rhyme.
He must not float upon his watery bier
Unwept, and welter to the parching wind,
Without the meed of some melodious tear.

Begin then, Sisters of the sacred well   15
That from beneath the seat of Jove doth spring,
Begin, and somewhat loudly sweep the string.
Hence with denial vain and coy excuse:
So may some gentle Muse
With lucky words favour my destined urn;   20
And as he passes, turn
And bid fair peace be to my sable shroud.

For we were nursed upon the self-same hill,
Fed the same flock by fountain, shade, and rill.
Together both, ere the high lawns appear'd   25
Under the opening eye-lids of the morn,
We drove a-field, and both together heard
What time the gray-fly winds her sultry horn,
Battening our flocks with the fresh dews of night,
Oft till the star, that rose at evening bright,   30

Toward heaven's descent had sloped his westering wheel.
Meanwhile the rural ditties were not mute,
Temper'd to the oaten flute;
Rough Satyrs danced, and Fauns with cloven heel
From the glad sound would not be absent long;   35
And old Damoetas loved to hear our song.

  But O the heavy change, now thou art gone,
Now thou art gone, and never must return!
Thee, Shepherd, thee the woods, and desert caves,
With wild thyme and the gadding vine o'ergrown,   40
And all their echoes, mourn:
The willows and the hazel copses green
Shall now no more be seen
Fanning their joyous leaves to thy soft lays.
As killing as the canker to the rose,   45
Or taint-worm to the weanling herds that graze,
Or frost to flowers, that their gay wardrobe wear
When first the white-thorn blows;
Such, Lycidas, thy loss to shepherd's ear.

  Where were ye, Nymphs, when the remorseless deep 50
Closed o'er the head of your loved Lycidas?
For neither were ye playing on the steep
Where your old bards, the famous Druids, lie,
Nor on the shaggy top of Mona high,
Nor yet where Deva spreads her wizard stream: 55
Ay me! I fondly dream—
Had ye been there—for what could that have done?
What could the Muse herself that Orpheus bore,
The Muse herself, for her enchanting son,
Whom universal nature did lament,   60
When by the rout that made the hideous roar
His gory visage down the stream was sent,
Down the swift Hebrus to the Lesbian shore?

  Alas! what boots it with uncessant care
To tend the homely, slighted, shepherd's trade   65
And strictly meditate the thankless Muse?
Were it not better done, as others use,

To sport with Amaryllis in the shade,
Or with the tangles of Neaera's hair?
Fame is the spur that the clear spirit doth raise   70
(That last infirmity of noble mind)
To scorn delights, and live laborious days;
But the fair guerdon when we hope to find,
And think to burst out into sudden blaze,
Comes the blind Fury with the abhorréd shears   75
And slits the thin-spun life.   'But not the praise'
Phoebus replied, and touch'd my trembling ears;
'Fame is no plant that grows on mortal soil,
Nor in the glistering foil
Set off to the world, nor in broad rumour lies: 80
But lives and spreads aloft by those pure eyes
And perfect witness of all-judging Jove;
As he pronounces lastly on each deed,
Of so much fame in heaven expect thy meed.'

Of fountain Arethuse, and thou honour'd flood   85
Smooth-sliding Mincius, crown'd with vocal reeds,
That strain I heard was of a higher mood:
But now my oat proceeds,
And listens to the herald of the sea
That came in Neptune's plea;   90
He ask'd the waves, and ask'd the felon winds,
What hard mishap hath doom'd this gentle swain?
And question'd every gust of rugged wings
That blows from off each beakéd promontory:
They knew not of his story;   95
And sage Hippotades their answer brings,
That not a blast was from his dungeon stray'd;
The air was calm, and on the level brine
Sleek Panope with all her sisters play'd.
It was that fatal and perfidious bark   100
Built in the eclipse, and rigg'd with curses dark,
That sunk so low that sacred head of thine.

Next Camus, reverend sire, went footing slow,
His mantle hairy, and his bonnet sedge,
Inwrought with figures dim, and on the edge   105
Like to that sanguine flower inscribed with woe:

c*

'Ah! who hath reft,' quoth he, 'my dearest pledge?'
Last came, and last did go
The pilot of the Galilean lake;
Two massy keys he bore of metals twain   110
(The golden opes, the iron shuts amain);
He shook his mitred locks, and stern bespake:
'How well could I have spared for thee, young
   swain,
Enow of such as for their bellies' sake
Creep and intrude and climb into the fold!   115
Of other care they little reckoning make
Than how to scramble at the shearers' feast,
And shove away the worthy bidden guest.
Blind mouths! that scarce themselves know how to
   hold
A sheep-hook, or have learn'd aught else the least   120
That to the faithful herdman's art belongs!
What recks it them? What need they? They are
   sped;
And when they list, their lean and flashy songs
Grate on their scrannel pipes of wretched straw;
The hungry sheep look up, and are not fed,   125
But swoln with wind and the rank mist they draw
Rot inwardly, and foul contagion spread:
Besides what the grim wolf with privy paw
Daily devours apace, and nothing said:
—But that two-handed engine at the door   130
Stands ready to smite once, and smite no more.'

   Return, Alpheus, the dread voice is past
That shrunk thy streams; return, Sicilian Muse,
And call the vales, and bid them hither cast
Their bells and flowerets of a thousand hues.   135
Ye valleys low, where the mild whispers use
Of shades, and wanton winds, and gushing brooks,
On whose fresh lap the swart star sparely looks,
Throw hither all your quaint enamell'd eyes
That on the green turf suck the honey'd showers   140
And purple all the ground with vernal flowers.
Bring the rathe primrose that forsaken dies,
The tufted crow-toe, and pale jessamine,

The white pink, and the pansy freak'd with jet,
The glowing violet,   145
The musk-rose, and the well-attired woodbine,
With cowslips wan that hang the pensive head,
And every flower that sad embroidery wears:
Bid amarantus all his beauty shed,
And daffadillies fill their cups with tears   150
To strew the laureat hearse where Lycid lies.
For, so to interpose a little ease,
Let our frail thoughts dally with false surmise;
Ay me! whilst thee the shores and sounding seas
Wash far away,—where'er thy bones are hurl'd,   155
Whether beyond the stormy Hebrides
Where thou perhaps, under the whelming tide,
Visitest the bottom of the monstrous world;
Or whether thou, to our moist vows denied,
Sleep'st by the fable of Bellerus old,   160
Where the great Vision of the guarded mount
Looks toward Namancos and Bayona's hold,
—Look homeward, Angel, now, and melt with ruth:
—And, O ye dolphins, waft the hapless youth!

　　Weep no more, woeful shepherds, weep no more,   165
For Lycidas, your sorrow, is not dead,
Sunk though he be beneath the watery floor;
So sinks the day-star in the ocean-bed,
And yet anon repairs his drooping head
And tricks his beams, and with new-spangled ore   170
Flames in the forehead of the morning sky:
So Lycidas sunk low, but mounted high
Through the dear might of Him that walk'd the
　　waves;
Where, other groves and other streams along,
With nectar pure his oozy locks he laves,   175
And hears the unexpressive nuptial song
In the blest kingdoms meek of joy and love.
There entertain him all the saints above
In solemn troops, and sweet societies,
That sing, and singing in their glory move,   180
And wipe the tears for ever from his eyes.

Now, Lycidas, the shepherds weep no more;
Henceforth thou art the Genius of the shore
In thy large recompense, and shalt be good
To all that wander in that perilous flood.   185

　　Thus sang the uncouth swain to the oaks and
　　　rills,
While the still morn went out with sandals grey;
He touch'd the tender stops of various quills,
With eager thought warbling his Doric lay:
And now the sun had stretch'd out all the hills,   190
And now was dropt into the western bay:
At last he rose, and twitch'd his mantle blue:
To-morrow to fresh woods, and pastures new.

                                                            J. Milton

67

ON THE TOMBS IN WESTMINSTER ABBEY

Mortality, behold and fear,
What a change of flesh is here!
Think how many royal bones
Sleep within these heaps of stones;
Here they lie, had realms and lands,   5
Who now want strength to stir their hands,
Where from their pulpits seal'd with dust
They preach, 'In greatness is no trust.'
Here's an acre sown indeed
With the richest royallest seed   10
That the earth did e'er suck in
Since the first man died for sin:
Here the bones of birth have cried
'Though gods they were, as men they died!'
Here are sands, ignoble things,   15
Dropt from the ruin'd sides of kings:
Here's a world of pomp and state
Buried in dust, once dead by fate.

                                                            F. Beaumont

68

THE LAST CONQUEROR

Victorious men of earth, no more
　Proclaim how wide your empires are;
Though you bind-in every shore,
　And your triumphs reach as far
　　As night or day,   5
　Yet you, proud monarchs, must obey
And mingle with forgotten ashes, when
Death calls ye to the crowd of common men.

Devouring Famine, Plague, and War,
　Each able to undo mankind,   10
Death's servile emissaries are;
　Nor to these alone confined,
　　He hath at will
More quaint and subtle ways to kill;
A smile or kiss, as he will use the art,   15
Shall have the cunning skill to break a heart.
                                        J. Shirley

69

DEATH THE LEVELLER

The glories of our blood and state
　Are shadows, not substantial things;
There is no armour against fate;
　Death lays his icy hand on kings:
　　Sceptre and Crown   5
　　Must tumble down,
And in the dust be equal made
With the poor crooked scythe and spade.

Some men with swords may reap the field,
　And plant fresh laurels where they kill: 10
But their strong nerves at last must yield;
　They tame but one another still:

                        Early or late
                        They stoop to fate,
        And must give up their murmuring breath   15
        When they, pale captives, creep to death.

        The garlands wither on your brow;
               Then boast no more your mighty deeds;
        Upon Death's purple altar now
               See where the victor-victim bleeds: 20
                        Your heads must come
                        To the cold tomb;
        Only the actions of the just
        Smell sweet, and blossom in their dust.

                                              J. Shirley

                              70

            WHEN THE ASSAULT WAS INTENDED
                        TO THE CITY

        Captain, or Colonel, or Knight in arms,
           Whose chance on these defenceless doors may seize,
           If deed of honour did thee ever please,
        Guard them, and him within protect from harms.

        He can requite thee; for he knows the charms   5
           That call fame on such gentle acts as these,
           And he can spread thy name o'er lands and seas,
        Whatever clime the sun's bright circle warms.

        Lift not thy spear against the Muses' bower:
           The great Emathian conqueror bid spare   10
        The house of Pindarus, when temple and tower

           Went to the ground: and the repeated air
        Of sad Electra's poet had the power
           To save the Athenian walls from ruin bare.

                                              J. Milton

71

ON HIS BLINDNESS

When I consider how my light is spent
  Ere half my days, in this dark world and wide,
  And that one talent which is death to hide
Lodged with me useless, though my soul more bent

To serve therewith my Maker, and present   5
  My true account, lest He returning chide,—
  Doth God exact day-labour, light denied?
I fondly ask:—But Patience, to prevent

That murmur, soon replies; God doth not need
  Either man's work, or His own gifts: who best   10
    Bear His mild yoke, they serve Him best: His
      state

Is kingly; thousands at His bidding speed
  And post o'er land and ocean without rest:—
    They also serve who only stand and wait.
                                        J. Milton

72

CHARACTER OF A HAPPY LIFE

How happy is he born or taught
  That serveth not another's will;
Whose armour is his honest thought,
  And silly truth his highest skill!

Whose passions not his masters are,   5
  Whose soul is still prepared for death;
Untied unto the world with care
  Of princely love or vulgar breath;

Who hath his life from rumours freed,
  Whose conscience is his strong retreat   10
Whose state can neither flatterers feed,
  Nor ruin make accusers great;

Who envieth none whom chance doth raise
   Or vice; who never understood
How deepest wounds are given with praise;   15
   Nor rules of state, but rules of good:

Who God doth late and early pray
   More of his grace than gifts to lend;
Who entertains the harmless day
   With a well-chosen book or friend;   20

—This man is free from servile bands
   Of hope to rise, or fear to fall;
Lord of himself, though not of lands;
   And having nothing, he hath all.
                        Sir H. Wotton

73

THE NOBLE NATURE

It is not growing like a tree
   In bulk, doth make Man better be;
Or standing long an oak, three hundred year,
To fall a log at last, dry, bald, and sere:
      A lily of a day   5
      Is fairer far in May,
   Although it fall and die that night;
   It was the plant and flower of Light.
In small proportions we just beauties see;
And in short measures life may perfect be.   10
                        B. Jonson

74

THE GIFTS OF GOD

When God at first made Man,
Having a glass of blessings standing by;
Let us (said He) pour on him all we can:
Let the world's riches, which dispersèd lie,
   Contract into a span.   5

       So strength first made a way;
Then beauty flow'd, then wisdom, honour, pleasure:
When almost all was out, God made a stay,
Perceiving that alone, of all His treasure,
       Rest in the bottom lay.   10

       For if I should (said He)
Bestow this jewel also on my creature,
He would adore my gifts instead of me,
And rest in Nature, not the God of Nature:
       So both should losers be.   15

       Yet let him keep the rest,
But keep them with repining restlessness:
Let him be rich and weary, that at least,
If goodness lead him not, yet weariness
       May toss him to my breast.   20

                                        G. Herbert

                      75

                 THE RETREAT

    Happy those early days, when I
    Shined in my Angel-infancy!
    Before I understood this place
    Appointed for my second race,
    Or taught my soul to fancy aught   5
    But a white, celestial thought;
    When yet I had not walk'd above
    A mile or two from my first Love,
    And looking back, at that short space
    Could see a glimpse of His bright face;   10
    When on some gilded cloud or flower
    My gazing soul would dwell an hour,
    And in those weaker glories spy
    Some shadows of eternity;
    Before I taught my tongue to wound   15
    My conscience with a sinful sound,
    Or had the black art to dispense
    A several sin to every sense,

But felt through all this fleshly dress
Bright shoots of everlastingness.   20

O how I long to travel back,
And tread again that ancient track!
That I might once more reach that plain,
Where first I left my glorious train;
From whence th' enlighten'd spirit sees   25
That shady City of Palm trees!
But ah! my soul with too much stay
Is drunk, and staggers in the way:—
Some men a forward motion love,
But I by backward steps would move;   30
And when this dust falls to the urn,
In that state I came, return.

H. Vaughan

76

TO MR. LAWRENCE

Lawrence, of virtuous father virtuous son,
    Now that the fields are dank and ways are mire,
    Where shall we sometimes meet, and by the fire
Help waste a sullen day, what may be won

From the hard season gaining?   Time will run   5
    On smoother, till Favonius re-inspire
    The frozen earth, and clothe in fresh attire
The lily and rose, that neither sow'd nor spun.

What neat repast shall feast us, light and choice,
    Of Attic taste, with wine, whence we may rise   10
To hear the lute well touch'd, or artful voice

    Warble immortal notes and Tuscan air?
    He who of those delights can judge, and spare
    To interpose them oft, is not unwise.

J. Milton

77

TO CYRIACK SKINNER

Cyriack, whose grandsire, on the royal bench
   Of British Themis, with no mean applause
   Pronounced, and in his volumes taught, our laws,
Which others at their bar so often wrench;

To-day deep thoughts resolve with me to drench   5
   In mirth, that after no repenting draws;
   Let Euclid rest, and Archimedes pause,
And what the Swede intend, and what the French.

To measure life learn thou betimes, and know
   Toward solid good what leads the nearest way;   10
     For other things mild Heaven a time ordains,

And disapproves that care, though wise in show,
   That with superfluous burden loads the day,
     And, when God sends a cheerful hour, refrains.

                                    J. Milton

78

HYMN TO DIANA

Queen and Huntress, chaste and fair,
   Now the sun is laid to sleep,
Seated in thy silver chair
   State in wonted manner keep:
     Hesperus entreats thy light,   5
     Goddess excellently bright.

Earth, let not thy envious shade
   Dare itself to interpose;
Cynthia's shining orb was made
   Heaven to clear when day did close: 10
     Bless us then with wishéd sight,
     Goddess excellently bright.

Lay thy bow of pearl apart
      And thy crystal-shining quiver;
Give unto the flying hart   15
      Space to breathe, how short soever:
            Thou that mak'st a day of night,
            Goddess excellently bright!

                                        B. Jonson

79

WISHES FOR THE SUPPOSED MISTRESS

      Whoe'er she be,
      That not impossible She
That shall command my heart and me;

      Where'er she lie,
      Lock'd up from mortal eye   5
In shady leaves of destiny:

      Till that ripe birth
      Of studied Fate stand forth,
And teach her fair steps tread our earth;

      Till that divine   10
      Idea take a shrine
Of crystal flesh, through which to shine:

      —Meet you her, my Wishes,
      Bespeak her to my blisses,
And be ye call'd, my absent kisses.   15

      I wish her beauty
      That owes not all its duty
To gaudy tire, or glist'ring shoe-tie:

      Something more than
      Taffata or tissue can,   20
Or rampant feather, or rich fan.

      A face that 's best
      By its own beauty drest,
And can alone commend the rest:

A face made up   25
Out of no other shop
Than what Nature's white hand sets ope.

Sidneian showers
Of sweet discourse, whose powers
Can crown old Winter's head with flowers.

Whate'er delight   31
Can make day's forehead bright
Or give down to the wings of night.

Soft silken hours,
Open suns, shady bowers;   35
'Bove all, nothing within that lowers.

Days, that need borrow
No part of their good morrow
From a fore-spent night of sorrow:

Days, that in spite   40
Of darkness, by the light
Of a clear mind are day all night.

Life, that dares send
A challenge to his end,
And when it comes, say, 'Welcome, friend.'   45

I wish her store
Of worth may leave her poor
Of wishes; and I wish——no more.

—Now, if Time knows
That Her, whose radiant brows   50
Weave them a garland of my vows;

Her that dares be
What these lines wish to see:
I seek no further, it is She.

'Tis She, and here   55
Lo! I unclothe and clear
My wishes' cloudy character.

Such worth as this is
Shall fix my flying wishes,
And determine them to kisses.   60

Let her full glory,
My fancies, fly before ye;
Be ye my fictions:—but her story.

                                                    R. Crashaw

80

THE GREAT ADVENTURER

Over the mountains
  And over the waves,
Under the fountains
  And under the graves;
Under floods that are deepest,   5
  Which Neptune obey;
Over rocks that are steepest
  Love will find out the way.

Where there is no place
  For the glow-worm to lie;   10
Where there is no space
  For receipt of a fly;
Where the midge dares not venture
  Lest herself fast she lay;
If love come, he will enter   15
  And soon find out his way.

You may esteem him
  A child for his might;
Or you may deem him
  A coward from his flight;   20
But if she whom love doth honour
  Be conceal'd from the day,
Set a thousand guards upon her,
  Love will find out the way.

Some think to lose him   25
  By having him confined;
And some do suppose him,
  Poor thing, to be blind;

But if ne'er so close ye wall him,
   Do the best that you may,   30
Blind love, if so ye call him,
   Will find out his way.

You may train the eagle
   To stoop to your fist;
Or you may inveigle   35
   The phoenix of the east;
The lioness, ye may move her
   To give o'er her prey;
But you'll ne'er stop a lover:
   He will find out his way.   40

Anon.

81

CHILD AND MAIDEN

Ah, Chloris! that I now could sit
   As unconcern'd as when
Your infant beauty could beget
   No pleasure, nor no pain!
When I the dawn used to admire,   5
   And praised the coming day,
I little thought the growing fire
   Must take my rest away.

Your charms in harmless childhood lay
   Like metals in the mine;   10
Age from no face took more away
   Than youth conceal'd in thine.
But as your charms insensibly
   To their perfection prest,
Fond love as unperceived did fly,   15
   And in my bosom rest.

My passion with your beauty grew,
   And Cupid at my heart,
Still as his mother favour'd you,
   Threw a new flaming dart: 20

Each gloried in their wanton part;
   To make a lover, he
Employ'd the utmost of his art—
   To make a beauty, she.

Sir C. Sedley

82

COUNSEL TO GIRLS

Gather ye rose-buds while ye may,
   Old Time is still a-flying:
And this same flower that smiles to-day,
   To-morrow will be dying.

The glorious Lamp of Heaven, the Sun,   5
   The higher he 's a-getting
The sooner will his race be run,
   And nearer he 's to setting.

That age is best which is the first,
   When youth and blood are warmer;   10
But being spent, the worse, and worst
   Times, still succeed the former.

Then be not coy, but use your time;
   And while ye may, go marry:
For having lost but once your prime,   15
   You may for ever tarry.

R. Herrick

83

TO LUCASTA, ON GOING TO THE WARS

Tell me not, Sweet, I am unkind
   That from the nunnery
Of thy chaste breast and quiet mind
   To war and arms I fly.

> True, a new mistress now I chase, 5
> The first foe in the field;
> And with a stronger faith embrace
> A sword, a horse, a shield.
>
> Yet this inconstancy is such
> As you too shall adore; 10
> I could not love thee, Dear, so much,
> Loved I not Honour more.

Colonel Lovelace

84

ELIZABETH OF BOHEMIA

You meaner beauties of the night,
 That poorly satisfy our eyes
More by your number than your light,
 You common people of the skies,
What are you, when the Moon shall rise? 5

You curious chanters of the wood
 That warble forth dame Nature's lays,
Thinking your passions understood
 By your weak accents; what 's your praise
When Philomel her voice shall raise? 10

You violets that first appear,
 By your pure purple mantles known
Like the proud virgins of the year,
 As if the spring were all your own,—
What are you, when the Rose is blown? 15

So when my Mistress shall be seen
 In form and beauty of her mind,
By virtue first, then choice, a Queen,
 Tell me, if she were not design'd
Th' eclipse and glory of her kind? 20

Sir H. Wotton

85

TO THE LADY MARGARET LEY

Daughter to that good Earl, once President
  Of England's Council and her Treasury,
  Who lived in both, unstain'd with gold or fee,
And left them both, more in himself content,

Till the sad breaking of that Parliament   5
  Broke him, as that dishonest victory
  At Chaeronea, fatal to liberty,
Kill'd with report that old man eloquent;—

Though later born than to have known the days
  Wherein your father flourish'd, yet by you,   10
    Madam, methinks I see him living yet;

So well your words his noble virtues praise,
  That all both judge you to relate them true,
    And to possess them, honour'd Margaret.

                                                    J. Milton

86

THE LOVELINESS OF LOVE

It is not Beauty I demand,
  A crystal brow, the moon's despair,
Nor the snow's daughter, a white hand,
  Nor mermaid's yellow pride of hair:

Tell me not of your starry eyes,   5
  Your lips that seem on roses fed,
Your breasts, where Cupid trembling lies
  Nor sleeps for kissing of his bed:—

A bloomy pair of vermeil cheeks
  Like Hebe's in her ruddiest hours,   10
A breath that softer music speaks
  Than summer winds a-wooing flowers,

These are but gauds: nay, what are lips?
  Coral beneath the ocean-stream,
Whose brink when your adventurer sips   15
  Full oft he perisheth on them.

And what are cheeks, but ensigns oft
  That wave hot youth to fields of blood?
Did Helen's breast, though ne'er so soft,
  Do Greece or Ilium any good?   20

Eyes can with baleful ardour burn;
  Poison can breath, that erst perfumed;
There's many a white hand holds an urn
  With lovers' hearts to dust consumed.

For crystal brows—there's nought within;   25
  They are but empty cells for pride;
He who the Syren's hair would win
  Is mostly strangled in the tide.

Give me, instead of Beauty's bust,
  A tender heart, a loyal mind   30
Which with temptation I could trust,
  Yet never link'd with error find,—

One in whose gentle bosom I
  Could pour my secret heart of woes,
Like the care-burthen'd honey-fly   35
  That hides his murmurs in the rose,—

My earthly Comforter! whose love
  So indefeasible might be
That, when my spirit won above,
  Hers could not stay, for sympathy.   40

G. Darley

87

THE TRUE BEAUTY

He that loves a rosy cheek
  Or a coral lip admires,
Or from star-like eyes doth seek
  Fuel to maintain his fires;

As old Time makes these decay,   5
So his flames must waste away.

But a smooth and steadfast mind,
    Gentle thoughts, and calm desires,
Hearts with equal love combined,
    Kindle never-dying fires:—   10
Where these are not, I despise
Lovely cheeks or lips or eyes.

T. Carew

88

TO DIANEME

Sweet, be not proud of those two eyes
Which starlike sparkle in their skies;
Nor be you proud, that you can see
All hearts your captives; yours yet free:
Be you not proud of that rich hair   5
Which wantons with the lovesick air;
Whenas that ruby which you wear,
Sunk from the tip of your soft ear,
Will last to be a precious stone
When all your world of beauty 's gone.   10

R. Herrick

89

Go, lovely Rose!
Tell her, that wastes her time and me,
    That now she knows,
When I resemble her to thee,
How sweet and fair she seems to be.   5

Tell her that's young
And shuns to have her graces spied,
    That hadst thou sprung
In deserts, where no men abide,
Thou must have uncommended died.   10

Small is the worth
Of beauty from the light retired :
    Bid her come forth,
Suffer herself to be desired,
And not blush so to be admired.   15

    Then die ! that she
The common fate of all things rare
    May read in thee :
How small a part of time they share
That are so wondrous sweet and fair !   20
                                    E. Waller

90

TO CELIA

Drink to me only with thine eyes,
    And I will pledge with mine ;
Or leave a kiss but in the cup
    And I'll not look for wine.
The thirst that from the soul doth rise   5
    Doth ask a drink divine ;
But might I of Jove's nectar sup,
    I would not change for thine.

I sent thee late a rosy wreath,
    Not so much honouring thee   10
As giving it a hope that there
    It could not wither'd be ;
But thou thereon didst only breathe
    And sent'st it back to me ;
Since when it grows, and smells, I swear,   15
    Not of itself but thee !
                                    B. Jonson

91

CHERRY-RIPE

There is a garden in her face
    Where roses and white lilies grow ;
A heavenly paradise is that place,
    Wherein all pleasant fruits do flow ;

There cherries grow which none may buy,   5
Till 'Cherry-Ripe' themselves do cry.

Those cherries fairly do enclose
   Of orient pearl a double row,
Which when her lovely laughter shows,
   They look like rose-buds fill'd with snow: 10
Yet them nor peer nor prince can buy,
Till 'Cherry-Ripe' themselves do cry.

Her eyes like angels watch them still;
   Her brows like bended bows do stand,
Threat'ning with piercing frowns to kill   15
   All that attempt with eye or hand
Those sacred cherries to come nigh,
—Till 'Cherry-Ripe' themselves do cry!

T. Campion

92

THE POETRY OF DRESS

I

A sweet disorder in the dress
Kindles in clothes a wantonness:—
A lawn about the shoulders thrown
Into a fine distractión,—
An erring lace, which here and there   5
Enthrals the crimson stomacher,—
A cuff neglectful, and thereby
Ribbands to flow confusedly,—
A winning wave, deserving note,
In the tempestuous petticoat,—   10
A careless shoe-string, in whose tie
I see a wild civility,—
Do more bewitch me, than when art
Is too precise in every part.

R. Herrick

93

II

Whenas in silks my Julia goes
Then, then (methinks) how sweetly flows
That liquefaction of her clothes.

Next, when I cast mine eyes and see
That brave vibration each way free;   5
O how that glittering taketh me!

R. Herrick

94

III

My Love in her attire doth shew her wit,
    It doth so well become her:
For every season she hath dressings fit,
    For Winter, Spring, and Summer,
    No beauty she doth miss   5
        When all her robes are on:
    But Beauty's self she is
        When all her robes are gone.

Anon.

95

ON A GIRDLE

That which her slender waist confined
Shall now my joyful temples bind:
No monarch but would give his crown
His arms might do what this has done.

It was my Heaven's extremest sphere,   5
The pale which held that lovely deer:
My joy, my grief, my hope, my love
Did all within this circle move.

A narrow compass! and yet there
Dwelt all that's good, and all that's fair: 10
Give me but what this ribband bound,
Take all the rest the Sun goes round.

                                        E. Waller

96

TO ANTHEA WHO MAY COMMAND HIM
ANY THING

Bid me to live, and I will live
   Thy Protestant to be:
Or bid me love, and I will give
   A loving heart to thee.

A heart as soft, a heart as kind,   5
   A heart as sound and free
As in the whole world thou canst find,
   That heart I'll give to thee.

Bid that heart stay, and it will stay,
   To honour thy decree: 10
Or bid it languish quite away,
   And 't shall do so for thee.

Bid me to weep, and I will weep
   While I have eyes to see:
And, having none, yet I will keep   15
   A heart to weep for thee.

Bid me despair, and I'll despair
   Under that cypress tree:
Or bid me die, and I will dare
   E'en Death, to die for thee.   20

Thou art my life, my love, my heart,
   The very eyes of me,
And hast command of every part,
   To live and die for thee.

                                        R. Herrick

97

Love not me for comely grace,
For my pleasing eye or face,
Nor for any outward part,
No, nor for my constant heart,—
 For those may fail, or turn to ill,   5
 ·So thou and I shall sever:
Keep therefore a true woman's eye,
And love me still, but know not why—
 So hast thou the same reason still
  To doat upon me ever!   10

          Anon.

98

Not, Celia, that I juster am
 Or better than the rest;
For I would change each hour, like them,
 Were not my heart at rest.

But I am tied to very thee   5
 By every thought I have;
Thy face I only care to see,
 Thy heart I only crave.

All that in woman is adored
 In thy dear self I find—   10
For the whole sex can but afford
 The handsome and the kind.

Why then should I seek further store,
 And still make love anew?
When change itself can give no more,   15
 'Tis easy to be true.

        Sir C. Sedley

          D

99

TO ALTHEA FROM PRISON

When Love with unconfinéd wings
   Hovers within my gates,
And my divine Althea brings
   To whisper at the grates;
When I lie tangled in her hair   5
   And fetter'd to her eye,
The Gods that wanton in the air
   Know no such liberty.

When flowing cups run swiftly round
   With no allaying Thames,   10
Our careless heads with roses crown'd,
   Our hearts with loyal flames;
When thirsty grief in wine we steep,
   When healths and draughts go free—
Fishes that tipple in the deep   15
   Know no such liberty.

When, like committed linnets, I
   With shriller throat shall sing
The sweetness, mercy, majesty
   And glories of my King;   20
When I shall voice aloud how good
   He is, how great should be,
Enlargéd winds, that curl the flood,
   Know no such liberty.

Stone walls do not a prison make   25
   Nor iron bars a cage;
Minds innocent and quiet take
   That for an heritage:
If I have freedom in my love
   And in my soul am free,   30
Angels alone, that soar above,
   Enjoy such liberty.

Colonel Lovelace

TO LUCASTA, ON GOING BEYOND THE
SEAS

If to be absent were to be
  Away from thee;
 Or that when I am gone
 You or I were alone;
Then, my Lucasta, might I crave   5
Pity from blustering wind, or swallowing wave.

Though seas and land betwixt us both,
  Our faith and troth,
 Like separated souls,
 All time and space controls: 10
Above the highest sphere we meet
Unseen, unknown, and greet as Angels greet.

So then we do anticipate
  Our after-fate,
 And are alive i' the skies,   15
 If thus our lips and eyes
Can speak like spirits unconfined
In Heaven, their earthy bodies left behind.

Colonel Lovelace

ENCOURAGEMENTS TO A LOVER

Why so pale and wan, fond lover?
  Prythee, why so pale?
Will, when looking well can't move her,
  Looking ill prevail?
  Prythee, why so pale?   5

Why so dull and mute, young sinner?
    Prythee, why so mute?
Will, when speaking well can't win her,
    Saying nothing do't?
    Prythee, why so mute?   10

Quit, quit, for shame! this will not move,
    This cannot take her;
If of herself she will not love,
    Nothing can make her:
    The devil take her!   15

                                    Sir J. Suckling

102

A SUPPLICATION

    Awake, awake, my Lyre!
And tell thy silent master's humble tale
    In sounds that may prevail;
  Sounds that gentle thoughts inspire:
    Though so exalted she   5
    And I so lowly be,
Tell her, such different notes make all thy harmony.

    Hark! how the strings awake:
And, though the moving hand approach not near,
    Themselves with awful fear   10
  A kind of numerous trembling make.
    Now all thy forces try;
    Now all thy charms apply;
Revenge upon her ear the conquests of her eye.

    Weak Lyre! thy virtue sure   15
Is useless here, since thou art only found
    To cure, but not to wound,
  And she to wound, but not to cure.
    Too weak too wilt thou prove
    My passion to remove;   20
Physic to other ills, thou'rt nourishment to love.

Sleep, sleep again, my Lyre!
For thou canst never tell my humble tale
    In sounds that will prevail,
  Nor gentle thoughts in her inspire;   25
    All thy vain mirth lay by,
    Bid thy strings silent lie,
Sleep, sleep again, my Lyre, and let thy master die.

                            A. Cowley

103

THE MANLY HEART

  Shall I, wasting in despair,
  Die because a woman's fair?
  Or make pale my cheeks with care
  'Cause another's rosy are?
  Be she fairer than the day   5
  Or the flowery meads in May—
    If she think not well of me,
    What care I how fair she be?

  Shall my silly heart be pined
  'Cause I see a woman kind;   10
  Or a well disposéd nature
  Joinéd with a lovely feature?
  Be she meeker, kinder, than
  Turtle-dove or pelican,
    If she be not so to me,   15
    What care I how kind she be?

  Shall a woman's virtues move
  Me to perish for her love?
  Or her well-deservings known
  Make me quite forget mine own?   20
  Be she with that goodness blest
  Which may merit name of Best;
    If she be not such to me,
    What care I how good she be?

'Cause her fortune seems too high,   25
Shall I play the fool and die?
She that bears a noble mind
If not outward helps she find,
Thinks what with them he would do
That without them dares her woo;   30
  And unless that mind I see,
  What care I how great she be?

Great or good, or kind or fair,
I will ne'er the more despair;
If she love me, this believe,   35
I will die ere she shall grieve;
If she slight me when I woo,
I can scorn and let her go;
  For if she be not for me,
  What care I for whom she be?   40

          G. Wither

104

MELANCHOLY

Hence, all you vain delights,
As short as are the nights
 Wherein you spend your folly:
There's nought in this life sweet,
If man were wise to see't,   5
 But only melancholy,
 O sweetest melancholy!
Welcome, folded arms, and fixéd eyes,
A sigh that piercing mortifies,
A look that's fasten'd to the ground,   10
A tongue chain'd up without a sound!
Fountain heads and pathless groves,
Places which pale passion loves!
Moonlight walks, when all the fowls
Are warmly housed, save bats and owls!   15

A midnight bell, a parting groan—
  These are the sounds we feed upon;
Then stretch our bones in a still gloomy valley;
Nothing 's so dainty sweet as lovely melancholy.

J. Fletcher

105

TO A LOCK OF HAIR

Thy hue, dear pledge, is pure and bright
As in that well-remember'd night
When first thy mystic braid was wove,
And first my Agnes whisper'd love.

  Since then how often hast thou prest   5
The torrid zone of this wild breast,
Whose wrath and hate have sworn to dwell
With the first sin that peopled hell;
A breast whose blood 's a troubled ocean,
Each throb the earthquake's wild commotion!   10
O if such clime thou canst endure
Yet keep thy hue unstain'd and pure,
What conquest o'er each erring thought
Of that fierce realm had Agnes wrought!
I had not wander'd far and wide   15
With such an angel for my guide;
Nor heaven nor earth could then reprove me
If she had lived, and lived to love me.

  Not then this world's wild joys had been
To me one savage hunting scene,   20
My sole delight the headlong race
And frantic hurry of the chase;
To start, pursue, and bring to bay,
Rush in, drag down, and rend my prey,
Then—from the carcass turn away!   25
Mine ireful mood had sweetness tamed,
And soothed each wound which pride inflamed:—
Yes, God and man might now approve me
If thou hadst lived, and lived to love me!

Sir W. Scott

106

THE FORSAKEN BRIDE

O waly waly up the bank,
  And waly waly down the brae,
And waly waly yon burn-side
  Where I and my Love wont to gae!
I leant my back unto an aik,   5
  I thought it was a trusty tree;
But first it bow'd, and syne it brak,
  Sae my true Love did lichtly me.

O waly waly, but love be bonny
  A little time while it is new;   10
But when 'tis auld, it waxeth cauld
  And fades awa' like morning dew.
O wherefore should I busk my head?
  Or wherefore should I kame my hair?
For my true Love has me forsook,   15
  And says he'll never loe me mair.

Now Arthur-seat sall be my bed;
  The sheets shall ne'er be 'fil'd by me:
Saint Anton's well sall be my drink,
  Since my true Love has forsaken me.   20
Marti'mas wind, when wilt thou blaw
  And shake the green leaves aff the tree?
O gentle Death, when wilt thou come?
  For of my life I am wearíe.

'Tis not the frost, that freezes fell,   25
  Nor blawing snaw's inclemencie;
'Tis not sic cauld that makes me cry,
  But my Love's heart grown cauld to me.
When we came in by Glasgow town
  We were a comely sight to see;   30
My Love was clad in the black velvét,
  And I myself in cramasie.

But had I wist, before I kist,
   That love had been sae ill to win;
I had lockt my heart in a case of gowd   35
   And pinn'd it with a siller pin.
And, O! if my young babe were born,
   And set upon the nurse's knee,
And I mysell were dead and gane,
   For a maid again I'll never be.   40

Anon.

107

FAIR HELEN

I wish I were where Helen lies;
Night and day on me she cries;
O that I were where Helen lies
   On fair Kirconnell lea!

Curst be the heart that thought the thought,   5
And curst the hand that fired the shot,
When in my arms burd Helen dropt,
   And died to succour me!

O think na but my heart was sair
When my Love dropt down and spak nae mair!   10
I laid her down wi' meikle care
   On fair Kirconnell lea.

As I went down the water-side,
None but my foe to be my guide,
None but my foe to be my guide,   15
   On fair Kirconnell lea;

I lighted down my sword to draw,
I hackéd him in pieces sma',
I hackéd him in pieces sma',
   For her sake that died for me.   20

O Helen fair, beyond compare!
I'll make a garland of thy hair
Shall bind my heart for evermair
   Until the day I die.

D*

O that I were where Helen lies!   25
Night and day on me she cries;
Out of my bed she bids me rise,
    Says, 'Haste and come to me!'

O Helen fair! O Helen chaste!
If I were with thee, I were blest,   30
Where thou lies low and takes thy rest
    On fair Kirconnell lea.

I wish my grave were growing green,
A winding-sheet drawn ower my een,
And I in Helen's arms lying,   35
    On fair Kirconnell lea.

I wish I were where Helen lies;
Night and day on me she cries;
And I am weary of the skies,
    Since my Love died for me.   40

Anon.

108

THE TWA CORBIES

As I was walking all alane
 I heard twa corbies making a mane;
The tane unto the t'other say,
'Where sall we gang and dine to-day?'

'—In behint yon auld fail dyke,   5
I wot there lies a new-slain Knight;
And naebody kens that he lies there,
But his hawk, his hound, and lady fair.

'His hound is to the hunting gane,
His hawk to fetch the wild-fowl hame,   10
His lady's ta'en another mate,
So we may make our dinner sweet.

'Ye'll sit on his white hause-bane,
And I'll pick out his bonny blue een:
Wi' ae lock o' his gowden hair   15
We'll theek our nest when it grows bare.

'Mony a one for him makes mane,
But nane sall ken where he is gane;
O'er his white banes, when they are bare,
The wind sall blaw for evermair.'   20

Anon.

109

TO BLOSSOMS

Fair pledges of a fruitful tree,
   Why do ye fall so fast?
   Your date is not so past,
But you may stay yet here awhile
   To blush and gently smile,   5
      And go at last.

What, were ye born to be
   An hour or half's delight,
   And so to bid good-night?
'Twas pity Nature brought ye forth   10
   Merely to show your worth,
      And lose you quite.

But you are lovely leaves, where we
   May read how soon things have
   Their end, though ne'er so brave: 15
And after they have shown their pride
   Like you awhile, they glide
      Into the grave.

R. Herrick

110

TO DAFFODILS

Fair Daffodils, we weep to see
   You haste away so soon:
As yet the early-rising Sun
   Has not attain'd his noon.

Stay, stay,   5
Until the hasting day
Has run
But to the even-song;
And, having pray'd together, we
Will go with you along.   10

We have short time to stay, as you,
We have as short a Spring;
As quick a growth to meet decay
As you, or any thing.
We die,   15
As your hours do, and dry
Away
Like to the Summer's rain;
Or as the pearls of morning's dew,
Ne'er to be found again.   20

R. Herrick

III

THOUGHTS IN A GARDEN

How vainly men themselves amaze
To win the palm, the oak, or bays,
And their uncessant labours see
Crown'd from some single herb or tree,
Whose short and narrow-vergéd shade   5
Does prudently their toils upbraid;
While all the flowers and trees do close
To weave the garlands of repose.

Fair Quiet, have I found thee here,
And Innocence thy sister dear!   10
Mistaken long, I sought you then
In busy companies of men:
Your sacred plants, if here below,
Only among the plants will grow:
Society is all but rude   15
To this delicious solitude.

No white nor red was ever seen
So amorous as this lovely green.
Fond lovers, cruel as their flame,
Cut in these trees their mistress' name: 20
Little, alas, they know or heed
How far these beauties hers exceed!
Fair trees! wheres'e'er your barks I wound,
No name shall but your own be found.

When we have run our passions' heat   25
Love hither makes his best retreat:
The gods, that mortal beauty chase,
Still in a tree did end their race:
Apollo hunted Daphne so,
Only that she might laurel grow: 30
And Pan did after Syrinx speed
Not as a nymph, but for a reed.

What wondrous life in this I lead!
Ripe apples drop about my head;
The luscious clusters of the vine   35
Upon my mouth do crush their wine;
The nectarine and curious peach
Into my hands themselves do reach;
Stumbling on melons, as I pass,
Ensnared with flowers, I fall on grass.   40

Meanwhile the mind, from pleasure less,
Withdraws into its happiness;
The mind, that ocean where each kind
Does straight its own resemblance find;
Yet it creates, transcending these,   45
Far other worlds, and other seas;
Annihilating all that 's made
To a green thought in a green shade.

Here at the fountain's sliding foot
Or at some fruit-tree's mossy root,   50
Casting the body's vest aside,
My soul into the boughs does glide;

There, like a bird, it sits and sings,
Then whets and combs its silver wings,
And, till prepared for longer flight,   55
Waves in its plumes the various light.

Such was that happy Garden-state
While man there walk'd without a mate:
After a place so pure and sweet,
What other help could yet be meet!   60
But 'twas beyond a mortal's share
To wander solitary there:
Two paradises 'twere in one,
To live in Paradise alone.

How well the skilful gardener drew   65
Of flowers and herbs this dial new!
Where, from above, the milder sun
Does through a fragrant zodiac run:
And, as it works, th' industrious bee
Computes its time as well as we.   70
How could such sweet and wholesome hours
Be reckon'd, but with herbs and flowers!

A. Marvell

112

L'ALLÉGRO

Hence, loathéd Melancholy,
Of Cerberus and blackest Midnight born
    In Stygian cave forlorn
'Mongst horrid shapes, and shrieks, and sights unholy!
    Find out some uncouth cell,   5
Where brooding Darkness spreads his jealous wings
    And the night-raven sings;
There, under ebon shades and low-brow'd rocks
    As ragged as thy locks,
In dark Cimmerian desert ever dwell.   10

    But come, thou Goddess fair and free,
    In heaven yclep'd Euphrosyne,

And by men, heart-easing Mirth,
Whom lovely Venus at a birth
With two sister Graces more   15
To ivy-crownéd Bacchus bore:
Or whether (as some sager sing)
The frolic wind that breathes the spring,
Zephyr, with Aurora playing,
As he met her once a-Maying—   20
There on beds of violets blue
And fresh-blown roses wash'd in dew
Fill'd her with thee, a daughter fair,
So buxom, blithe, and debonair.
    Haste thee, Nymph, and bring with thee   25
Jest, and youthful jollity,
Quips, and cranks, and wanton wiles,
Nods, and becks, and wreathéd smiles,
Such as hang on Hebe's cheek,
And love to live in dimple sleek;   30
Sport that wrinkled Care derides,
And Laughter holding both his sides.
Come, and trip it as you go
On the light fantastic toe;
And in thy right hand lead with thee   35
The mountain nymph, sweet Liberty;
And if I give thee honour due,
Mirth, admit me of thy crew,
To live with her, and live with thee
In unreprovéd pleasures free;   40
To hear the lark begin his flight
And singing startle the dull night
From his watch-tower in the skies,
Till the dappled dawn doth rise;
Then to come, in spite of sorrow,   45
And at my window bid good-morrow
Through the sweetbriar, or the vine,
Or the twisted eglantine:
While the cock with lively din
Scatters the rear of darkness thin,   50
And to the stack, or the barn-door,
Stoutly struts his dames before:

Oft listening how the hounds and horn
Cheerly rouse the slumbering morn,
From the side of some hoar hill,   55
Through the high wood echoing shrill.
Sometime walking, not unseen,
By hedge-row elms, on hillocks green,
Right against the eastern gate
Where the great Sun begins his state   60
Robed in flames and amber light,
The clouds in thousand liveries dight;
While the ploughman, near at hand,
Whistles o'er the furrow'd land,
And the milkmaid singeth blithe,   65
And the mower whets his scythe,
And every shepherd tells his tale
Under the hawthorn in the dale.
    Straight mine eye hath caught new pleasures
Whilst the landscape round it measures;   70
Russet lawns, and fallows grey,
Where the nibbling flocks do stray;
Mountains, on whose barren breast
The labouring clouds do often rest;
Meadows trim with daisies pied,   75
Shallow brooks, and rivers wide;
Towers and battlements it sees
Bosom'd high in tufted trees,
Where perhaps some Beauty lies,
The Cynosure of neighbouring eyes.   80
    Hard by, a cottage chimney smokes
From betwixt two aged oaks,
Where Corydon and Thyrsis, met,
Are at their savoury dinner set
Of herbs, and other country messes   85
Which the neat-handed Phillis dresses;
And then in haste her bower she leaves
With Thestylis to bind the sheaves;
Or, if the earlier season lead,
To the tann'd haycock in the mead.   90
    Sometimes with secure delight
The upland hamlets will invite,

When the merry bells ring round,
And the jocund rebecks sound
To many a youth and many a maid,   95
Dancing in the chequer'd shade;
And young and old come forth to play
On a sunshine holy-day,
Till the live-long daylight fail:
Then to the spicy nut-brown ale,   100
With stories told of many a feat,
How Faery Mab the junkets eat;
She was pinch'd, and pull'd, she said;
And he, by Friar's lantern led;
Tells how the drudging Goblin sweat   105
To earn his cream-bowl duly set,
When in one night, ere glimpse of morn,
His shadowy flail hath thresh'd the corn
That ten day-labourers could not end;
Then lies him down the lubber fiend,   110
And, stretch'd out all the chimney's length,
Basks at the fire his hairy strength;
And crop-full out of doors he flings,
Ere the first cock his matin rings.
Thus done the tales, to bed they creep,   115
By whispering winds soon lull'd asleep.
    Tower'd cities please us then
And the busy hum of men,
Where throngs of knights and barons bold,
In weeds of peace high triumphs hold,   120
With store of ladies, whose bright eyes
Rain influence, and judge the prize
Of wit or arms, while both contend
To win her grace, whom all commend.
There let Hymen oft appear   125
In saffron robe, with taper clear,
And pomp, and feast, and revelry,
With mask, and antique pageantry;
Such sights as youthful poets dream
On summer eves by haunted stream.   130
Then to the well-trod stage anon,
If Jonson's learned sock be on,

Or sweetest Shakespeare, Fancy's child,
Warble his native wood-notes wild.
   And ever against eating cares   135
Lap me in soft Lydian airs
Married to immortal verse,
Such as the meeting soul may pierce
In notes, with many a winding bout
Of linkéd sweetness long drawn out,   140
With wanton heed and giddy cunning,
The melting voice through mazes running,
Untwisting all the chains that tie
The hidden soul of harmony;
That Orpheus' self may heave his head   145
From golden slumber, on a bed
Of heap'd Elysian flowers, and hear
Such strains as would have won the ear
Of Pluto, to have quite set free
His half-regain'd Eurydice.   150

    These delights if thou canst give,
Mirth, with thee I mean to live.

                            J. Milton

113

IL PENSEROSO

    Hence, vain deluding Joys,
The brood of Folly without father bred!
    How little you bestead
Or fill the fixéd mind with all your toys!
    Dwell in some idle brain,   5
And fancies fond with gaudy shapes possess
    As thick and numberless
As the gay motes that people the sunbeams,
    Or likest hovering dreams
The fickle pensioners of Morpheus' train.   10

    But hail, thou goddess sage and holy,
Hail, divinest Melancholy!

Whose saintly visage is too bright
To hit the sense of human sight,
And therefore to our weaker view   15
O'erlaid with black, staid Wisdom's hue;
Black, but such as in esteem
Prince Memnon's sister might beseem,
Or that starr'd Ethiop queen that strove
To set her beauty's praise above   20
The sea-nymphs, and their powers offended:
Yet thou art higher far descended:
Thee bright-hair'd Vesta, long of yore,
To solitary Saturn bore;
His daughter she; in Saturn's reign   25
Such mixture was not held a stain:
Oft in glimmering bowers and glades
He met her, and in secret shades
Of woody Ida's inmost grove,
Whilst yet there was no fear of Jove.   30
   Come, pensive nun, devout and pure,
Sober, steadfast, and demure,
All in a robe of darkest grain
Flowing with majestic train,
And sable stole of cypres lawn   35
Over thy decent shoulders drawn
Come, but keep thy wonted state,
With even step, and musing gait,
And looks commercing with the skies,
Thy rapt soul sitting in thine eyes: 40
There, held in holy passion still,
Forget thyself to marble, till
With a sad leaden downward cast
Thou fix them on the earth as fast:
And join with thee calm Peace, and Quiet,   45
Spare Fast, that oft with gods doth diet,
And hears the Muses in a ring
Ay round about Jove's altar sing:
And add to these retired Leisure
That in trim gardens takes his pleasure:—   50
But first, and chiefest, with thee bring
Him that yon soars on golden wing

Guiding the fiery-wheeléd throne,
The cherub Contemplatión;
And the mute Silence hist along,   55
'Less Philomel will deign a song
In her sweetest saddest plight,
Smoothing the rugged brow of Night,
While Cynthia checks her dragon yoke
Gently o'er the accustom'd oak.   60
—Sweet bird, that shunn'st the noise of folly,
Most musical, most melancholy!
Thee, chauntress, oft, the woods among
I woo, to hear thy even-song;
And missing thee, I walk unseen   65
On the dry smooth-shaven green,
To behold the wandering Moon
Riding near her highest noon,
Like one that had been led astray
Through the heaven's wide pathless way,   70
And oft, as if her head she bow'd,
Stooping through a fleecy cloud.
    Oft, on a plat of rising ground
I hear the far-off curfeu sound
Over some wide-water'd shore,   75
Swinging slow with sullen roar:
Or, if the air will not permit,
Some still removéd place will fit,
Where glowing embers through the room
Teach light to counterfeit a gloom;   80
Far from all resort of mirth,
Save the cricket on the hearth,
Or the bellman's drowsy charm
To bless the doors from nightly harm.
    Or let my lamp at midnight hour   85
Be seen in some high lonely tower,
Where I may oft out-watch the Bear
With thrice-great Hermes, or unsphere
The spirit of Plato, to unfold
What worlds or what vast regions hold   90
The immortal mind, that hath forsook
Her mansion in this fleshly nook:

And of those demons that are found
In fire, air, flood, or under ground,
Whose power hath a true consent   95
With planet, or with element.
Sometime let gorgeous Tragedy
In scepter'd pall come sweeping by,
Presenting Thebes, or Pelops' line,
Or the tale of Troy divine;   100
Or what (though rare) of later age
Ennobled hath the buskin'd stage.
   But, O sad Virgin, that thy power
Might raise Musaeus from his bower,
Or bid the soul of Orpheus sing   105
Such notes as, warbled to the string,
Drew iron tears down Pluto's cheek
And made Hell grant what Love did seek!
Or call up him that left half-told
The story of Cambuscan bold,   110
Of Camball, and of Algarsife,
And who had Canacé to wife,
That own'd the virtuous ring and glass;
And of the wondrous horse of brass
On which the Tartar king did ride: 115
And if aught else great bards beside
In sage and solemn tunes have sung
Of turneys, and of trophies hung,
Of forests, and enchantments drear,
Where more is meant than meets the ear.   120
   Thus, Night, oft see me in thy pale career,
Till civil-suited Morn appear,
Not trick'd and frounced as she was wont
With the Attic Boy to hunt,
But kercheft in a comely cloud   125
While rocking winds are piping loud,
Or usher'd with a shower still,
When the gust hath blown his fill,
Ending on the rustling leaves
With minute drops from off the eaves.   130
And when the sun begins to fling
His flaring beams, me, goddess, bring

To archéd walks of twilight groves,
And shadows brown, that Sylvan loves,
Of pine, or monumental oak,   135
Where the rude axe, with heavéd stroke,
Was never heard the nymphs to daunt
Or fright them from their hallow'd haunt.
There in close covert by some brook
Where no profaner eye may look,   140
Hide me from day's garish eye,
While the bee with honey'd thigh,
That at her flowery work doth sing,
And the waters murmuring,
With such consort as they keep   145
Entice the dewy-feather'd Sleep;
And let some strange mysterious dream
Wave at his wings in airy stream
Of lively portraiture display'd,
Softly on my eyelids laid: 150
And, as I wake, sweet music breathe
Above, about, or underneath,
Sent by some Spirit to mortals good,
Or the unseen Genius of the wood.
    But let my due feet never fail   155
To walk the studious cloister's pale,
And love the high-embowéd roof,
With antique pillars massy-proof,
And storied windows richly dight
Casting a dim religious light: 160
There let the pealing organ blow
To the full-voiced quire below
In service high and anthems clear,
As may with sweetness, through mine ear,
Dissolve me into ecstasies,   165
And bring all Heaven before mine eyes.
    And may at last my weary age
Find out the peaceful hermitage,
The hairy gown and mossy cell
Where I may sit and rightly spell   170
Of every star that heaven doth show,
And every herb that sips the dew;

Till old experience do attain
To something like prophetic strain.

These pleasures, Melancholy, give,   175
And I with thee will choose to live.

J. Milton

114

SONG OF THE EMIGRANTS IN BERMUDA

Where the remote Bermudas ride
In the ocean's bosom unespied,
From a small boat that row'd along
The listening winds received this song:
    'What should we do but sing His praise   5
That led us through the watery maze
Unto an isle so long unknown,
And yet far kinder than our own?
Where He the huge sea-monsters wracks,
That lift the deep upon their backs,   10
He lands us on a grassy stage,
Safe from the storms and prelate's rage:
He gave us this eternal spring
Which here enamels everything,
And sends the fowls to us in care   15
On daily visits through the air;
He hangs in shades the orange bright
Like golden lamps in a green night,
And does in the pomegranates close
Jewels more rich than Ormus shows: 20
He makes the figs our mouths to meet,
And throws the melons at our feet;
But apples plants of such a price,
No tree could ever bear them twice.
With cedars chosen by His hand   25
From Lebanon He stores the land;
And makes the hollow seas that roar
Proclaim the ambergris on shore.
He cast (of which we rather boast)
The Gospel's pearl upon our coast;   30

And in these rocks for us did frame
A temple where to sound His name.
Oh! let our voice His praise exalt
Till it arrive at Heaven's vault,
Which thence (perhaps) rebounding may   35
Echo beyond the Mexique bay!'
Thus sung they in the English boat
An holy and a cheerful note:
And all the way, to guide their chime,
With falling oars they kept the time.   40

A. Marvell

115

AT A SOLEMN MUSIC

Blest pair of Sirens, pledges of Heaven's joy,
   Sphere-born harmonious Sisters, Voice and Verse!
Wed your divine sounds, and mixt power employ
   Dead things with inbreathed sense able to pierce;
And to our high-raised phantasy present   5
That undisturbéd Song of pure concent
Ay sung before the sapphire-colour'd throne
      To Him that sits thereon,
With saintly shout and solemn jubilee;
Where the bright Seraphim in burning row   10
Their loud uplifted angel-trumpets blow;
And the Cherubic host in thousand quires
Touch their immortal harps of golden wires,
With those just Spirits that wear victorious palms,
      Hymns devout and holy psalms   15
      Singing everlastingly:
That we on earth, with undiscording voice
May rightly answer that melodious noise;
As once we did, till disproportion'd sin
Jarr'd against nature's chime, and with harsh din   20
Broke the fair music that all creatures made
To their great Lord, whose love their motion sway'd
In perfect diapason, whilst they stood
In first obedience, and their state of good.

O may we soon again renew that Song,   25
And keep in tune with Heaven, till God ere long
To His celestial consort us unite,
To live with Him, and sing in endless morn of light.

J. Milton

116

ALEXANDER'S FEAST, OR, THE POWER OF MUSIC

'Twas at the royal feast for Persia won
  By Philip's warlike son—
  Aloft in awful state
  The godlike hero sate
  On his imperial throne;   5
 His valiant peers were placed around,
Their brows with roses and with myrtles bound
  (So should desert in arms be crown'd);
  The lovely Thais by his side
  Sate like a blooming eastern bride   10
  In flower of youth and beauty's pride:—
   Happy, happy, happy pair!
    None but the brave
    None but the brave
  None but the brave deserves the fair!   15

  Timotheus placed on high
  Amid the tuneful quire
With flying fingers touch'd the lyre:
The trembling notes ascend the sky
  And heavenly joys inspire.   20
 The song began from Jove
Who left his blissful seats above—
Such is the power of mighty love!
A dragon's fiery form belied the god;
Sublime on radiant spires he rode   25
When he to fair Olympia prest,
And while he sought her snowy breast,

Then round her slender waist he curl'd,
And stamp'd an image of himself, a sovereign of the
    world.
—The listening crowd admire the lofty sound;   30
A present deity! they shout around:
A present deity! the vaulted roofs rebound:
        With ravish'd ears
        The monarch hears,
        Assumes the god,   35
        Affects to nod
    And seems to shake the spheres.

The praise of Bacchus then the sweet musician sung,
    Of Bacchus ever fair and ever young:
      The jolly god in triumph comes!   40
      Sound the trumpets, beat the drums!
        Flush'd with a purple grace
        He shows his honest face:
Now give the hautboys breath; he comes, he comes!
      Bacchus, ever fair and young,   45
      Drinking joys did first ordain;
      Bacchus' blessings are a treasure,
      Drinking is the soldier's pleasure:
        Rich the treasure,
        Sweet the pleasure,   50
      Sweet is pleasure after pain.

  Soothed with the sound, the king grew vain;
  Fought all his battles o'er again,
And thrice he routed all his foes, and thrice he slew the
    slain.
The master saw the madness rise,   55
His glowing cheeks, his ardent eyes;
And while he Heaven and Earth defied
Changed his hand and check'd his pride.
    He chose a mournful Muse
    Soft pity to infuse: 60
He sung Darius great and good,
    By too severe a fate
Fallen, fallen, fallen, fallen,
    Fallen from his high estate,

And weltering in his blood;   65
Deserted, at his utmost need,
By those his former bounty fed;
On the bare earth exposed he lies
With not a friend to close his eyes.
—With downcast looks the joyless victor sate,   70
Revolving in his alter'd soul
  The various turns of Chance below;
And now and then a sigh he stole,
  And tears began to flow.

The mighty master smiled to see   75
That love was in the next degree;
'Twas but a kindred-sound to move,
For pity melts the mind to love.
Softly sweet, in Lydian measures
Soon he soothed his soul to pleasures.   80
War, he sung, is toil and trouble,
Honour but an empty bubble;
Never ending, still beginning,
  Fighting still, and still destroying;
If the world be worth thy winning,   85
  Think, O think, it worth enjoying:
Lovely Thais sits beside thee,
Take the good the gods provide thee!
—The many rend the skies with loud applause;
So Love was crown'd, but Music won the cause.   90
The prince, unable to conceal his pain,
    Gazed on the fair
    Who caused his care,
And sigh'd and look'd, sigh'd and look'd,
Sigh'd and look'd, and sigh'd again: 95
At length with love and wine at once opprest
The vanquish'd victor sunk upon her breast.

Now strike the golden lyre again:
A louder yet, and yet a louder strain!
Break his bands of sleep asunder   100
And rouse him like a rattling peal of thunder.
Hark, hark! the horrid sound
  Has raised up his head:

As awaked from the dead
And amazed he stares around.   105
Revenge, revenge, Timotheus cries,
See the Furies arise!
  See the snakes that they rear
  How they hiss in their hair,
And the sparkles that flash from their eyes!   110
    Behold a ghastly band,
    Each a torch in his hand!
Those are Grecian ghosts, that in battle were slain
    And unburied remain
    Inglorious on the plain: 115
    Give the vengeance due
    To the valiant crew!
Behold how they toss their torches on high,
How they point to the Persian abodes
And glittering temples of their hostile gods.   120
—The princes applaud with a furious joy:
And the King seized a flambeau with zeal to destroy;
    Thais led the way
    To light him to his prey,
And like another Helen, fired another Troy!   125

    —Thus, long ago,
Ere heaving bellows learn'd to blow,
  While organs yet were mute,
  Timotheus, to his breathing flute
    And sounding lyre,   130
Could swell the soul to rage, or kindle soft desire.
  At last divine Cecilia came,
  Inventress of the vocal frame;
The sweet enthusiast from her sacred store
  Enlarged the former narrow bounds,   135
  And added length to solemn sounds,
With Nature's mother-wit, and arts unknown before.
  —Let old Timotheus yield the prize
  Or both divide the crown;
He raised a mortal to the skies;   140
  She drew an angel down!

                      J. Dryden

THE GOLDEN TREASURY

BOOK THIRD

ODE ON THE PLEASURE ARISING FROM VICISSITUDE

Now the golden Morn aloft
  Waves her dew-bespangled wing,
With vermeil cheek and whisper soft
  She woos the tardy Spring:
Till April starts, and calls around   5
The sleeping fragrance from the ground,
And lightly o'er the living scene
Scatters his freshest, tenderest green.

New-born flocks, in rustic dance,
  Frisking ply their feeble feet;   10
Forgetful of their wintry trance
  The birds his presence greet:
But chief, the sky-lark warbles high
His trembling thrilling ecstasy;
And lessening from the dazzled sight,   15
Melts into air and liquid light.

Yesterday the sullen year
  Saw the snowy whirlwind fly;
Mute was the music of the air,
  The herd stood drooping by: 20
Their raptures now that wildly flow
No yesterday nor morrow know;
'Tis Man alone that joy descries
With forward and reverted eyes.

Smiles on past Misfortune's brow   25
   Soft Reflection's hand can trace,
And o'er the cheek of Sorrow throw
   A melancholy grace;
While Hope prolongs our happier hour,
Or deepest shades, that dimly lour   30
And blacken round our weary way,
Gilds with a gleam of distant day.

Still, where rosy Pleasure leads,
   See a kindred Grief pursue;
Behind the steps that Misery treads   35
   Approaching Comfort view:
The hues of bliss more brightly glow
Chastised by sabler tints of woe,
And blended form, with artful strife,
The strength and harmony of life.   40

See the wretch that long has tost
   On the thorny bed of pain,
At length repair his vigour lost
   And breathe and walk again:
The meanest floweret of the vale,   45
The simplest note that swells the gale,
The common sun, the air, the skies,
To him are opening Paradise.
                            T. Gray

118

THE QUIET LIFE

Happy the man, whose wish and care
   A few paternal acres bound,
Content to breathe his native air
          In his own ground.

Whose herds with milk, whose fields with bread,   5
   Whose flocks supply him with attire;
Whose trees in summer yield him shade,
          In winter fire.

Blest, who can unconcern'dly find
    Hours, days, and years slide soft away   10
In health of body, peace of mind,
            Quiet by day,

Sound sleep by night; study and ease
    Together mix'd; sweet recreation,
And innocence, which most does please   15
           With meditation.

Thus let me live, unseen, unknown;
    Thus unlamented let me die;
Steal from the world, and not a stone
           Tell where I lie.   20

                    A. Pope

119

THE BLIND BOY

O say what is that thing call'd Light,
    Which I must ne'er enjoy;
What are the blessings of the sight,
    O tell your poor blind boy!

You talk of wondrous things you see,   5
    You say the sun shines bright;
I feel him warm, but how can he
    Or make it day or night?

My day or night myself I make
    Whene'er I sleep or play;   10
And could I ever keep awake
    With me 'twere always day.

With heavy sighs I often hear
    You mourn my hapless woe;
But sure with patience I can bear   15
    A loss I ne'er can know.

Then let not what I cannot have
    My cheer of mind destroy:
Whilst thus I sing, I am a king,
    Although a poor blind boy.   20

                  C. Cibber

120

ON A FAVOURITE CAT, DROWNED IN A TUB OF GOLDFISHES

'Twas on a lofty vase's side,
Where China's gayest art had dyed
  The azure flowers that blow,
Demurest of the tabby kind,
The pensive Selima, reclined,   5
  Gazed on the lake below.

Her conscious tail her joy declared:
The fair round face, the snowy beard,
  The velvet of her paws,
Her coat that with the tortoise vies,   10
Her ears of jet, and emerald eyes,
  She saw; and purr'd applause.

Still had she gazed, but 'midst the tide
Two angel forms were seen to glide,
  The Genii of the stream: 15
Their scaly armour's Tyrian hue
Through richest purple to the view
  Betray'd a golden gleam.

The hapless Nymph with wonder saw:
A whisker first, and then a claw   20
  With many an ardent wish
She stretch'd, in vain, to reach the prize—
What female heart can gold despise?
  What Cat 's averse to Fish?

Presumptuous maid! with looks intent   25
Again she stretch'd, again she bent,
  Nor knew the gulf between—
Malignant Fate sat by and smiled—
The slippery verge her feet beguiled;
  She tumbled headlong in!   30

Eight times emerging from the flood
She mew'd to every watery God
   Some speedy aid to send:—
No Dolphin came, no Nereid stirr'd,
Nor cruel Tom nor Susan heard—   35
   A favourite has no friend!

From hence, ye Beauties, undeceived,
Know one false step is ne'er retrieved,
   And be with caution bold:
Not all that tempts your wandering eyes   40
And heedless hearts, is lawful prize,
   Nor all that glisters, gold!

T. Gray

121

TO CHARLOTTE PULTENEY

Timely blossom, Infant fair,
Fondling of a happy pair,
Every morn and every night
Their solicitous delight,
Sleeping, waking, still at ease,   5
Pleasing, without skill to please;
Little gossip, blithe and hale,
Tattling many a broken tale,
Singing many a tuneless song,
Lavish of a heedless tongue;   10
Simple maiden, void of art,
Babbling out the very heart,
Yet abandon'd to thy will,
Yet imagining no ill,
Yet too innocent to blush;   15
Like the linnet in the bush
To the mother-linnet's note
Moduling her slender throat;
Chirping forth thy petty joys,
Wanton in the change of toys,   20
Like the linnet green, in May
Flitting to each bloomy spray;

Wearied then and glad of rest,
Like the linnet in the nest:—
This thy present happy lot,   25
This, in time will be forgot:
Other pleasures, other cares,
Ever-busy Time prepares;
And thou shalt in thy daughter see,
This picture, once, resembled thee.   30
A. Philips

122

RULE, BRITANNIA

When Britain first at Heaven's command
    Arose from out the azure main,
This was the charter of the land,
    And guardian angels sung this strain:
Rule, Britannia! rule the waves!   5
    Britons never will be slaves.

The nations not so blest as thee
    Must in their turns to tyrants fall,
While thou shalt flourish great and free,
    The dread and envy of them all.   10

Still more majestic shalt thou rise,
    More dreadful from each foreign stroke;
As the loud blast that tears the skies
    Serves but to root thy native oak.

Thee haughty tyrants ne'er shall tame;   15
    All their attempts to bend thee down
Will but arouse thy generous flame,
    But work their woe and thy renown.

To thee belongs the rural reign;
    Thy cities shall with commerce shine;   20
All thine shall be the subject main,
    And every shore it circles thine!

The Muses, still with Freedom found,
    Shall to thy happy coast repair;

Blest Isle, with matchless beauty crown'd, 25
    And manly hearts to guard the fair:—
Rule, Britannia! rule the waves!
    Britons never will be slaves!

J. Thomson

123

THE BARD

A Pindaric Ode

'Ruin seize thee, ruthless King!
    Confusion on thy banners wait!
Tho' fann'd by Conquest's crimson wing
    They mock the air with idle state.
Helm, nor hauberk's twisted mail, 5
Nor e'en thy virtues, tyrant, shall avail
To save thy secret soul from nightly fears,
From Cambria's curse, from Cambria's tears!'
—Such were the sounds that o'er the crested pride
    Of the first Edward scatter'd wild dismay, 10
As down the steep of Snowdon's shaggy side
    He wound with toilsome march his long array:—
Stout Glo'ster stood aghast in speechless trance;
'To arms!' cried Mortimer, and couch'd his quivering
    lance.

On a rock, whose haughty brow 15
Frowns o'er old Conway's foaming flood,
    Robed in the sable garb of woe,
With haggard eyes the Poet stood;
(Loose his beard and hoary hair
Stream'd like a meteor to the troubled air;) 20
And with a master's hand and prophet's fire
Struck the deep sorrows of his lyre:
'Hark, how each giant oak and desert cave
    Sighs to the torrent's awful voice beneath!
O'er thee, O King, their hundred arms they wave, 25
    Revenge on thee in hoarser murmurs breathe;

Vocal no more, since Cambria's fatal day,
To high-born Hoel's harp, or soft Llewellyn's lay.

'Cold is Cadwallo's tongue,
   That hush'd the stormy main: 30
Brave Urien sleeps upon his craggy bed:
   Mountains, ye mourn in vain
   Modred, whose magic song
Made huge Plinlimmon bow his cloud-topt head.
   On dreary Arvon's shore they lie   35
Smear'd with gore and ghastly pale:
Far, far aloof the affrighted ravens sail;
   The famish'd eagle screams, and passes by.
Dear lost companions of my tuneful art,
   Dear as the light that visits these sad eyes,   40
Dear as the ruddy drops that warm my heart,
   Ye died amidst your dying country's cries—
No more I weep. They do not sleep;
   On yonder cliffs, a griesly band,
I see them sit; they linger yet,   45
   Avengers of their native land:
With me in dreadful harmony they join,
And weave with bloody hands the tissue of thy line.'

"Weave the warp and weave the woof,
   The winding-sheet of Edward's race: 50
Give ample room and verge enough
   The characters of hell to trace.
Mark the year and mark the night
When Severn shall re-echo with affright
The shrieks of death thro' Berkley's roofs that ring,
Shrieks of an agonizing king!   56
   She-wolf of France, with unrelenting fangs
That tear'st the bowels of thy mangled mate,
   From thee be born, who o'er thy country hangs
The scourge of Heaven! What terrors round him
     wait!   60
Amazement in his van, with Flight combined,
And Sorrow's faded form, and Solitude behind.

"Mighty victor, mighty lord,
   Low on his funeral couch he lies!

No pitying heart, no eye, afford 65
   A tear to grace his obsequies.
Is the sable warrior fled?
Thy son is gone.   He rests among the dead.
The swarm that in thy noon-tide beam were born?
—Gone to salute the rising morn. 70
Fair laughs the Morn, and soft the zephyr blows,
   While proudly riding o'er the azure realm
In gallant trim the gilded Vessel goes:
   Youth on the prow, and Pleasure at the helm:
Regardless of the sweeping Whirlwind's sway, 75
That, hush'd in grim repose, expects his evening prey.

   "Fill high the sparkling bowl,
The rich repast prepare;
   Reft of a crown, he yet may share the feast:
Close by the regal chair 80
   Fell Thirst and Famine scowl
   A baleful smile upon their baffled guest.
Heard ye the din of battle bray,
   Lance to lance, and horse to horse?
   Long years of havoc urge their destined course, 85
And thro' the kindred squadrons mow their way.
   Ye towers of Julius, London's lasting shame,
With many a foul and midnight murder fed,
   Revere his Consort's faith, his Father's fame,
And spare the meek usurper's holy head! 90
Above, below, the rose of snow
   Twined with her blushing foe, we spread:
The bristled boar in infant-gore
   Wallows beneath the thorny shade.
Now, brothers, bending o'er the accursèd loom, 95
Stamp we our vengeance deep, and ratify his doom.

"Edward, lo! to sudden fate
   (Weave we the woof; The thread is spun;)
Half of thy heart we consecrate.
   (The web is wove; The work is done.)" 100
'Stay, O stay! nor thus forlorn
Leave me unbless'd, unpitied, here to mourn:

In yon bright track that fires the western skies
They melt, they vanish from my eyes.   104
But O! what solemn scenes on Snowdon's height
   Descending slow their glittering skirts unroll?
Visions of glory, spare my aching sight,
   Ye unborn ages, crowd not on my soul!
No more our long-lost Arthur we bewail:—   109
All hail, ye genuine kings! Britannia's issue, hail!

   'Girt with many a baron bold
Sublime their starry fronts they rear;
   And gorgeous dames, and statesmen old
In bearded majesty, appear.
In the midst a form divine!   115
Her eye proclaims her of the Briton-Line:
Her lion-port, her awe-commanding face
Attemper'd sweet to virgin-grace.
What strings symphonious tremble in the air,
   What strains of vocal transport round her play?
Hear from the grave, great Taliessin, hear;   121
   They breathe a soul to animate thy clay.
Bright Rapture calls, and soaring as she sings,
Waves in the eye of Heaven her many-colour'd wings.

   The verse adorn again   125
   Fierce War, and faithful Love,
And Truth severe, by fairy Fiction drest.
   In buskin'd measures move
Pale Grief, and pleasing Pain,
With Horror, tyrant of the throbbing breast.   130
A voice as of the cherub-choir
   Gales from blooming Eden bear,
   And distant warblings lessen on my ear,
That lost in long futurity expire.   134
Fond impious man, think'st thou yon sanguine cloud
   Raised by thy breath, has quench'd the orb of day?
To-morrow he repairs the golden flood
   And warms the nations with redoubled ray.
Enough for me: with joy I see
   The different doom our fates assign: 140

Be thine Despair and sceptred Care;
    To triumph and to die are mine.'
—He spoke, and headlong from the mountain's height
Deep in the roaring tide he plunged to endless night.

                                                    T. Gray

124

ODE WRITTEN IN MDCCXLVI

How sleep the Brave who sink to rest
By all their Country's wishes blest!
When Spring, with dewy fingers cold,
Returns to deck their hallow'd mould,
She there shall dress a sweeter sod   5
Than Fancy's feet have ever trod.

By fairy hands their knell is rung,
By forms unseen their dirge is sung:
There Honour comes, a pilgrim grey,
To bless the turf that wraps their clay;   10
And Freedom shall awhile repair
To dwell, a weeping hermit, there!

                                                  W. Collins

125

LAMENT FOR CULLODEN

The lovely lass o' Inverness,
    Nae joy nor pleasure can she see;
For e'en and morn she cries, Alas!
    And ay the saut tear blin's her ee:
Drumossie moor—Drumossie day—   5
    A waefu' day it was to me!
For there I lost my father dear,
    My father dear, and brethren three.

Their winding-sheet the bluidy clay,
    Their graves are growing green to see: 10

And by them lies the dearest lad
  That ever blest a woman's ee!
Now wae to thee, thou cruel lord,
  A bluidy man I trow thou be;
For mony a heart thou hast made sair   15
  That ne'er did wrang to thine or thee.

                                        R. Burns

126

LAMENT FOR FLODDEN

I've heard them lilting at the ewe-milking,
  Lasses a' lilting before dawn of day;
But now they are moaning on ilka green loaning—
  The Flowers of the Forest are a' wede away.   4

At bughts, in the morning, nae blythe lads are scorning,
  Lasses are lonely and dowie and wae;
Nae daffing, nae gabbing, but sighing and sabbing,
  Ilk ane lifts her leglin and hies her away.

In har'st, at the shearing, nae youths now are jeering,
  Bandsters are runkled, and lyart, or grey;   10
At fair or at preaching, nae wooing, nae fleeching—
  The Flowers of the Forest are a' wede away.

At e'en, in the gloaming, nae younkers are roaming
  'Bout stacks with the lasses at bogle to play;
But ilk maid sits dreary, lamenting her dearie—   15
  The Flowers of the Forest are weded away.

Dool and wae for the order, sent our lads to the Border!
  The English, for ance, by guile wan the day;
The Flowers of the Forest, that fought aye the foremost,
  The prime of our land, are cauld in the clay.   20

We'll hear nae mair lilting at the ewe-milking;
  Women and bairns are heartless and wae;
Sighing and moaning on ilka green loaning—
  The Flowers of the Forest are a' wede away.

                                        J. Elliot

127

THE BRAES OF YARROW

'Thy braes were bonny, Yarrow stream,
  When first on them I met my lover;
Thy braes how dreary, Yarrow stream,
  When now thy waves his body cover!
For ever now, O Yarrow stream,   5
  Thou art to me a stream of sorrow;
For never on thy banks shall I
  Behold my love, the flower of Yarrow.

'He promised me a milk-white steed
  To bear me to his father's bowers;   10
He promised me a little page
  To squire me to his father's towers;
He promised me a wedding-ring,—
  The wedding-day was fix'd to-morrow;—
Now he is wedded to his grave,   15
  Alas, his watery grave, in Yarrow!

'Sweet were his words when last we met;
  My passion I as freely told him;
Clasp'd in his arms, I little thought
  That I should never more behold him!   20
Scarce was he gone, I saw his ghost;
  It vanish'd with a shriek of sorrow;
Thrice did the water-wraith ascend,
  And gave a doleful groan thro' Yarrow.

'His mother from the window look'd   25
  With all the longing of a mother;
His little sister weeping walk'd
  The green-wood path to meet her brother;
They sought him east, they sought him west,
  They sought him all the forest thorough;   30
They only saw the cloud of night,
  They only heard the roar of Yarrow.

E*

'No longer from thy window look—
   Thou hast no son, thou tender mother!
No longer walk, thou lovely maid;   35
   Alas, thou hast no more a brother!
No longer seek him east or west
   And search no more the forest thorough;
For, wandering in the night so dark,
   He fell a lifeless corpse in Yarrow.   40

'The tear shall never leave my cheek,
   No other youth shall be my marrow—
I'll seek thy body in the stream,
   And then with thee I'll sleep in Yarrow.'
—The tear did never leave her cheek,   45
   No other youth became her marrow;
She found his body in the stream,
   And now with him she sleeps in Yarrow.
                    J. Logan

128

WILLY DROWNED IN YARROW

Down in yon garden sweet and gay
   Where bonnie grows the lily,
I heard a fair maid sighing say,
   'My wish be wi' sweet Willie!

'Willie's rare, and Willie's fair,   5
   And Willie's wondrous bonny;
And Willie hecht to marry me
   Gin e'er he married ony.

'O gentle wind, that bloweth south
   From where my Love repaireth,
Convey a kiss frae his dear mouth   10
   And tell me how he fareth!

'O tell sweet Willie to come doun
   And hear the mavis singing,
And see the birds on ilka bush   15
   And leaves around them hinging.

'The lav'rock there, wi' her white breast
   And gentle throat sae narrow;
There's sport eneuch for gentlemen
   On Leader haughs and Yarrow.   20

'O Leader haughs are wide and braid
   And Yarrow haughs are bonny;
There Willie hecht to marry me
   If e'er he married ony.

'But Willie's gone, whom I thought on,   25
   And does not hear me weeping;
Draws many a tear frae 's true love's e'e
   When other maids are sleeping.

'Yestreen I made my bed fu' braid,
   The night I'll mak' it narrow,   30
For a' the live-lang winter night
   I lie twined o' my marrow.

'O came ye by yon water-side?
   Pou'd you the rose or lily?
Or came you by yon meadow green,   35
   Or saw you my sweet Willie?'

She sought him up, she sought him down,
   She sought him braid and narrow;
Syne, in the cleaving of a craig,
   She found him drown'd in Yarrow!   40

Anon.

129

LOSS OF THE ROYAL GEORGE

Toll for the Brave!
The brave that are no more!
   All sunk beneath the wave
Fast by their native shore!

   Eight hundred of the brave,   5
Whose courage well was tried,
   Had made the vessel heel
And laid her on her side.

A land-breeze shook the shrouds
And she was overset;   10
 Down went the Royal George,
With all her crew complete.

 Toll for the brave!
Brave Kempenfelt is gone;
 His last sea-fight is fought,   15
His work of glory done.

 It was not in the battle;
No tempest gave the shock;
 She sprang no fatal leak,
She ran upon no rock.   20

 His sword was in the sheath,
His fingers held the pen,
 When Kempenfelt went down
With twice four hundred men.

 Weigh the vessel up   25
Once dreaded by our foes,
 And mingle with your cup
The tears that England owes.

 Her timbers yet are sound,
And she may float again   30
 Full charged with England's thunder,
And plough the distant main:

 But Kempenfelt is gone,
His victories are o'er;
 And he and his eight hundred   35
Must plough the wave no more.

       W. Cowper

130

BLACK-EYED SUSAN

All in the Downs the fleet was moor'd,
 The streamers waving in the wind,
When black-eyed Susan came aboard;
 'O! where shall I my true-love find?

Tell me, ye jovial sailors, tell me true   5
If my sweet William sails among the crew.'

William, who high upon the yard
  Rock'd with the billow to and fro,
Soon as her well-known voice he heard,
  He sigh'd, and cast his eyes below: 10
The cord slides swiftly through his glowing hands,
And quick as lightning on the deck he stands.

So the sweet lark, high poised in air,
  Shuts close his pinions to his breast
If chance his mate's shrill call he hear,   15
  And drops at once into her nest:—
The noblest captain in the British fleet
Might envy William's lips those kisses sweet.

'O Susan, Susan, lovely dear,
  My vows shall ever true remain;   20
Let me kiss off that falling tear;
  We only part to meet again.
Change as ye list, ye winds; my heart shall be
The faithful compass that still points to thee.

'Believe not what the landmen say   25
  Who tempt with doubts thy constant mind:
They'll tell thee, sailors, when away,
  In every port a mistress find:
Yes, yes, believe them when they tell thee so,
For Thou art present wheresoe'er I go.   30

'If to far India's coast we sail,
  Thy eyes are seen in diamonds bright,
Thy breath is Afric's spicy gale,
  Thy skin is ivory so white.
Thus every beauteous object that I view   35
Wakes in my soul some charm of lovely Sue.

'Though battle call me from thy arms
  Let not my pretty Susan mourn;
Though cannons roar, yet safe from harms
  William shall to his Dear return.   40
Love turns aside the balls that round me fly,
Lest precious tears should drop from Susan' eye.'

The boatswain gave the dreadful word,
   The sails their swelling bosom spread;
No longer must she stay aboard;   45
   They kiss'd, she sigh'd, he hung his head.
Her lessening boat unwilling rows to land;
'Adieu!' she cries; and waved her lily hand.

                                        J. Gay

                    131

          SALLY IN OUR ALLEY

Of all the girls that are so smart
   There's none like pretty Sally;
She is the darling of my heart,
   And she lives in our alley.
There is no lady in the land   5
   Is half so sweet as Sally;
She is the darling of my heart,
   And she lives in our alley.

Her father he makes cabbage-nets
   And through the streets does cry 'em;   10
Her mother she sells laces long
   To such as please to buy 'em:
But sure such folks could ne'er beget
   So sweet a girl as Sally!
She is the darling of my heart,   15
   And she lives in our alley.

When she is by, I leave my work,
   I love her so sincerely;
My master comes like any Turk,
   And bangs me most severely—   20
But let him bang his bellyful,
   I'll bear it all for Sally;
She is the darling of my heart,
   And she lives in our alley.

Of all the days that 's in the week   25
   I dearly love but one day—

And that's the day that comes betwixt
   A Saturday and Monday;
For then I'm drest all in my best
   To walk abroad with Sally;   30
She is the darling of my heart,
   And she lives in our alley.

My master carries me to church,
   And often am I blamed
Because I leave him in the lurch   35
   As soon as text is named;
I leave the church in sermon-time
   And slink away to Sally;
She is the darling of my heart,
   And she lives in our alley.   40

When Christmas comes about again
   O then I shall have money;
I'll hoard it up, and box and all,
   I'll give it to my honey:
Would it were ten thousand pound,   45
   I'd give it all to Sally;
She is the darling of my heart,
   And she lives in our alley.

My master and the neighbours all
   Make game of me and Sally,   50
And, but for her, I'd better be
   A slave and row a galley;
But when my seven long years are out
   O then I'll marry Sally,—
O then we'll wed, and then we'll bed,   55
   But not in our alley!

                            H. Carey

132

A FAREWELL

Go fetch to me a pint o' wine,
   An' fill it in a silver tassie;
That I may drink before I go
   A service to my bonnie lassie:

The boat rocks at the pier o' Leith,   5
    Fu' loud the wind blaws frae the Ferry,
The ship rides by the Berwick-law,
    And I maun leave my bonnie Mary.

The trumpets sound, the banners fly,
    The glittering spears are rankéd ready;   10
The shouts o' war are heard afar,
    The battle closes thick and bloody;
But it's not the roar o' sea or shore
    Wad make me langer wish to tarry;
Nor shout o' war that 's heard afar—   15
    It's leaving thee, my bonnie Mary.

                                            R. Burns

133

If doughty deeds my lady please
    Right soon I'll mount my steed;
And strong his arm, and fast his seat,
    That bears frae me the meed.
I'll wear thy colours in my cap,   5
    Thy picture in my heart;
And he that bends not to thine eye
    Shall rue it to his smart.
        Then tell me how to woo thee, love;
            O tell me how to woo thee!   10
        For thy dear sake, nae care I'll take,
            Tho' ne'er another trow me.

If gay attire delight thine eye
    I'll dight me in array;
I'll tend thy chamber door all night,   15
    And squire thee all the day.
If sweetest sounds can win thine ear,
    These sounds I'll strive to catch;
Thy voice I'll steal to woo thysell,
    That voice that nane can match.   20

But if fond love thy heart can gain,
    I never broke a vow;

Nae maiden lays her skaith to me,
  I never loved but you.
For you alone I ride the ring,   25
  For you I wear the blue;
For you alone I strive to sing,
    O tell me how to woo!
      Then tell me how to woo thee, love;
        O tell me how to woo thee!   30
    For thy dear sake, nae care I'll take,
    Tho' ne'er another trow me.

R. Graham of Gartmore

134

TO A YOUNG LADY

Sweet stream, that winds through yonder glade,
Apt emblem of a virtuous maid—
Silent and chaste she steals along,
Far from the world's gay busy throng:
With gentle yet prevailing force,   5
Intent upon her destined course;
Graceful and useful all she does,
Blessing and blest where'er she goes;
Pure-bosom'd as that watery glass,
And Heaven reflected in her face.   10

W. Cowper

135

THE SLEEPING BEAUTY

Sleep on, and dream of Heaven awhile—
  Tho' shut so close thy laughing eyes,
Thy rosy lips still wear a smile
  And move, and breathe delicious sighs!

Ah, now soft blushes tinge her cheeks   5
  And mantle o'er her neck of snow:
Ah, now she murmurs, now she speaks
  What most I wish—and fear to know!

She starts, she trembles, and she weeps!
  Her fair hands folded on her breast: 10
—And now, how like a saint she sleeps!
  A seraph in the realms of rest!

Sleep on secure!   Above control
  Thy thoughts belong to Heaven and thee:
And may the secret of thy soul   15
  Remain within its sanctuary!

                         S. Rogers

136

For ever, Fortune, wilt thou prove
An unrelenting foe to Love,
And when we meet a mutual heart
Come in between, and bid us part?

Bid us sigh on from day to day,   5
And wish and wish the soul away;
Till youth and genial years are flown,
And all the life of life is gone?

But busy, busy, still art thou,
To bind the loveless joyless vow,   10
The heart from pleasure to delude,
And join the gentle to the rude.

For once, O Fortune, hear my prayer,
And I absolve thy future care;
All other blessings I resign,   15
Make but the dear Amanda mine.

                         J. Thomson

137

The merchant, to secure his treasure,
  Conveys it in a borrow'd name:
Euphelia serves to grace my measure
  But Cloe is my real flame.

My softest verse, my darling lyre   5
  Upon Euphelia's toilet lay—
When Cloe noted her desire
  That I should sing, that I should play.

My lyre I tune, my voice I raise,
  But with my numbers mix my sighs;   10
And whilst I sing Euphelia's praise,
  I fix my soul on Cloe's eyes.

Fair Cloe blush'd: Euphelia frown'd:
  I sung, and gazed; I play'd, and trembled:
And Venus to the Loves around   15
  Remark'd how ill we all dissembled.

M. Prior

138

When lovely woman stoops to folly
  And finds too late that men betray,—
What charm can soothe her melancholy,
  What art can wash her guilt away?

The only art her guilt to cover,   5
  To hide her shame from every eye,
To give repentance to her lover
  And wring his bosom, is—to die.

O. Goldsmith

139

Ye flowery banks o' bonnie Doon,
How can ye bloom sae fair!
How can ye chant, ye little birds,
  And I sae fu' o' care!

Thou'll break my heart, thou bonnie bird   5
  That sings upon the bough;
Thou minds me o' the happy days
  When my fause Luve was true.

Thou'll break my heart, thou bonnie bird
   That sings beside thy mate;   10
For sae I sat, and sae I sang,
   And wist na o' my fate.

Aft hae I roved by bonnie Doon
   To see the woodbine twine;
And ilka bird sang o' its love,   15
   And sae did I o' mine.

Wi' lightsome heart I pu'd a rose,
   Frae aff its thorny tree;
And my fause luver staw the rose,
   But left the thorn wi' me.   20

                             R. Burns

140

THE PROGRESS OF POESY

A Pindaric Ode

Awake, Aeolian lyre, awake,
And give to rapture all thy trembling strings.
From Helicon's harmonious springs
   A thousand rills their mazy progress take:
The laughing flowers that round them blow   5
Drink life and fragrance as they flow.
Now the rich stream of Music winds along
Deep, majestic, smooth, and strong,
Through verdant vales and Ceres' golden reign;
Now rolling down the steep amain,   10
Headlong, impetuous, see it pour:
The rocks and nodding groves rebellow to the roar.

O Sovereign of the willing soul,
Parent of sweet and solemn-breathing airs,
Enchanting shell! the sullen Cares   15
   And frantic Passions hear thy soft control.
On Thracia's hills the Lord of War
Has curb'd the fury of his car

And dropt his thirsty lance at thy command.
Perching on the sceptred hand   20
Of Jove, thy magic lulls the feather'd king
With ruffled plumes, and flagging wing:
Quench'd in dark clouds of slumber lie
The terror of his beak, and lightnings of his eye.

Thee the voice, the dance, obey   25
Temper'd to thy warbled lay.
    O'er Idalia's velvet green
    The rosy-crownéd Loves are seen
On Cytherea's day,
    With antic Sports, and blue-eyed Pleasures,   30
    Frisking light in frolic measures;
Now pursuing, now retreating,
    Now in circling troops they meet:
To brisk notes in cadence beating
    Glance their many-twinkling feet.   35
Slow melting strains their Queen's approach
        declare:
    Where'er she turns the Graces homage pay:
With arms sublime that float upon the air
    In gliding state she wins her easy way:
O'er her warm cheek and rising bosom move   40
The bloom of young Desire and purple light of
        Love.

Man's feeble race what ills await!
Labour, and Penury, the racks of Pain,
Disease, and Sorrow's weeping train,
    And Death, sad refuge from the storms of Fate!   45
The fond complaint, my song, disprove,
And justify the laws of Jove.
Say, has he given in vain the heavenly Muse?
Night, and all her sickly dews,
Her spectres wan, and birds of boding cry   50
He gives to range the dreary sky:
Till down the eastern cliffs afar
Hyperion's march they spy, and glittering shafts of
        war.

In climes beyond the solar road,
Where shaggy forms o'er ice-built mountains roam,   55
The Muse has broke the twilight gloom
    To cheer the shivering native's dull abode.
And oft, beneath the odorous shade
Of Chili's boundless forests laid,
She deigns to hear the savage youth repeat   60
In loose numbers wildly sweet
Their feather-cinctured chiefs, and dusky loves.
Her track, where'er the Goddess roves,
Glory pursue, and generous Shame,
Th' unconquerable Mind, and Freedom's holy flame.   65

Woods, that wave o'er Delphi's steep,
Isles, that crown th' Aegean deep,
    Fields that cool Ilissus laves,
    Or where Maeander's amber waves
In lingering lab'rinths creep,   70
    How do your tuneful echoes languish,
    Mute, but to the voice of anguish!
Where each old poetic mountain
    Inspiration breath'd around;
Every shade and hallow'd fountain   75
    Murmur'd deep a solemn sound:
Till the sad Nine, in Greece's evil hour,
    Left their Parnassus for the Latian plains.
Alike they scorn the pomp of tyrant Power,
    And coward Vice, that revels in her chains.   80
When Latium had her lofty spirit lost,
They sought, O Albion, next thy sea-encircled coast.

    Far from the sun and summer-gale
In thy green lap was Nature's Darling laid,
What time, where lucid Avon stray'd,   85
    To him the mighty Mother did unveil
Her awful face: the dauntless Child
Stretch'd forth his little arms, and smiled.

This pencil take (she said), whose colours clear
Richly paint the vernal year: 90
Thine, too, these golden keys, immortal Boy!
This can unlock the gates of Joy;
Of Horror that, and thrilling Fears,
Or ope the sacred source of sympathetic Tears.

   Nor second He, that rode sublime   95
Upon the seraph-wings of Ecstasy,
The secrets of the Abyss to spy:
   He pass'd the flaming bounds of Place and Time:
The living Throne, the sapphire-blaze,
Where Angels tremble while they gaze,   100
He saw; but blasted with excess of light,
Closed his eyes in endless night.
Behold where Dryden's less presumptuous car
Wide o'er the fields of Glory bear
Two coursers of ethereal race   105
With necks in thunder clothed, and long-resounding
    pace.

Hark, his hands the lyre explore!
Bright-eyed Fancy, hovering o'er,
   Scatters from her pictur'd urn
   Thoughts that breathe, and words that burn.   110
But ah! 'tis heard no more——
   O! Lyre divine, what daring Spirit
   Wakes thee now? Tho' he inherit
Nor the pride, nor ample pinion,
   That the Theban Eagle bear,   115
Sailing with supreme dominion
   Thro' the azure deep of air:
Yet oft before his infant eyes would run
   Such forms as glitter in the Muse's ray
With orient hues, unborrow'd of the sun: 120
   Yet shall he mount, and keep his distant way
Beyond the limits of a vulgar fate:
Beneath the Good how far—but far above the Great.

                          T. Gray

141

THE PASSIONS

An Ode for Music

When Music, heavenly maid, was young,
While yet in early Greece she sung,
The Passions oft, to hear her shell,
Throng'd around her magic cell
Exulting, trembling, raging, fainting,   5
Possest beyond the Muse's painting;
By turns they felt the glowing mind
Disturb'd, delighted, rais'd, refin'd:
Till once, 'tis said, when all were fir'd,
Fill'd with fury, rapt, inspir'd,   10
From the supporting myrtles round
They snatch'd her instruments of sound,
And, as they oft had heard apart
Sweet lessons of her forceful art,
Each, for Madness ruled the hour,   15
Would prove his own expressive power.

First Fear his hand, its skill to try,
    Amid the chords bewilder'd laid,
And back recoil'd, he knew not why,
    E'en at the sound himself had made.   20

Next Anger rush'd, his eyes on fire,
    In lightnings own'd his secret stings;
In one rude clash he struck the lyre
    And swept with hurried hand the strings.

With woeful measures wan Despair,   25
    Low sullen sounds, his grief beguiled,
A solemn, strange, and mingled air,
    'Twas sad by fits, by starts 'twas wild.

But thou, O Hope, with eyes so fair,
    What was thy delightful measure?   30
Still it whisper'd promised pleasure
    And bade the lovely scenes at distance hail!

Still would her touch the strain prolong;
   And from the rocks, the woods, the vale,
She call'd on Echo still through all the song;   35
   And, where her sweetest theme she chose,
   A soft responsive voice was heard at every close;
And Hope enchanted smiled, and waved her golden hair.

And longer had she sung,—but with a frown
   Revenge impatient rose: 40
He threw his blood-stain'd sword in thunder down;
   And with a withering look
   The war-denouncing trumpet took,
And blew a blast so loud and dread,
Were ne'er prophetic sounds so full of woe.   45
   And ever and anon he beat
   The doubling drum with furious heat;
And, though sometimes, each dreary pause between,
   Dejected Pity at his side
   Her soul-subduing voice applied,   50
   Yet still he kept his wild unalter'd mien,
While each strain'd ball of sight seem'd bursting from
     his head.

Thy numbers, Jealousy, to nought were fix'd:
   Sad proof of thy distressful state!
Of differing themes the veering song was mix'd;   55
   And now it courted Love, now raving call'd on Hate.

With eyes up-rais'd, as one inspir'd,
Pale Melancholy sat retir'd;
And from her wild sequester'd seat,
In notes by distance made more sweet,   60
Pour'd through the mellow horn her pensive soul:
   And dashing soft from rocks around
   Bubbling runnels join'd the sound;
Through glades and glooms the mingled measure stole,
   Or, o'er some haunted stream, with fond delay,   65
   Round an holy calm diffusing,
   Love of peace and lonely musing,
In hollow murmurs died away.

But O! how alter'd was its sprightlier tone,
When Cheerfulness, a nymph of healthiest hue,   70
   Her bow across her shoulder flung,
   Her buskins gemm'd with morning dew,
Blew an inspiring air, that dale and thicket rung,
   The hunter's call to Faun and Dryad known!   74
The oak-crown'd Sisters and their chaste-eyed Queen,
   Satyrs and Sylvan Boys, were seen
   Peeping from forth their alleys green:
Brown Exercise rejoic'd to hear;
   And Sport leap'd up, and seiz'd his beechen spear.

Last came Joy's ecstatic trial: 80
He, with viny crown advancing,
   First to the lively pipe his hand addrest:
But soon he saw the brisk awak'ning viol,
   Whose sweet entrancing voice he lov'd the best:
They would have thought who heard the strain   85
     They saw, in Tempe's vale, her native maids
     Amidst the festal-sounding shades
To some unwearied minstrel dancing;
While, as his flying fingers kiss'd the strings,
   Love fram'd with Mirth a gay fantastic round: 90
   Loose were her tresses seen, her zone unbound;
   And he, amidst his frolic play,
   As if he would the charming air repay,
Shook thousand odours from his dewy wings.

O Music! sphere-descended maid,   95
Friend of Pleasure, Wisdom's aid!
Why, goddess, why, to us denied,
Lay'st thou thy ancient lyre aside?
As in that lov'd Athenian bower
You learn'd an all-commanding power,   100
Thy mimic soul, O nymph endear'd,
Can well recall what then it heard.
Where is thy native simple heart
Devote to Virtue, Fancy, Art?
Arise, as in that elder time,   105

Warm, energic, chaste, sublime!
Thy wonders in that god-like age
Fill thy recording Sister's page;—
'Tis said, and I believe the tale,
Thy humblest reed could more prevail,   110
Had more of strength, diviner rage,
Than all which charms this laggard age,
E'en all at once together found,
Cecilia's mingled world of cease:—
O bid our vain endeavours cease: 115
Revive the just designs of Greece:
Return in all thy simple state!
Confirm the tales her sons relate!

W. Collins

142

ODE ON THE SPRING

Lo! where the rosy-bosom'd Hours,
    Fair Venus' train, appear,
Disclose the long-expecting flowers
    And wake the purple year!
The Attic warbler pours her throat   5
Responsive to the cuckoo's note,
The untaught harmony of Spring:
    While, whispering pleasure as they fly,
    Cool Zephyrs through the clear blue sky
Their gather'd fragrance fling.   10

Where'er the oak's thick branches stretch
    A broader, browner shade,
Where'er the rude and moss-grown beech
    O'er-canopies the glade,
Beside some water's rushy brink   15
With me the Muse shall sit, and think
(At ease reclined in rustic state)
    How vain the ardour of the Crowd,
    How low, how little are the Proud,
How indigent the Great!   20

Still is the toiling hand of Care;
    The panting herds repose:
Yet hark, how through the peopled air
    The busy murmur glows!
The insect youth are on the wing,   25
Eager to taste the honied spring
And float amid the liquid noon:
    Some lightly o'er the current skim,
    Some show their gaily-gilded trim
Quick-glancing to the sun.   30

To Contemplation's sober eye
    Such is the race of Man:
And they that creep, and they that fly,
    Shall end where they began.
Alike the busy and the gay   35
But flutter through life's little day,
In Fortune's varying colours drest:
    Brush'd by the hand of rough Mischance,
    Or chill'd by Age, their airy dance
They leave, in dust to rest.   40

Methinks I hear in accents low
    The sportive kind reply:
Poor moralist! and what art thou?
    A solitary fly!
Thy joys no glittering female meets,   45
No hive hast thou of hoarded sweets,
No painted plumage to display:
    On hasty wings thy youth is flown;
    Thy sun is set, thy spring is gone—
We frolic while 'tis May.   50
                                        T. Gray

143

THE POPLAR FIELD

The poplars are fell'd; farewell to the shade
And the whispering sound of the cool colonnade;
The winds play no longer and sing in the leaves,
Nor Ouse on his bosom their image receives.

Twelve years have elapsed since I first took a view   5
Of my favourite field, and the bank where they grew:
And now in the grass behold they are laid,
And the tree is my seat that once lent me a shade.

The blackbird has fled to another retreat,   9
Where the hazels afford him a screen from the heat;
And the scene where his melody charm'd me before
Resounds with his sweet-flowing ditty no more.

My fugitive years are all hasting away,
And I must ere long lie as lowly as they,   14
With a turf on my breast and a stone at my head,
Ere another such grove shall arise in its stead.

'Tis a sight to engage me, if anything can,
To muse on the perishing pleasures of man;
Though his life be a dream, his enjoyments, I see,
Have a being less durable even than he.   20

W. Cowper

144

TO A MOUSE

On turning her up in her nest with the plough,
November 1785

Wee, sleekit, cow'rin', tim'rous beastie,
O what a panic 's in thy breastie!
Thou need na start awa sae hasty,
   Wi' bickering brattle!
I wad be laith to rin an' chase thee   5
   Wi' murd'ring pattle!

I'm truly sorry man's dominion
Has broken nature's social union,
An' justifies that ill opinion
   Which makes thee startle   10
At me, thy poor earth-born companion,
   An' fellow-mortal!

I doubt na, whiles, but thou may thieve;
What then? poor beastie, thou maun live!

A daimen-icker in a thrave   15
   'S a sma' request:
I'll get a blessin' wi' the lave,
   And never miss't!

Thy wee bit housie, too, in ruin!
Its silly wa's the win's are strewin':   20
And naething, now, to big a new ane,
   O' foggage green!
An' bleak December's winds ensuin'
   Baith snell an' keen!

Thou saw the fields laid bare and waste 25
An' weary winter comin' fast,
An' cozie here, beneath the blast,
   Thou thought to dwell,
Till, crash! the cruel coulter past
   Out thro' thy cell.   30

That wee bit heap o' leaves a' stibble
Hast cost thee mony a weary nibble!
Now thou's turn'd out, for a' thy trouble,
   But house or hald,
To thole the winter's sleety dribble   35
   An' cranreuch cauld!

But, Mousie, thou art no thy lane
In proving foresight may be vain:
The best laid schemes o' mice an' men
   Gang aft a-gley,   40
An' lea'e us nought but grief an' pain,
   For promised joy.

Still thou art blest, compared wi' me!
The present only toucheth thee:
But, och! I backward cast my e'e   45
   On prospects drear!
An' forward, tho' I canna see,
   I guess an' fear!

                                    R. Burns

145

A WISH

Mine be a cot beside the hill;
  A bee-hive's hum shall soothe my ear;
A willowy brook that turns a mill,
  With many a fall shall linger near.

The swallow, oft, beneath my thatch   5
  Shall twitter from her clay-built nest;
Oft shall the pilgrim lift the latch,
  And share my meal, a welcome guest.

Around my ivied porch shall spring
  Each fragrant flower that drinks the dew;   10
And Lucy, at her wheel, shall sing
  In russet gown and apron blue.

The village-church among the trees,
  Where first our marriage-vows were given,
With merry peals shall swell the breeze   15
  And point with taper spire to Heaven.

S. Rogers

146

TO EVENING

If aught of oaten stop or pastoral song
May hope, O pensive Eve, to soothe thine ear,
  Like thy own brawling springs,
  Thy springs, and dying gales;

O Nymph reserved,—while now the bright-hair'd sun   5
Sits in yon western tent, whose cloudy skirts
  With brede ethereal wove
  O'erhang his wavy bed;

Now air is hush'd, save where the weak-ey'd bat
With short shrill shriek flits by on leathern wing,   10
  Or where the beetle winds
  His small but sullen horn,

As oft he rises 'midst the twilight path,
Against the pilgrim borne in heedless hum,—
    Now teach me, maid composed,   15
    To breathe some soften'd strain,

Whose numbers, stealing through thy dark'ning vale,
May not unseemly with its stillness suit;
    As musing slow I hail
    Thy genial loved return.   20

For when thy folding-star arising shows
His paly circlet, at his warning lamp
    The fragrant Hours, and Elves
    Who slept in buds the day,

And many a Nymph who wreathes her brows with
    sedge   25
And sheds the freshening dew, and lovelier still
    The pensive Pleasures sweet,
    Prepare thy shadowy car.

Then let me rove some wild and heathy scene;
Or find some ruin midst its dreary dells,   30
    Whose walls more awful nod
    By thy religious gleams.

Or if chill blustering winds or driving rain
Prevent my willing feet, be mine the hut
    That, from the mountain's side,   35
    Views wilds and swelling floods,

And hamlets brown, and dim-discover'd spires;
And hears their simple bell; and marks o'er all
    Thy dewy fingers draw
    The gradual dusky veil.   40

While Spring shall pour his showers, as oft he wont,
And bathe thy breathing tresses, meekest Eve!
    While Summer loves to sport
    Beneath thy lingering light;

While sallow Autumn fills thy lap with leaves;   45
Or Winter, yelling through the troublous air,
    Affrights thy shrinking train
    And rudely rends thy robes;

So long, regardful of thy quiet rule,
Shall Fancy, Friendship, Science, smiling Peace,   50
    Thy gentlest influence own,
    And love thy favourite name!

                    W. Collins

147

ELEGY
WRITTEN IN A COUNTRY CHURCH-YARD

The curfew tolls the knell of parting day,
    The lowing herd wind slowly o'er the lea,
The ploughman homeward plods his weary way,
    And leaves the world to darkness, and to me.

Now fades the glimmering landscape on the sight,   5
    And all the air a solemn stillness holds,
Save where the beetle wheels his droning flight,
    And drowsy tinklings lull the distant folds:

Save that from yonder ivy-mantled tower
    The moping owl does to the moon complain   10
Of such as, wandering near her secret bower,
    Molest her ancient solitary reign.

Beneath those rugged elms, that yew-tree's shade,
    Where heaves the turf in many a mouldering heap,
Each in his narrow cell for ever laid,   15
    The rude Forefathers of the hamlet sleep.

The breezy call of incense-breathing morn,
    The swallow twittering from the straw-built shed,
The cock's shrill clarion, or the echoing horn,
    No more shall rouse them from their lowly bed.   20

For them no more the blazing hearth shall burn,
    Or busy housewife ply her evening care:
No children run to lisp their sire's return,
    Or climb his knees the envied kiss to share.

Oft did the harvest to their sickle yield,   25
    Their furrow oft the stubborn glebe has broke;
How jocund did they drive their team afield!
    How bow'd the woods beneath their sturdy stroke!

                                        F

Let not Ambition mock their useful toil,
 Their homely joys, and destiny obscure;   30
Nor Grandeur hear with a disdainful smile
 The short and simple annals of the Poor.

The boast of heraldry, the pomp of power,
 And all that beauty, all that wealth e'er gave,
Awaits alike th' inevitable hour:—   35
 The paths of glory lead but to the grave.

Nor you, ye Proud, impute to these the fault
 If Memory o'er their tomb no trophies raise,
Where through the long-drawn aisle and fretted vault
 The pealing anthem swells the note of praise. 40

Can storied urn or animated bust
 Back to its mansion call the fleeting breath?
Can Honour's voice provoke the silent dust,
 Or Flattery soothe the dull cold ear of Death?

Perhaps in this neglected spot is laid   45
 Some heart once pregnant with celestial fire;
Hands, that the rod of empire might have sway'd,
 Or waked to ecstasy the living lyre:

But Knowledge to their eyes her ample page
 Rich with the spoils of time, did ne'er unroll; 50
Chill Penury repress'd their noble rage,
 And froze the genial current of the soul.

Full many a gem of purest ray serene
 The dark unfathom'd caves of ocean bear:
Full many a flower is born to blush unseen, 55
 And waste its sweetness on the desert air.

Some village-Hampden, that with dauntless breast
 The little tyrant of his fields withstood,
Some mute inglorious Milton here may rest,
 Some Cromwell, guiltless of his country's blood. 60

Th' applause of list'ning senates to command,
 The threats of pain and ruin to despise,
To scatter plenty o'er a smiling land,
 And read their history in a nation's eyes,

Their lot forbad: nor circumscribed alone   65
   Their growing virtues, but their crimes confined;
Forbad to wade through slaughter to a throne,
   And shut the gates of mercy on mankind,

The struggling pangs of conscious truth to hide.
   To quench the blushes of ingenuous shame,   70
Or heap the shrine of Luxury and Pride
   With incense kindled at the Muse's flame.

Far from the madding crowd's ignoble strife,
   Their sober wishes never learn'd to stray;
Along the cool sequester'd vale of life   75
   They kept the noiseless tenour of their way.

Yet e'en these bones from insult to protect
   Some frail memorial still erected nigh,
With uncouth rhymes and shapeless sculpture deck'd,
   Implores the passing tribute of a sigh.   80

Their name, their years, spelt by th' unletter'd Muse,
   The place of fame and elegy supply:
And many a holy text around she strews,
   That teach the rustic moralist to die.

For who, to dumb forgetfulness a prey,   85
   This pleasing anxious being e'er resign'd,
Left the warm precincts of the cheerful day,
   Nor cast one longing lingering look behind?

On some fond breast the parting soul relies,
   Some pious drops the closing eye requires;   90
E'en from the tomb the voice of Nature cries,
   E'en in our ashes live their wonted fires.

For thee, who, mindful of th' unhonour'd dead,
   Dost in these lines their artless tale relate;
If chance, by lonely contemplation led,   95
   Some kindred spirit shall inquire thy fate,

Haply some hoary-headed swain may say,
   'Oft have we seen him at the peep of dawn
Brushing with hasty steps the dews away,
   To meet the sun upon the upland lawn;   100

'There at the foot of yonder nodding beech
    That wreathes its old fantastic roots so high,
His listless length at noontide would be stretch,
    And pore upon the brook that babbles by.

'Hard by yon wood, now smiling as in scorn,   105
    Muttering his wayward fancies he would rove;
Now drooping, woeful wan, like one forlorn,
    Or crazed with care, or cross'd in hopeless love.

'One morn I miss'd him on the custom'd hill,
    Along the heath, and near his favourite tree;   110
Another came; nor yet beside the rill,
    Nor up the lawn, nor at the wood was he;

'The next with dirges due in sad array
    Slow through the church-way path we saw him
        borne,—
Approach and read (for thou canst read) the lay   115
    Graved on the stone beneath yon aged thorn.'

THE EPITAPH

Here rests his head upon the lap of Earth
    A Youth, to Fortune and to Fame unknown;
Fair Science frown'd not on his humble birth,
    And Melancholy mark'd him for her own.   120

Large was his bounty, and his soul sincere;
    Heaven did a recompense as largely send:
He gave to Misery all he had, a tear,
    He gain'd from Heaven, 'twas all he wish'd, a friend.

No farther seeks his merits to disclose,   125
    Or draw his frailties from their dread abode,
(There they alike in trembling hope repose,)
    The bosom of his Father and his God.

                                                    T. Gray

148

MARY MORISON

O Mary, at thy window be,
  It is the wish'd, the trysted hour!
Those smiles and glances let me see
  That make the miser's treasure poor:
  How blythely wad I bide the stoure,   5
A weary slave frae sun to sun,
  Could I the rich reward secure,
The lovely Mary Morison.

Yestreen, when to the trembling string
  The dance gaed thro' the lighted ha',   10
To thee my fancy took its wing,—
  I sat, but neither heard nor saw:
  Tho' this was fair, and that was braw,
And yon the toast of a' the town,
  I sigh'd, and said amang them a',   15
'Ye arena Mary Morison.'

O Mary, canst thou wreck his peace
  Wha for thy sake wad gladly dee?
Or canst thou break that heart of his,
  Whase only faut is loving thee?   20
  If love for love thou wiltna gie,
At least be pity to me shown;
  A thought ungentle canna be
The thought o' Mary Morison.

R. Burns

149

BONNIE LESLEY

  O saw ye bonnie Lesley
    As she gaed o'er the border?
  She 's gane, like Alexander,
    To spread her conquests farther.

To see her is to love her,   5
  And love but her for ever;
For nature made her what she is,
  And never made anither!

Thou art a queen, fair Lesley,
  Thy subjects we, before thee;   10
Thou art divine, fair Lesley,
  The hearts o' men adore thee.

The deil he couldna scaith thee,
  Or aught that wad belang thee;
He'd look into thy bonnie face,   15
  And say 'I canna wrang thee!'

The Powers aboon will tent thee;
  Misfortune sha'na steer thee;
Thou'rt like themselves sae lovely,
  That ill they'll ne'er let near thee.   20

Return again, fair Lesley,
  Return to Caledonie!
That we may brag we hae a lass
  There's nane again sae bonnie.

                                                          R. Burns

150

O my Luve's like a red, red rose
  That's newly sprung in June:
O my Luve's like the melodie
  That's sweetly play'd in tune.

As fair art thou, my bonnie lass,   5
  So deep in luve am I:
And I will luve thee still, my dear,
  Till a' the seas gang dry:

Till a' the seas gang dry, my dear,
  And the rocks melt wi' the sun;   10
I will luve thee still, my dear,
  While the sands o' life shall run.

And fare thee weel, my only Luve!
   And fare thee weel a while!
And I will come again, my Luve,   15
   Tho' it were ten thousand mile.

                        R. Burns

151

HIGHLAND MARY

Ye banks and braes and streams around
   The castle o' Montgomery,
Green be your woods, and fair your flowers,
   Your waters never drumlie!
There simmer first unfauld her robes,   5
   And there the langest tarry;
For there I took the last fareweel
   O' my sweet Highland Mary.

How sweetly bloom'd the gay green birk,
   How rich the hawthorn's blossom,   10
As underneath their fragrant shade
   I clasp'd her to my bosom!
The golden hours on angel wings
   Flew o'er me and my dearie;
For dear to me as light and life   15
   Was my sweet Highland Mary.

Wi' mony a vow and lock'd embrace
   Our parting was fu' tender;
And pledging aft to meet again,
   We tore oursels asunder;   20
But, oh! fell Death's untimely frost,
   That nipt my flower sae early!
Now green 's the sod, and cauld 's the clay,
   That wraps my Highland Mary!

O pale, pale now, those rosy lips,   25
   I aft hae kiss'd sae fondly!
And closed for ay the sparkling glance
   That dwelt on me sae kindly;

And mouldering now in silent dust
   That heart that lo'ed me dearly!   30
But still within my bosom's core
   Shall live my Highland Mary.

R. Burns

152

AULD ROBIN GRAY

When the sheep are in the fauld, and the kye at hame,
And a' the warld to rest are gane,
The waes o' my heart fa' in showers frae my e'e,
While my gudeman lies sound by me.

Young Jamie lo'ed me weel, and sought me for his
    bride;   5
But saving a croun he had naething else beside:
To make the croun a pund, young Jamie gaed to sea;
And the croun and the pund were baith for me.

He hadna been awa' a week but only twa,
When my father brak his arm, and the cow was stown
    awa';   10
My mother she fell sick, and my Jamie at the sea—
And auld Robin Gray came a-courtin' me.

My father couldna work, and my mother couldna spin;
I toil'd day and night, but their bread I couldna win;
Auld Rob maintain'd them baith, and wi' tears in his
    e'e   15
Said, Jennie, for their sakes, O, marry me!

My heart it said nay; I look'd for Jamie back;
But the wind it blew high, and the ship it was a wrack;
His ship it was a wrack—why didna Jamie dee?
Or why do I live to cry, Wae's me?   20

My father urgit sair: my mother didna speak;
But she look'd in my face till my heart was like to break:
They gi'ed him my hand, but my heart was at the sea;
Sae auld Robin Gray he was gudeman to me.

I hadna been a wife a week but only four,   25
When mournfu' as I sat on the stane at the door,
I saw my Jamie's wraith, for I couldna think it he—
Till he said, I'm come hame to marry thee.

O sair, sair did we greet, and muckle did we say;
We took but ae kiss, and I bad him gang away: 30
I wish that I were dead, but I'm no like to dee;
And why was I born to say, Wae's me!

I gang like a ghaist, and I carena to spin;
I daurna think on Jamie, for that wad be a sin;
But I'll do my best a gude wife ay to be,   35
For auld Robin Gray he is kind unto me.

                                    Lady A. Lindsay

153

DUNCAN GRAY

Duncan Gray cam here to woo,
      Ha, ha, the wooing o't,
On blythe Yule night when we were fou,
      Ha, ha, the wooing o't:
Maggie coost her head fu' high,   5
Look'd asklent and unco skeigh,
Gart poor Duncan stand abeigh;
      Ha, ha, the wooing o't!

Duncan fleech'd, and Duncan pray'd;
Meg was deaf as Ailsa Craig;   10
Duncan sigh'd baith out and in,
Grat his een baith bleer't and blin',
Spak o' lowpin ower a linn!

Time and chance are but a tide,
Slighted love is sair to bide;   15
Shall I, like a fool, quoth he,
For a haughty hizzie dee?
She may gae to—France for me!

F*

How it comes let doctors tell,
Meg grew sick—as he grew heal;   20
Something in her bosom wrings,
For relief a sigh she brings;
And O, her een, they spak sic things!

Duncan was a lad o' grace;
   Ha, ha, the wooing o't!   25
Maggie's was a piteous case;
   Ha, ha, the wooing o't!
Duncan couldna be her death,
Swelling pity smoor'd his wrath;
Now they're crouse and canty baith: 30
   Ha, ha, the wooing o't!

                             R. Burns

154

THE SAILOR'S WIFE

And are ye sure the news is true?
   And are ye sure he 's weel?
Is this a time to think o' wark?
   Ye jades, lay by your wheel;
Is this the time to spin a thread,   5
   When Colin 's at the door?
Reach down my cloak, I'll to the quay,
   And see him come ashore.
For there 's nae luck about the house,
   There 's nae luck at a';   10
There 's little pleasure in the house
   When our gudeman 's awa'.

And gie to me my bigonet,
   My bishop's satin gown;
For I maun tell the baillie's wife   15
   That Colin 's in the town.
My Turkey slippers maun gae on,
   My stockins pearly blue;
It's a' to pleasure our gudeman,
   For he 's baith leal and true.   20

Rise, lass, and mak a clean fireside,
  Put on the muckle pot;
Gie little Kate her button gown
  And Jock his Sunday coat;
And mak their shoon as black as slaes,   25
  Their hose as white as snaw;
It's a' to please my ain gudeman,
  For he's been long awa'.

There's twa fat hens upo' the coop
  Been fed this month and mair;   30
Mak haste and thraw their necks about,
  That Colin weel may fare;
And spread the table neat and clean,
  Gar ilka thing look braw,
For wha can tell how Colin fared   35
  When he was far awa'?

Sae true his heart, sae smooth his speech,
  His breath like caller air;
His very foot has music in't
  As he comes up the stair—   40
And will I see his face again?
  And will I hear him speak?
I'm downright dizzy wi' the thought,
  In troth I'm like to greet!

If Colin's weel, and weel content,   45
  I hae nae mair to crave:
And gin I live to keep him sae,
  I'm blest aboon the lave:
And will I see his face again,
  And will I hear him speak?   50
I'm downright dizzy wi' the thought,
  In troth I'm like to greet.
For there's nae luck about the house,
  There's nae luck at a';
There's little pleasure in the house   55
  When our gudeman's awa'.

W. J. Mickle

155

JEAN

Of a' the airts the wind can blaw
   I dearly like the West,
For there the bonnie lassie lives,
   The lassie I lo'e best:
There's wild woods grow, and rivers row,   5
   And mony a hill between;
But day and night my fancy's flight
   Is ever wi' my Jean.

I see her in the dewy flowers,
   I see her sweet and fair: 10
I hear her in the tunefu' birds,
   I hear her charm the air:
There's not a bonnie flower that springs
   By fountain, shaw, or green,
There's not a bonnie bird that sings   15
   But minds me o' my Jean.

O blaw ye westlin winds, blaw saft
   Amang the leafy trees;
Wi' balmy gale, frae hill and dale
   Bring hame the laden bees;   20
And bring the lassie back to me
   That's ay sae neat and clean;
Ae smile o' her wad banish care,
   Sae charming is my Jean.

What sighs and vows amang the knowes   25
   Hae pass'd atween us twa!
How fond to meet, how wae to part
   That night she gaed awa!
The Powers aboon can only ken
   To whom the heart is seen,   30
That nane can be sae dear to me
   As my sweet lovely Jean!

R. Burns

156

JOHN ANDERSON

John Anderson my jo, John,
  When we were first acquent
Your locks were like the raven,
  Your bonnie brow was brent;
But now your brow is beld, John,   5
  Your locks are like the snow;
But blessings on your frosty pow,
  John Anderson my jo.

John Anderson my jo, John,
  We clamb the hill thegither,   10
And mony a canty day, John,
  We've had wi' ane anither:
Now we maun totter down, John,
  But hand in hand we'll go,
And sleep thegither at the foot,   15
  John Anderson my jo.

R. Burns

157

THE LAND O' THE LEAL

I'm wearing awa', Jean,
Like snaw when it's thaw, Jean,
I'm wearing awa'
  To the land o' the leal.
There 's nae sorrow there, Jean,   5
There 's neither cauld nor care, Jean,
The day is ay fair
  In the land o' the leal.

Ye were ay leal and true, Jean,
Your task 's ended noo, Jean,   10
And I'll welcome you
  To the land o' the leal.

Our bonnie bairn 's there, Jean,
She was baith guid and fair, Jean;
O we grudged her right sair   15
    To the land o' the leal!

Then dry that tearfu' e'e, Jean,
My soul langs to be free, Jean,
And angels wait on me
    To the land o' the leal.   20
Now fare ye weel, my ain Jean,
This warld's care is vain, Jean;
We'll meet and ay be fain
    In the land o' the leal.

Lady Nairne

158

ODE ON A DISTANT PROSPECT OF ETON COLLEGE

Ye distant spires, ye antique towers
    That crown the watery glade,
Where grateful Science still adores
    Her Henry's holy shade;
And ye, that from the stately brow   5
Of Windsor's heights th' expanse below
    Of grove, of lawn, of mead survey,
Whose turf, whose shade, whose flowers among
Wanders the hoary Thames along
    His silver-winding way: 10

Ah happy hills! ah pleasing shade!
    Ah fields beloved in vain!
Where once my careless childhood stray'd,
    A stranger yet to pain!
I feel the gales that from ye blow   15
A momentary bliss bestow,
    As waving fresh their gladsome wing
My weary soul they seem to soothe,
And, redolent of joy and youth,
    To breathe a second spring.   20

Say, Father Thames, for thou hast seen
   Full many a sprightly race
Disporting on thy margent green
   The paths of pleasure trace;
Who foremost now delight to cleave   25
With pliant arm, thy glassy wave?
   The captive linnet which enthral?
What idle progeny succeed
To chase the rolling circle's speed
   Or urge the flying ball?   30

While some on earnest business bent
   Their murmuring labours ply
'Gainst graver hours, that bring constraint
   To sweeten liberty:
Some bold adventurers disdain   35
The limits of their little reign
   And unknown regions dare descry:
Still as they run they look behind,
They hear a voice in every wind,
   And snatch a fearful joy.   40

Gay hope is theirs by fancy fed,
   Less pleasing when possest;
The tear forgot as soon as shed,
   The sunshine of the breast:
Theirs buxom health, of rosy hue,   45
Wild wit, invention ever new,
   And lively cheer, of vigour born;
The thoughtless day, the easy night,
The spirits pure, the slumbers light
   That fly th' approach of morn.   50

Alas! regardless of their doom
   The little victims play!
No sense have they of ills to come
   Nor care beyond to-day:
Yet see how all around them wait   55
The Ministers of human fate
   And black Misfortune's baleful train!

Ah show them where in ambush stand
To seize their prey, the murderous band!
   Ah, tell them they are men!   60

These shall the fury Passions tear,
   The vultures of the mind,
Disdainful Anger, pallid Fear,
   And Shame that skulks behind;
Or pining Love shall waste their youth,   65
Or Jealousy with rankling tooth
   That inly gnaws the secret heart,
And Envy wan, and faded Care,
Grim-visaged comfortless Despair,
   And Sorrow's piercing dart.   70

Ambition this shall tempt to rise,
   Then whirl the wretch from high,
To bitter Scorn a sacrifice
   And grinning Infamy.
The stings of Falsehood those shall try,   75
And hard Unkindness' alter'd eye,
   That mocks the tear it forced to flow;
And keen Remorse with blood defiled,
And moody Madness laughing wild
   Amid severest woe.   80

Lo, in the vale of years beneath
   A griesly troop are seen,
The painful family of Death,
   More hideous than their Queen:
This racks the joints, this fires the veins,   85
That every labouring sinew strains,
   Those in the deeper vitals rage:
Lo, Poverty, to fill the band,
That numbs the soul with icy hand,
   And slow-consuming Age.   90

To each his sufferings: all are men,
   Condemn'd alike to groan;
The tender for another's pain,
   Th' unfeeling for his own.   94
Yet, ah! why should they know their fate,
Since sorrow never comes too late,

And happiness too swiftly flies?
Thought would destroy their paradise.
No more;—where ignorance is bliss,
	'Tis folly to be wise.				100

								T. Gray

159

HYMN TO ADVERSITY

Daughter of Jove, relentless power,
	Thou tamer of the human breast,
Whose iron scourge and torturing hour
	The bad affright, afflict the best!
Bound in thy adamantine chain				5
The proud are taught to taste of pain,
And purple tyrants vainly groan
With pangs unfelt before, unpitied and alone.

When first thy Sire to send on earth
	Virtue, his darling child, design'd,			10
To thee he gave the heavenly birth
	And bade to form her infant mind.
Stern, rugged Nurse! thy rigid lore
With patience many a year she bore:
What sorrow was, thou bad'st her know,			15
And from her own she learn'd to melt at others' woe.

Scared at thy frown terrific, fly
	Self-pleasing Folly's idle brood,
Wild Laughter, Noise, and thoughtless Joy,
	And leave us leisure to be good.			20
Light they disperse, and with them go
The summer Friend, the flattering Foe;
By vain Prosperity received,
To her they vow their truth, and are again believed.

Wisdom in sable garb array'd				25
	Immersed in rapturous thought profound,
And Melancholy, silent maid,
	With leaden eye, that loves the ground,

Still on thy solemn steps attend:
Warm Charity, the general friend,   30
With Justice, to herself severe,
And Pity dropping soft the sadly-pleasing tear.

O, gently on thy suppliant's head
    Dread Goddess, lay thy chastening hand!
Not in thy Gorgon terrors clad,   35
    Nor circled with the vengeful band
(As by the impious thou art seen)
With thundering voice, and threatening mien,
With screaming Horror's funeral cry,
Despair, and fell Disease, and ghastly Poverty: 40

Thy form benign, O Goddess, wear,
    Thy milder influence impart,
Thy philosophic train be there
    To soften, not to wound my heart.
The generous spark extinct revive,   45
Teach me to love and to forgive,
Exact my own defects to scan,
What others are to feel, and know myself a Man.
                                                   T. Gray

160

THE SOLITUDE OF ALEXANDER SELKIRK

I am monarch of all I survey,
    My right there is none to dispute;
From the centre all round to the sea
    I am lord of the fowl and the brute.
O solitude! where are the charms   5
    That sages have seen in thy face?
Better dwell in the midst of alarms
    Than reign in this horrible place.

I am out of humanity's reach.
    I must finish my journey alone,   10
Never hear the sweet music of speech;
    I start at the sound of my own.

The beasts that roam over the plain
  My form with indifference see;
They are so unacquainted with man,   15
  Their tameness is shocking to me.

Society, friendship, and love
  Divinely bestow'd upon man,
O had I the wings of a dove
  How soon would I taste you again!   20
My sorrows I then might assuage
  In the ways of religion and truth,
Might learn from the wisdom of age,
  And be cheer'd by the sallies of youth.

Ye winds that have made me your sport,   25
  Convey to this desolate shore
Some cordial endearing report
  Of a land I shall visit no more:
My friends, do they now and then send
  A wish or a thought after me?   30
O tell me I yet have a friend,
  Though a friend I am never to see.

How fleet is a glance of the mind!
  Compared with the speed of its flight,
The tempest itself lags behind,   35
  And the swift-wingéd arrows of light.
When I think of my own native land
  In a moment I seem to be there;
But, alas! recollection at hand
  Soon hurries me back to despair.   40

But the seafowl is gone to her nest,
  The beast is laid down in his lair;
Even here is a season of rest,
  And I to my cabin repair.
There is mercy in every place,   45
  And mercy, encouraging thought!
Gives even affliction a grace
  And reconciles man to his lot.

                                    W. Cowper

161

TO MARY UNWIN

Mary! I want a lyre with other strings,
   Such aid from heaven as some have feign'd they drew,
   An eloquence scarce given to mortals, new
And undebased by praise of meaner things,

That ere through age or woe I shed my wings   5
   I may record thy worth with honour due,
   In verse as musical as thou art true,
Verse that immortalizes whom it sings:—

But thou hast little need. There is a Book
   By seraphs writ with beams of heavenly light,   10
On which the eyes of God not rarely look,
   A chronicle of actions just and bright—

There all thy deeds, my faithful Mary, shine;
And since thou own'st that praise, I spare thee mine.
                          W. Cowper

162

TO THE SAME

   The twentieth year is well-nigh past
   Since first our sky was overcast;
   Ah, would that this might be the last!
       My Mary!

   Thy spirits have a fainter flow,   5
   I see thee daily weaker grow—
   'Twas my distress that brought thee low,
       My Mary!

   Thy needles, once a shining store,
   For my sake restless heretofore,   10
   Now rust disused, and shine no more;
       My Mary!

For though thou gladly wouldst fulfil
The same kind office for me still,
Thy sight now seconds not thy will,   15
    My Mary!

But well thou play'dst the housewife's part,
And all thy threads with magic art
Have wound themselves about this heart,
    My Mary!   20

Thy indistinct expressions seem
Like language utter'd in a dream;
Yet me they charm, whate'er the theme,
    My Mary!

Thy silver locks, once auburn bright,   25
Are still more lovely in my sight
Than golden beams of orient light,
    My Mary!

For could I view nor them nor thee,
What sight worth seeing could I see?   30
The sun would rise in vain for me,
    My Mary!

Partakers of thy sad decline
Thy hands their little force resign;
Yet, gently press'd, press gently mine,   35
    My Mary!

Such feebleness of limbs thou prov'st
That now at every step thou mov'st
Upheld by two; yet still thou lov'st,
    My Mary!   40

And still to love, though press'd with ill,
In wintry age to feel no chill,
With me is to be lovely still,
    My Mary!

But ah! by constant heed I know   45
How oft the sadness that I show
Transforms thy smiles to looks of woe,
    My Mary!

And should my future lot be cast
With much resemblance of the past,   50
Thy worn-out heart will break at last—
    My Mary!

                  W. Cowper

163

THE DYING MAN IN HIS GARDEN

Why, Damon, with the forward day
Dost thou thy little spot survey,
From tree to tree, with doubtful cheer,
Observe the progress of the year,
What winds arise, what rains descend,   5
When thou before that year shalt end?

What do thy noonday walks avail,
To clear the leaf, and pick the snail
Then wantonly to death decree
An insect usefuller than thee?   10
Thou and the worm are brother-kind,
As low, as earthy, and as blind.

Vain wretch! canst thou expect to see
The downy peach make court to thee?
Or that thy sense shall ever meet   15
The bean-flower's deep-embosom'd sweet
Exhaling with an evening's blast?
Thy evenings then will all be past!

Thy narrow pride, thy fancied green
(For vanity 's in little seen),   20
All must be left when Death appears,
In spite of wishes, groans, and tears;
Nor one of all thy plants that grow
But Rosemary will with thee go.

                  G. Sewell

164

TO-MORROW

In the downhill of life, when I find I'm declining,
   May my lot no less fortunate be
Than a snug elbow-chair can afford for reclining,
   And a cot that o'erlooks the wide sea;
With an ambling pad-pony to pace o'er the lawn,   5
   While I carol away idle sorrow,
And blithe as the lark that each day hails the dawn
   Look forward with hope for to-morrow.

With a porch at my door, both for shelter and shade
   too,
   As the sunshine or rain may prevail;   10
And a small spot of ground for the use of the spade
   too,
   With a barn for the use of the flail:
A cow for my dairy, a dog for my game,
   And a purse when a friend wants to borrow;
I'll envy no nabob his riches or fame,   15
   Nor what honours await him to-morrow.

From the bleak northern blast may my cot be completely
   Secured by a neighbouring hill;
And at night may repose steal upon me more sweetly
   By the sound of a murmuring rill: 20
And while peace and plenty I find at my board,
   With a heart free from sickness and sorrow,
With my friends may I share what to-day may
   afford,
   And let them spread the table to-morrow.   24

And when I at last must throw off this frail covering
   Which I've worn for three-score years and ten,
On the brink of the grave I'll not seek to keep
   hovering,
   Nor my thread wish to spin o'er again:

But my face in the glass I'll serenely survey,
  And with smiles count each wrinkle and furrow;   30
As this old worn-out stuff, which is threadbare to-day,
  May become everlasting to-morrow.

J. Collins

165

Life! I know not what thou art,
But know that thou and I must part;
And when, or how, or where we met
I own to me 's a secret yet.

Life! we've been long together   5
Through pleasant and through cloudy weather;
'Tis hard to part when friends are dear—
Perhaps 'twill cost a sigh, a tear;
—Then steal away, give little warning,
  Choose thine own time;   10
Say not Good Night,—but in some brighter clime
  Bid me Good Morning.

A. L. Barbauld

THE GOLDEN TREASURY

BOOK FOURTH

166

ON FIRST LOOKING INTO CHAPMAN'S HOMER

Much have I travell'd in the realms of gold
  And many goodly states and kingdoms seen;
  Round many western islands have I been
Which bards in fealty to Apollo hold.

Oft of one wide expanse had I been told   5
  That deep-brow'd Homer ruled as his demesne;
  Yet did I never breathe its pure serene
Till I heard Chapman speak out loud and bold:

Then felt I like some watcher of the skies
  When a new planet swims into his ken;   10
Or like stout Cortez, when with eagle eyes

  He stared at the Pacific—and all his men
Look'd at each other with a wild surmise—
  Silent, upon a peak of Darien.

J. Keats

167

ODE ON THE POETS

Bards of Passion and of Mirth
Ye have left your souls on earth!
Have ye souls in heaven too,
Double-lived in regions new?

Yes, and those of heaven commune   5
With the spheres of sun and moon;
With the noise of fountains wond'rous
And the parle of voices thund'rous;
With the whisper of heaven's trees
And one another, in soft ease   10
Seated on Elysian lawns
Brows'd by none but Dian's fawns;
Underneath large blue-bells tented,
Where the daisies are rose-scented,
And the rose herself has got   15
Perfume which on earth is not;
Where the nightingale doth sing
Not a senseless, trancéd thing,
But divine melodious truth;
Philosophic numbers smooth;   20
Tales and golden histories
Of heaven and its mysteries.

Thus ye live on high, and then
On the earth ye live again;
And the souls ye left behind you   25
Teach us, here, the way to find you,
Where your other souls are joying,
Never slumber'd, never cloying.
Here, your earth-born souls still speak
To mortals, of their little week;   30
Of their sorrows and delights;
Of their passions and their spites;
Of their glory and their shame;
What doth strengthen and what maim:—
Thus ye teach us, every day,   35
Wisdom, though fled far away.

Bards of Passion and of Mirth
Ye have left your souls on earth!
Ye have souls in heaven too,
Double-lived in regions new!   40
                                    J. Keats

168

LOVE

All thoughts, all passions, all delights,
   Whatever stirs this mortal frame,
All are but ministers of Love,
      And feed his sacred flame.

Oft in my waking dreams do I   5
   Live o'er again that happy hour,
When midway on the mount I lay
      Beside the ruin'd tower.

The moonshine stealing o'er the scene
   Had blended with the lights of eve;   10
And she was there, my hope, my joy,
      My own dear Genevieve!

She lean'd against the arméd man,
   The statue of the arméd knight;
She stood and listen'd to my lay,   15
      Amid the lingering light.

Few sorrows hath she of her own,
   My hope! my joy! my Genevieve!
She loves me best whene'er I sing
      The songs that make her grieve.   20

I play'd a soft and doleful air,
   I sang an old and moving story—
An old rude song, that suited well
      That ruin wild and hoary.

She listen'd with a flitting blush,   25
   With downcast eyes and modest grace;
For well she knew I could not choose
      But gaze upon her face.

I told her of the Knight that wore
   Upon his shield a burning brand;   30
And that for ten long years he woo'd
      The Lady of the Land.

I told her how he pined; and ah!
  The deep, the low, the pleading tone
With which I sang another's love   35
    Interpreted my own.

She listen'd with a flitting blush,
  With downcast eyes and modest grace;
And she forgave me, that I gazed
    Too fondly on her face.   40

But when I told the cruel scorn
  That crazed that bold and lovely Knight,
And that he cross'd the mountain-woods,
    Nor rested day nor night;

That sometimes from the savage den,   45
  And sometimes from the darksome shade,
And sometimes starting up at once
    In green and sunny glade

There came and look'd him in the face
  An angel beautiful and bright;   50
And that he knew it was a Fiend,
    This miserable Knight!

And that, unknowing what he did,
  He leap'd amid a murderous band,
And saved from outrage worse than death   55
    The Lady of the Land;

And how she wept, and clasp'd his knees
  And how she tended him in vain;
And ever strove to expiate
    The scorn that crazed his brain;   60

And that she nursed him in a cave,
  And how his madness went away,
When on the yellow forest leaves
    A dying man he lay;

—His dying words—but when I reach'd   65
  That tenderest strain of all the ditty,
My faltering voice and pausing harp
    Disturb'd her soul with pity!

All impulses of soul and sense
   Had thrill'd my guileless Genevieve;   70
The music and the doleful tale,
     The rich and balmy eve;

And hopes, and fears that kindle hope,
   An undistinguishable throng,
And gentle wishes long subdued,   75
     Subdued and cherish'd long!

She wept with pity and delight,
   She blush'd with love and virgin shame;
And like the murmur of a dream,
     I heard her breathe my name.   80

Her bosom heaved—she stepp'd aside,
   As conscious of my look she stept—
Then suddenly, with timorous eye
     She fled to me and wept.

She half enclosed me with her arms,   85
   She press'd me with a meek embrace;
And bending back her head, look'd up,
     And gazed upon my face.

'Twas partly love, and partly fear,
   And partly 'twas a bashful art,   90
That I might rather feel, than see,
     The swelling of her heart.

I calm'd her fears, and she was calm,
   And told her love with virgin pride;
And so I won my Genevieve,   95
     My bright and beauteous Bride.

S. T. Coleridge

169

ALL FOR LOVE

O talk not to me of a name great in story;
The days of our youth are the days of our glory;
And the myrtle and ivy of sweet two-and-twenty
Are worth all your laurels, though ever so plenty.

What are garlands and crowns to the brow that is
    wrinkled?   5
'Tis but as a dead flower with May-dew besprinkled:
Then away with all such from the head that is hoary—
What care I for the wreaths that can only give glory?

O Fame!—if I e'er took delight in thy praises,
'Twas less for the sake of thy high-sounding phrases,   10
Than to see the bright eyes of the dear one discover
She thought that I was not unworthy to love her.

There chiefly I sought thee, there only I found thee;
Her glance was the best of the rays that surround thee;
When it sparkled o'er aught that was bright in my
    story,   15
I knew it was love, and I felt it was glory.

                                                    Lord Byron

                            170

                        THE OUTLAW

        O Brignall banks are wild and fair,
            And Greta woods are green,
        And you may gather garlands there
            Would grace a summer queen.
        And as I rode by Dalton Hall   5
            Beneath the turrets high,
        A Maiden on the castle-wall
            Was singing merrily:
        'O Brignall banks are fresh and fair,
            And Greta woods are green;   10
        I'd rather rove with Edmund there
            Than reign our English queen.'

        'If, Maiden, thou wouldst wend with me,
            To leave both tower and town,
        Thou first must guess what life lead we   15
            That dwell by dale and down.
        And if thou canst that riddle read,
            As read full well you may,

Then to the greenwood shalt thou speed
  As blithe as Queen of May.'   20
Yet sung she, 'Brignall banks are fair
  And Greta woods are green;
I'd rather rove with Edmund there
  Than reign our English queen.

'I read you by your bugle-horn   25
  And by your palfrey good,
I read you for a ranger sworn
  To keep the king's greenwood.'
'A ranger, lady, winds his horn,
  And 'tis at peep of light;   30
His blast is heard at merry morn,
  And mine at dead of night.'
Yet sung she, 'Brignall banks are fair,
  And Greta woods are gay;
I would I were with Edmund there   35
  To reign his Queen of May!

'With burnish'd brand and musketoon
  So gallantly you come,
I read you for a bold Dragoon
  That lists the tuck of drum.'   40
'I list no more the tuck of drum,
  No more the trumpet hear;
But when the beetle sounds his hum
  My comrades take the spear.
And O! though Brignall banks be fair   45
  And Greta woods be gay,
Yet mickle must the maiden dare
  Would reign my Queen of May!

'Maiden! a nameless life I lead,
  A nameless death I'll die;   50
The fiend whose lantern lights the mead
  Were better mate than I!
And when I'm with my comrades met
  Beneath the greenwood bough,—
What once we were we all forget,   55
  Nor think what we are now.'

Chorus

Yet Brignall banks are fresh and fair,
  And Greta woods are green,
And you may gather garlands there
  Would grace a summer queen.   60
                                    Sir W. Scott

171

There be none of Beauty's daughters
  With a magic like thee;
And like music on the waters
  Is thy sweet voice to me:
When, as if its sound were causing   5
The charméd ocean's pausing,
The waves lie still and gleaming,
And the lull'd winds seem dreaming:

And the midnight moon is weaving
  Her bright chain o'er the deep,   10
Whose breast is gently heaving
  As an infant's asleep:
So the spirit bows before thee
To listen and adore thee;
With a full but soft emotion,   15
Like the swell of Summer's ocean.
                                    Lord Byron

172

LINES TO AN INDIAN AIR

I arise from dreams of thee
  In the first sweet sleep of night,
When the winds are breathing low
  And the stars are shining bright:
I arise from dreams of thee,   5
  And a spirit in my feet
Has led me—who knows how?
  To thy chamber-window, sweet!

The wandering airs they faint
  On the dark, the silent stream—   10
The champak odours fail
  Like sweet thoughts in a dream;
The nightingale's complaint
  It dies upon her heart,
As I must die on thine,   15
  O belovéd as thou art!

O lift me from the grass!
  I die, I faint, I fail!
Let thy love in kisses rain
  On my lips and eyelids pale.   20
My cheek is cold and white, alas!
  My heart beats loud and fast;
O! press it close to thine again
  Where it will break at last.

              P. B. Shelley

173

She walks in beauty, like the night
  Of cloudless climes and starry skies,
And all that 's best of dark and bright
  Meet in her aspect and her eyes,
Thus mellow'd to that tender light   5
  Which heaven to gaudy day denies.

One shade the more, one ray the less,
  Had half impair'd the nameless grace
Which waves in every raven tress,
  Of softly lightens o'er her face,   10
Where thoughts serenely sweet express
  How pure, how dear their dwelling-place.

And on that cheek and o'er that brow
  So soft, so calm, yet eloquent,
The smiles that win, the tints that glow   15
  But tell of days in goodness spent,
A mind at peace with all below,
  A heart whose love is innocent.

              Lord Byron

G

174

She was a phantom of delight
When first she gleam'd upon my sight;
A lovely apparition, sent
To be a moment's ornament;
Her eyes as stars of Twilight fair;   5
Like Twilight's, too, her dusky hair;
But all things else about her drawn
From May-time and the cheerful dawn;
A dancing shape, an image gay,
To haunt, to startle, and waylay.   10

I saw her upon nearer view,
A spirit, yet a woman too!
Her household motions light and free,
And steps of virgin-liberty;
A countenance in which did meet   15
Sweet records, promises as sweet;
A creature not too bright or good
For human nature's daily food,
For transient sorrows, simple wiles,
Praise, blame, love, kisses, tears, and smiles.   20

And now I see with eye serene
The very pulse of the machine;
A being breathing thoughtful breath,
A traveller between life and death:
The reason firm, the temperate will,   25
Endurance, foresight, strength, and skill;
A perfect woman, nobly plann'd
To warn, to comfort, and command;
And yet a Spirit still, and bright
With something of angelic light.   30
                                      W. Wordsworth

175

She is not fair to outward view
    As many maidens be;
Her loveliness I never knew
    Until she smiled on me.

O then I saw her eye was bright,   5
A well of love, a spring of light.

But now her looks are coy and cold,
    To mine they ne'er reply,
And yet I cease not to behold
    The love-light in her eye: 10
Her very frowns are fairer far
Than smiles of other maidens are.

H. Coleridge

176

I fear thy kisses, gentle maiden;
    Thou needest not fear mine;
My spirit is too deeply laden
    Ever to burthen thine.

I fear thy mien, thy tones, thy motion;   5
    Thou needest not fear mine;
Innocent is the heart's devotion
    With which I worship thine.

P. B. Shelley

177

THE LOST LOVE

She dwelt among the untrodden ways
    Beside the springs of Dove;
A maid whom there were none to praise,
    And very few to love:

A violet by a mossy stone   5
    Half hidden from the eye!
—Fair as a star, when only one
    Is shining in the sky.

She lived unknown, and few could know
    When Lucy ceased to be;   10
But she is in her grave, and oh,
    The difference to me!

W. Wordsworth

178

I travell'd among unknown men
  In lands beyond the sea;
Nor, England! did I know till then
  What love I bore to thee.

'Tis past, that melancholy dream!   5
  Nor will I quit thy shore
A second time; for still I seem
  To love thee more and more.

Among thy mountains did I feel
  The joy of my desire;   10
And she I cherish'd turn'd her wheel
  Beside an English fire.

Thy mornings show'd, thy nights conceal'd
  The bowers where Lucy play'd;
And thine too is the last green field   15
  That Lucy's eyes survey'd.

                                        W. Wordsworth

179

THE EDUCATION OF NATURE

Three years she grew in sun and shower;
Then Nature said, 'A lovelier flower
  On earth was never sown:
This child I to myself will take;
She shall be mine, and I will make   5
  A lady of my own.

'Myself will to my darling be
Both law and impulse: and with me
  The girl, in rock and plain,
In earth and heaven, in glade and bower,   10
Shall feel an overseeing power
  To kindle or restrain.

'She shall be sportive as the fawn
That wild with glee across the lawn
   Or up the mountain springs;   15
And hers shall be the breathing balm,
And hers the silence and the calm
   Of mute insensate things.

'The floating clouds their state shall lend
To her; for her the willow bend;   20
   Nor shall she fail to see
E'en in the motions of the storm
Grace that shall mould the maiden's form
   By silent sympathy.

'The stars of midnight shall be dear   25
To her; and she shall lean her ear
   In many a secret place
Where rivulets dance their wayward round,
And beauty born of murmuring sound
   Shall pass into her face.   30

'And vital feelings of delight
Shall rear her form to stately height,
   Her virgin bosom swell;
Such thoughts to Lucy I will give
While she and I together live   35
   Here in this happy dell.'

Thus Nature spake—The work was done—
How soon my Lucy's race was run!
   She died, and left to me
This heath, this calm and quiet scene;   40
The memory of what has been,
   And never more will be.

                 W. Wordsworth

180

A slumber did my spirit seal;
   I had no human fears:
She seem'd a thing that could not feel
   The touch of earthly years.

No motion has she now, no force;   5
  She neither hears nor sees;
Roll'd round in earth's diurnal course
  With rocks, and stones, and trees.

W. Wordsworth

181

LORD ULLIN'S DAUGHTER

A Chieftain to the Highlands bound
  Cries 'Boatman, do not tarry!
And I'll give thee a silver pound
  To row us o'er the ferry!'

'Now who be ye, would cross Lochgyle   5
  This dark and stormy water?'
'O I'm the chief of Ulva's isle,
  And this, Lord Ullin's daughter.

'And fast before her father's men
  Three days we've fled together,   10
For should he find us in the glen,
  My blood would stain the heather.

'His horsemen hard behind us ride—
  Should they our steps discover,
Then who will cheer my bonny bride   15
  When they have slain her lover?'

Out spoke the hardy Highland wight,
  'I'll go, my chief, I'm ready:
It is not for your silver bright,
  But for your winsome lady:—   20

'And by my word; the bonny bird
  In danger shall not tarry;
So though the waves are raging white
  I'll row you o'er the ferry.'

By this the storm grew loud apace,   25
  The water-wraith was shrieking;
And in the scowl of heaven each face
  Grew dark as they were speaking.

But still as wilder blew the wind
   And as the night grew drearer,   30
Adown the glen rode arméd men,
   The trampling sounded nearer.

'O haste thee, haste!' the lady cries,
   'Though tempests round us gather;
I'll meet the raging of the skies,   35
   But not an angry father.'

The boat has left a stormy land,
   A stormy sea before her,—
When, oh! too strong for human hand
   The tempest gather'd o'er her.   40

And still they row'd amidst the roar
   Of waters fast prevailing:
Lord Ullin reach'd that fatal shore,—
   His wrath was changed to wailing.

For, sore dismay'd, through storm and shade   45
   His child he did discover:—
One lovely hand she stretch'd for aid,
   And one was round her lover.

'Come back! come back!' he cried in grief,
   'Across this stormy water: 50
And I'll forgive your Highland chief,
   My daughter!—O my daughter!'

'Twas vain: the loud waves lash'd the shore,
   Return or aid preventing:
The waters wild went o'er his child,   55
   And he was left lamenting.

T. Campbell

182

JOCK O' HAZELDEAN

'Why weep ye by the tide, ladie?
   Why weep ye by the tide?
I'll wed ye to my youngest son,
   And ye sall be his bride:

And ye sall be his bride, ladie,   5
  Sae comely to be seen'—
But aye she loot the tears down fa'
  For Jock o' Hazeldean.

'Now let this wilfu' grief be done,
  And dry that cheek so pale;   10
Young Frank is chief of Errington
  And lord of Langley-dale;
His step is first in peaceful ha',
  His sword in battle keen'—
But aye she loot the tears down fa'   15
  For Jock o' Hazeldean.

'A chain of gold ye sall not lack,
  Nor braid to bind your hair;
Nor mettled hound, nor managed hawk,
  Nor palfrey fresh and fair;   20
And you, the foremost o' them a',
  Shall ride our forest queen'—
But aye she loot the tears down fa'
  For Jock o' Hazeldean.

The kirk was deck'd at morning-tide,   25
  The tapers glimmer'd fair;
The priest and bridegroom wait the bride,
  And dame and knight are there.
They sought her baith by bower and ha';
  The ladie was not seen!   30
She 's o'er the Border, and awa'
  Wi' Jock o' Hazeldean.

                  Sir W. Scott

183

FREEDOM AND LOVE

How delicious is the winning
Of a kiss at love's beginning,
When two mutual hearts are sighing
For the knot there 's no untying!

Yet remember, 'midst your wooing,   5
Love has bliss, but Love has ruing;
Other smiles may make you fickle,
Tears for other charms may trickle.

Love he comes, and Love he tarries,
Just as fate or fancy carries;   10
Longest stays, when sorest chidden;
Laughs and flies, when press'd and bidden.

Bind the sea to slumber stilly,
Bind its odour to the lily,
Bind the aspen ne'er to quiver,   15
Then bind Love to last for ever.

Love's a fire that needs renewal
Of fresh beauty for its fuel:
Love's wing moults when caged and captured,
Only free, he soars enraptured.   20

Can you keep the bee from ranging
Or the ringdove's neck from changing?
No! nor fetter'd Love from dying
In the knot there's no untying.

                                    T. Campbell

184

LOVE'S PHILOSOPHY

The fountains mingle with the river
    And the rivers with the ocean,
The winds of heaven mix for ever
    With a sweet emotion;
Nothing in the world is single,   5
    All things by a law divine
In one another's being mingle—
    Why not I with thine?

See the mountains kiss high heaven
    And the waves clasp one another;   10
No sister-flower would be forgiven
    If it disdain'd its brother:

                                              G*

And the sunlight clasps the earth,
   And the moonbeams kiss the sea—
What are all these kissings worth,   15
   If thou kiss not me?

                          P. B. Shelley

185

ECHOES

How sweet the answer Echo makes
   To Music at night,
When, roused by lute or horn, she wakes,
And far away o'er lawns and lakes
   Goes answering light!   5

Yet Love hath echoes truer far
   And far more sweet
Than e'er, beneath the moonlight's star,
Of horn or lute or soft guitar
   The songs repeat.   10

'Tis when the sigh,—in youth sincere
   And only then—
The sigh that 's breathed for one to hear,
Is by that one, that only Dear
   Breathed back again.   15

                          T. Moore

186

A SERENADE

Ah! County Guy, the hour is nigh,
   The sun has left the lea,
The orange flower perfumes the bower,
   The breeze is on the sea.
The lark, his lay who trill'd all day,   5
   Sits hush'd his partner nigh;
Breeze, bird, and flower confess the hour,
   But where is County Guy?

The village maid steals through the shade
  Her shepherd's suit to hear;   10
To beauty shy, by lattice high,
  Sings high-born Cavalier.
The star of Love, all stars above,
  Now reigns o'er earth and sky,
And high and low the influence know—   15
  But where is County Guy?

                      Sir W. Scott

187

TO THE EVENING STAR

Gem of the crimson-colour'd Even,
  Companion of retiring day,
Why at the closing gates of heaven,
  Belovéd Star, dost thou delay?

So fair thy pensile beauty burns   5
  When soft the tear of twilight flows;
So due thy plighted love returns
  To chambers brighter than the rose;

To Peace, to Pleasure, and to Love
  So kind a star thou seem'st to be,   10
Sure some enamour'd orb above
  Descends and burns to meet with thee.

Thine is the breathing, blushing hour,
  When all unheavenly passions fly,
Chased by the soul-subduing power   15
  Of Love's delicious witchery.

O! sacred to the fall of day,
  Queen of propitious stars, appear,
And early rise, and long delay,
  When Caroline herself is here!   20

Shine on her chosen green resort,
  Whose trees the sunward summit crown,
And wanton flowers, that well may court
  An angel's feet to tread them down.

Shine on her sweetly-scented road,   25
  Thou star of evening's purple dome,
That lead'st the nightingale abroad,
  And guid'st the pilgrim to his home.

Shine where my charmer's sweeter breath
  Embalms the soft exhaling dew,   30
Where dying winds a sigh bequeath
  To kiss the cheek of rosy hue.

Where, winnow'd by the gentle air,
  Her silken tresses darkly flow,
And fall upon her brow so fair,   35
  Like shadows on the mountain snow.

Thus, ever thus, at day's decline
  In converse sweet to wander far—
O bring with thee my Caroline,
  And thou shalt be my Ruling Star!   40

T. Campbell

188

TO THE NIGHT

Swiftly walk over the western wave
      Spirit of Night!
Out of the misty eastern cave,
  Where, all the long and lone daylight,
Thou wovest dreams of joy and fear   5
Which make thee terrible and dear,—
      Swift be thy flight!

Wrap thy form in a mantle grey
      Star-inwrought!
Blind with thine hair the eyes of Day,   10
  Kiss her until she be wearied out,
Then wander o'er city, and sea, and land,
Touching all with thine opiate wand—
      Come, long-sought!

When I arose and saw the dawn,   15
       I sigh'd for thee;
When light rode high, and the dew was gone,
  And noon lay heavy on flower and tree,
And the weary Day turn'd to his rest,
Lingering like an unloved guest,   20
       I sigh'd for thee.

Thy brother Death came, and cried,
      'Wouldst thou me?'
Thy sweet child Sleep, the filmy-eyed,
  Murmur'd like a noontide bee,   25
'Shall I nestle near thy side?
Wouldst thou me?'—And I replied,
      'No, not thee!'

Death will come when thou art dead,
      Soon, too soon—   30
Sleep will come when thou art fled;
  Of neither would I ask the boon
I ask of thee, belovéd Night—
Swift be thine approaching flight,
      Come soon, soon!   35

P. B. Shelley

189

TO A DISTANT FRIEND

Why art thou silent?   Is thy love a plant
  Of such weak fibre that the treacherous air
  Of absence withers what was once so fair?
Is there no debt to pay, no boon to grant?

Yet have my thoughts for thee been vigilant,   5
  Bound to thy service with unceasing care—
The mind's least generous wish a mendicant
  For nought but what thy happiness could spare.

Speak!—though this soft warm heart, once free to hold
  A thousand tender pleasures, thine and mine,   10
Be left more desolate, more dreary cold

Than a forsaken bird's-nest fill'd with snow
  'Mid its own bush of leafless eglantine—
Speak, that my torturing doubts their end may know!
W. Wordsworth

190

When we two parted
  In silence and tears,
Half broken-hearted,
  To sever for years,
Pale grew thy cheek and cold,   5
  Colder thy kiss;
Truly that hour foretold
  Sorrow to this!

The dew of the morning
  Sunk chill on my brow;   10
It felt like the warning
  Of what I feel now.
Thy vows are all broken,
  And light is thy fame:
I hear thy name spoken   15
  And share in its shame.

They name thee before me,
  A knell to mine ear;
A shudder comes o'er me—
  Why wert thou so dear?   20
They know not I knew thee
  Who knew thee too well:
Long, long shall I rue thee
  Too deeply to tell.

In secret we met: 25
  In silence I grieve
That thy heart could forget,
  Thy spirit deceive.
If I should meet thee
  After long years,   30
How should I greet thee?—
  With silence and tears.
Lord Byron

191

HAPPY INSENSIBILITY

In a drear-nighted December,
  Too happy, happy tree,
Thy branches ne'er remember
  Their green felicity:
The north cannot undo them   5
With a sleety whistle through them,
Nor frozen thawings glue them
  From budding at the prime.

In a drear-nighted December,
  Too happy, happy brook,   10
Thy bubblings ne'er remember
  Apollo's summer look;
But with a sweet forgetting
They stay their crystal fretting,
Never, never petting   15
  About the frozen time.

Ah, would 'twere so with many
  A gentle girl and boy!
But were there ever any
  Writhed not at passéd joy?   20
To know the change and feel it,
When there is none to heal it
Nor numbéd sense to steel it—
  Was never said in rhyme.

J. Keats

192

Where shall the lover rest
  Whom the fates sever
From his true maiden's breast,
  Parted for ever?

Where, through groves deep and high,   5
  Sounds the far billow,
Where early violets die
  Under the willow.
    Eleu loro!
Soft shall be his pillow.   10

There, through the summer day,
  Cool streams are laving:
There, while the tempests sway,
  Scarce are boughs waving;
There thy rest shalt thou take,   15
  Parted for ever,
Never again to wake,
  Never, O never!
    Eleu loro!
  Never, O never!   20

Where shall the traitor rest,
  He, the deceiver,
Who could win maiden's breast,
  Ruin, and leave her?
In the lost battle,   25
  Borne down by the flying,
Where mingles war's rattle
  With groans of the dying;
    Eleu loro!
  There shall he be lying.   30

Her wing shall the eagle flap
  O'er the falsehearted;
His warm blood the wolf shall lap
  Ere life be parted:
Shame and dishonour sit   35
  By his grave ever;
Blessing shall hallow it
  Never, O never!
    Eleu loro!
  Never, O never!   40

Sir W. Scott

193

LA BELLE DAME SANS MERCI

'O what can ail thee, knight-at-arms,
    Alone and palely loitering?
The sedge has wither'd from the Lake,
    And no birds sing.

'O what can ail thee, knight-at-arms!   5
    So haggard and so woebegone?
The squirrel's granary is full,
    And the harvest's done.

'I see a lily on thy brow
    With anguish moist and fever dew,   10
And on thy cheeks a fading rose
    Fast withereth too.'

'I met a Lady in the Meads,
    Full beautiful—a fairy's child,
Her hair was long, her foot was light,   15
    And her eyes were wild.

'I made a garland for her head,
    And bracelets too, and fragrant zone;
She look'd at me as she did love,
    And made sweet moan.   20

'I set her on my pacing steed
    And nothing else saw all day long,
For sidelong would she bend, and sing
    A fairy's song.

'She found me roots of relish sweet,   25
    And honey wild and manna dew,
And sure in language strange she said
    "I love thee true."

'She took me to her elfin grot,
    And there she wept, and sigh'd full sore, 30
And there I shut her wild wild eyes
    With kisses four.

'And there she lulléd me asleep,
   And there I dream'd—Ah! woe betide!
The latest dream I ever dreamt   35
   On the cold hill side.

'I saw pale Kings and Princes too,
   Pale warriors, death-pale were they all;
They cried—"La belle Dame sans Merci
   Thee hath in thrall!"   40

'I saw their starved lips in the gloom
   With horrid warning gapéd wide,
And I awoke and found me here
   On the cold hill's side.

'And this is why I sojourn here   45
   Alone and palely loitering,
Though the sedge is wither'd from the Lake
   And no birds sing.'

J. Keats

194

THE ROVER

'A weary lot is thine, fair maid,
   A weary lot is thine!
To pull the thorn thy brow to braid,
   And press the rue for wine.
A lightsome eye, a soldier's mien,   5
   A feather of the blue,
A doublet of the Lincoln green—
   No more of me you knew
               My love!
No more of me you knew.   10

'This morn is merry June, I trow,
   The rose is budding fain;
But she shall bloom in winter snow
   Ere we two meet again.'
He turn'd his charger as he spake   15
   Upon the river shore,

He gave his bridle-reins a shake,
　Said 'Adieu for evermore
　　　　　　　　My Love!
And adieu for evermore.'   20
　　　　　　　　　　　Sir W. Scott

195

THE FLIGHT OF LOVE

When the lamp is shattered,
　The light in the dust lies dead—
When the cloud is shattered,
　The rainbow's glory is shed.
When the lute is broken,   5
　Sweet tones are remembered not;
When the lips have spoken,
　Loved accents are soon forgot.

As music and splendour
　Survive not the lamp and the lute,   10
The heart's echoes render
　No song when the spirit is mute—
No song but sad dirges,
　Like the wind through a ruined cell,
Or the mournful surges   15
　That ring the dead seaman's knell.

When hearts have once mingled,
　Love first leaves the well-built nest;
The weak one is singled
　To endure what it once possest.   20
O Love! who bewailest
　The frailty of all things here,
Why choose you the frailest
　For your cradle, your home, and your bier?

Its passions will rock thee   25
　As the storms rock the ravens on high;
Bright reason will mock thee
　Like the sun from a wintry sky.

From thy nest every rafter
  Will rot, and thine eagle home   30
Leave thee naked to laughter,
  When leaves fall and cold winds come.

                                        P. B. Shelley

                        196

            THE MAID OF NEIDPATH

O lovers' eyes are sharp to see,
  And lovers' ears in hearing;
And love, in life's extremity,
  Can lend an hour of cheering.
Disease had been in Mary's bower   5
  And slow decay from mourning,
Though now she sits on Neidpath's tower
  To watch her love's returning.

All sunk and dim her eyes so bright,
  Her form decay'd by pining,   10
Till through her wasted hand, at night,
  You saw the taper shining.
By fits a sultry hectic hue
  Across her cheek was flying;
By fits so ashy pale she grew   15
  Her maidens thought her dying.

Yet keenest powers to see and hear
  Seem'd in her frame residing;
Before the watch-dog prick'd his ear
  She heard her lover's riding;   20
Ere scarce a distant form was kenn'd
  She knew and waved to greet him,
And o'er the battlement did bend
  As on the wing to meet him.

He came—he pass'd—an heedless gaze,   25
  As o'er some stranger glancing;
Her welcome, spoke in faltering phrase,
  Lost in his courser's prancing—

The castle-arch, whose hollow tone
   Returns each whisper spoken,   30
Could scarcely catch the feeble moan
   Which told her heart was broken.

Sir W. Scott

197

THE MAID OF NEIDPATH

Earl March look'd on his dying child,
   And, smit with grief to view her—
'The youth,' he cried, 'whom I exiled
   Shall be restored to woo her.'

She's at the window many an hour   5
   His coming to discover:
And he look'd up to Ellen's bower
   And she look'd on her lover—

But ah! so pale, he knew her not,
   Though her smile on him was dwelling—   10
'And am I then forgot—forgot?'
   It broke the heart of Ellen.

In vain he weeps, in vain he sighs,
   Her cheek is cold as ashes;
Nor love's own kiss shall wake those eyes   15
   To lift their silken lashes.

T. Campbell

198

Bright Star, would I were steadfast as thou art—
   Not in lone splendour hung aloft the night,
And watching, with eternal lids apart,
   Like nature's patient sleepless Eremite,

The moving waters at their priestlike task   5
   Of pure ablution round earth's human shores,
Or gazing on the new soft-fallen mask
   Of snow upon the mountains and the moors—

No—yet still steadfast, still unchangeable,
  Pillow'd upon my fair love's ripening breast,   10
To feel for ever its soft fall and swell,
  Awake for ever in a sweet unrest;

Still, still to hear her tender-taken breath,
And so live ever,—or else swoon to death.

                                                   J. Keats

199

THE TERROR OF DEATH

When I have fears that I may cease to be
  Before my pen has glean'd my teeming brain,
Before high-piléd books, in charact'ry
  Hold like rich garners the full-ripen'd grain;

When I behold, upon the night's starr'd face,   5
  Huge cloudy symbols of a high romance,
And think that I may never live to trace
  Their shadows, with the magic hand of chance;

And when I feel, fair creature of an hour!
  That I shall never look upon thee more,   10
Never have relish in the fairy power
  Of unreflecting love—then on the shore

Of the wide world I stand alone, and think
Till love and fame to nothingness do sink.

                                                   J. Keats

200

DESIDERIA

Surprised by joy—impatient as the wind—
  I turn'd to share the transport—O with whom
  But Thee—deep buried in the silent tomb,
That spot which no vicissitude can find?

Love, faithful love recall'd thee to my mind—   5
   But how could I forget thee? Through what power
   Even for the least division of an hour
Have I been so beguiled as to be blind

To my most grievous loss?—That thought's return
   Was the worst pang that sorrow ever bore,   10
Save one, one only, when I stood forlorn,

   Knowing my heart's best treasure was no more;
That neither present time, nor years unborn
   Could to my sight that heavenly face restore.

                                        W. Wordsworth

201

At the mid hour of night, when stars are weeping, I fly
To the lone vale we loved, when life shone warm in
      thine eye;
And I think oft, if spirits can steal from the regions of air
To revisit past scenes of delight, thou wilt come to me
      there
And tell me our love is remember'd, even in the sky! 5

Then I sing the wild song it once was rapture to hear,
When our voices, commingling, breathed like one on the
      ear;
And as Echo far off through the vale my sad orison rolls,
I think, O my Love! 'tis thy voice, from the Kingdom
      of Souls
Faintly answering still the notes that once were so dear. 10

                                            T. Moore

202

ELEGY ON THYRZA

And thou art dead, as young and fair
   As aught of mortal birth;
And form so soft and charms so rare
   Too soon return'd to Earth!

Though Earth received them in her bed,   5
And o'er the spot the crowd may tread
    In carelessness or mirth,
There is an eye which could not brook
A moment on that grave to look.

I will not ask where thou liest low,   10
    Nor gaze upon the spot;
There flowers or weeds at will may grow,
    So I behold them not:
It is enough for me to prove
That what I loved and long must love   15
    Like common earth can rot;
To me there needs no stone to tell
'Tis Nothing that I loved so well.

Yet did I love thee to the last,
    As fervently as thou,   20
Who didst not change through all the past
    And canst not alter now.
The love where Death has set his seal
Nor age can chill, nor rival steal,
    Nor falsehood disavow: 25
And, what were worse, thou canst not see
Or wrong, or change, or fault in me.

The better days of life were ours;
    The worst can be but mine:
The sun that cheers, the storm that lours,   30
    Shall never more be thine.
The silence of that dreamless sleep
I envy now too much to weep;
    Nor need I to repine
That all those charms have pass'd away   35
I might have watch'd through long decay.

The flower in ripen'd bloom unmatch'd
    Must fall the earliest prey;
Though by no hand untimely snatch'd,
    The leaves must drop away,   40
And yet it were a greater grief

To watch it withering, leaf by leaf,
　　Than see it pluck'd to-day;
Since earthly eye but ill can bear
To trace the change to foul from fair.   45

I know not if I could have borne
　　To see thy beauties fade;
The night that follow'd such a morn
　　Had worn a deeper shade:
Thy day without a cloud hath past,   50
And thou wert lovely to the last,
　　Extinguish'd, not decay'd;
As stars that shoot along the sky
Shine brightest as they fall from high.

As once I wept, if I could weep,   55
　　My tears might well be shed,
To think I was not near, to keep
　　One vigil o'er thy bed:
To gaze, how fondly! on thy face,
To fold thee in a faint embrace,   60
　　Uphold thy drooping head;
And show that love, however vain,
Nor thou nor I can feel again.

Yet how much less it were to gain,
　　Though thou hast left me free,   65
The loveliest things that still remain
　　Than thus remember thee!
The all of thine that cannot die
Through dark and dread Eternity
　　Returns again to me,   70
And more thy buried love endears
Than aught except its living years.

Lord Byron

203

One word is too often profaned
　　For me to profane it,
One feeling too falsely disdain'd
　　For thee to disdain it;

One hope is too like despair   5
  For prudence to smother,
And Pity from thee more dear
  Than that from another.

I can give not what men call love;
  But wilt thou accept not   10
The worship the heart lifts above
  And the Heavens reject not,—
The desire of the moth for the star,
  Of the night for the morrow,
The devotion to something afar   15
  From the sphere of our sorrow?
                                    P. B. Shelley

204

GATHERING SONG OF DONALD
THE BLACK

Pibroch of Donuil Dhu,
  Pibroch of Donuil,
Wake thy wild voice anew,
  Summon Clan Conuil.
Come away, come away,   5
  Hark to the summons!
Come in your war-array,
  Gentles and commons.

Come from deep glen, and
  From mountain so rocky;   10
The war-pipe and pennon
  Are at Inverlocky.
Come every hill-plaid, and
  True heart that wears one,
Come every steel blade, and   15
  Strong hand that bears one.

Leave untended the herd,
  The flock without shelter;
Leave the corpse uninterr'd,
  The bride at the altar;   20

Leave the deer, leave the steer,
   Leave nets and barges:
Come with your fighting gear,
   Broadswords and targes.

Come as the winds come, when   25
   Forests are rended;
Come as the waves come, when
   Navies are stranded:
Faster come, faster come,
   Faster and faster,   30
Chief, vassal, page and groom,
   Tenant and master.

Fast they come, fast they come;
   See how they gather!
Wide waves the eagle plume,   35
   Blended with heather.
Cast your plaids, draw your blades,
   Forward each man set!
Pibroch of Donuil Dhu
   Knell for the onset!   40

                              Sir W. Scott

                    205

A wet sheet and a flowing sea,
   A wind that follows fast
And fills the white and rustling sail
   And bends the gallant mast;
And bends the gallant mast, my boys,   5
   While like the eagle free
Away the good ship flies, and leaves
   Old England on the lee.

O for a soft and gentle wind!
   I heard a fair one cry;   10
But give to me the snoring breeze
   And white waves heaving high;

And white waves heaving high, my lads,
   The good ship tight and free—
The world of waters is our home,   15
   And merry men are we.

There's tempest in yon hornéd moon,
   And lightning in yon cloud;
But hark the music, mariners!
   The wind is piping loud;   20
The wind is piping loud, my boys,
   The lightning flashes free—
While the hollow oak our palace is,
   Our heritage the sea.

                         A. Cunningham

206

Ye Mariners of England
   That guard our native seas,
Whose flag has braved, a thousand years,
   The battle and the breeze,
Your glorious standard launch again   5
   To match another foe:
And sweep through the deep,
   While the stormy winds do blow;
While the battle rages loud and long
   And the stormy winds do blow.   10

The spirits of your fathers
   Shall start from every wave—
For the deck it was their field of fame,
   And Ocean was their grave.
Where Blake and mighty Nelson fell   15
   Your manly hearts shall glow,
As ye sweep through the deep,
   While the stormy winds do blow;
While the battle rages loud and long
   And the stormy winds do blow.   20

Britannia needs no bulwarks,
   No towers along the steep;
Her march is o'er the mountain waves,
   Her home is on the deep.

With thunders from her native oak   25
  She quells the floods below—
As they roar on the shore,
  When the stormy winds do blow;
When the battle rages loud and long,
  And the stormy winds do blow.   30

The meteor flag of England
  Shall yet terrific burn;
Till danger's troubled night depart
  And the star of peace return.
Then, then, ye ocean warriors!   35
  Our song and feast shall flow
To the fame of your name,
  When the storm has ceased to blow;
When the fiery fight is heard no more,
  And the storm has ceased to blow.   40

T. Campbell

207

BATTLE OF THE BALTIC

Of Nelson and the North
Sing the glorious day's renown,
  When to battle fierce came forth
All the might of Denmark's crown,
And her arms along the deep proudly shone;   5
  By each gun the lighted brand
  In a bold, determined hand,
  And the Prince of all the land
    Led them on.

Like leviathans afloat   10
Lay their bulwarks on the brine;
  While the sign of battle flew
On the lofty British line:
It was ten of April morn by the chime:
  As they drifted on their path   15
  There was silence deep as death;
  And the boldest held his breath
    For a time.

But the might of England flush'd
To anticipate the scene;   20
   And her van the fleeter rush'd
O'er the deadly space between.
'Hearts of oak!' our captains cried, when each gun
  From its adamantine lips
Spread a death-shade round the ships,   25
  Like the hurricane eclipse
    Of the sun.

   Again! again! again!
And the havoc did not slack,
   Till a feeble cheer the Dane   30
To our cheering sent us back;
Their shots along the deep slowly boom:
  Then ceased—and all is wail,
As they strike the shatter'd sail;
  Or in conflagration pale   35
    Light the gloom.

   Out spoke the victor then
As he hail'd them o'er the wave,
   'Ye are brothers! ye are men!
And we conquer but to save: 40
So peace instead of death let us bring:
  But yield, proud foe, thy fleet
With the crews, at England's feet,
  And make submission meet
    To our King.'   45

   Then Denmark blest our chief
That he gave her wounds repose;
   And the sounds of joy and grief
From her people wildly rose,
As death withdrew his shades from the day: 50
  While the sun look'd smiling bright
O'er a wide and woeful sight,
  Where the fires of funeral light
    Died away.

Now joy, old England, raise   55
For the tidings of thy might,
    By the festal cities' blaze,
    Whilst the wine cup shines in light;
And yet amidst that joy and uproar,
    Let us think of them that sleep   60
Full many a fathom deep
By thy wild and stormy steep,
    Elsinore!

Brave hearts! to Britain's pride
Once so faithful and so true,   65
    On the deck of fame that died
    With the gallant good Riou:
Soft sigh the winds of heaven o'er their grave!
    While the billow mournful rolls
And the mermaid's song condoles,   70
Singing glory to the souls
    Of the brave!

T. Campbell

208
ODE TO DUTY

Stern Daughter of the Voice of God!
    O Duty! if that name thou love
Who art a light to guide, a rod
    To check the erring, and reprove;
Thou, who art victory and law   5
When empty terrors overawe,
From vain temptations dost set free,
And calm'st the weary strife of frail humanity!

There are who ask not if thine eye
    Be on them; who, in love and truth   10
Where no misgiving is, rely
    Upon the genial sense of youth:
Glad hearts! without reproach or blot,
Who do thy work, and know it not:
O! if through confidence misplaced   15
They fail, thy saving arms, dread Power! around them
    cast.

Serene will be our days and bright,
    And happy will our nature be,
When love is an unerring light,
    And joy its own security.   20
And they a blissful course may hold
Ev'n now, who, not unwisely bold,
Live in the spirit of this creed,
Yet seek thy firm support, according to their need.

I, loving freedom, and untried,   25
    No sport of every random gust,
Yet being to myself a guide,
    Too blindly have reposed my trust:
And oft, when in my heart was heard
Thy timely mandate, I deferr'd   30
The task, in smoother walks to stray;
But thee I now would serve more strictly, if I may.

Through no disturbance of my soul
    Or strong compunction in me wrought,
I supplicate for thy control,   35
    But in the quietness of thought:
Me this uncharter'd freedom tires;
I feel the weight of chance desires:
My hopes no more must change their name;
I long for a respose that ever is the same.   40

Stern Lawgiver! yet thou dost wear
    The Godhead's most benignant grace;
Nor know we anything so fair
    As is the smile upon thy face:
Flowers laugh before thee on their beds,   45
And fragrance in thy footing treads;
Thou dost preserve the stars from wrong;
And the most ancient heavens, through thee, are fresh
    and strong.

To humbler functions, awful Power!
    I call thee: I myself commend   50
Unto thy guidance from this hour;
    O let my weakness have an end!

Give unto me, made lowly wise,
  The spirit of self-sacrifice;
  The confidence of reason give;   55
And in the light of Truth thy bondman let me live.
                                  W. Wordsworth

209

ON THE CASTLE OF CHILLON

Eternal Spirit of the chainless Mind!
  Brightest in dungeons, Liberty, thou art—
  For there thy habitation is the heart—
The heart which love of Thee alone can bind;

And when thy sons to fetters are consign'd,   5
  To fetters, and the damp vault's dayless gloom,
  Their country conquers with their martyrdom,
And Freedom's fame finds wings on every wind.

Chillon! thy prison is a holy place
  And thy sad floor an altar, for 'twas trod,   10
Until his very steps have left a trace

  Worn, as if thy cold pavement were a sod,
By Bonnivard! May none those marks efface!
  For they appeal from tyranny to God.
                                  Lord Byron

210

ENGLAND AND SWITZERLAND

1802

Two Voices are there, one is of the Sea,
  One of the Mountains, each a mighty voice:
  In both from age to age thou didst rejoice,
They were thy chosen music, Liberty!

There came a tyrant, and with holy glee   5
  Thou fought'st against him,—but hast vainly striven:
  Thou from thy Alpine holds at length art driven,
Where not a torrent murmurs heard by thee.

                                        H

Of one deep bliss thine ear hath been bereft;
Then cleave, O cleave to that which still is left;   10
   For, high-soul'd Maid, what sorrow would it be

   That Mountain floods should thunder as before,
   And Ocean bellow from his rocky shore,
And neither awful Voice be heard by Thee!

                                        W. Wordsworth

211

ON THE EXTINCTION OF THE VENETIAN REPUBLIC

Once did She hold the gorgeous East in fee,
   And was the safeguard of the West; the worth
   Of Venice did not fall below her birth,
Venice, the eldest child of liberty.

She was a maiden city, bright and free;   5
   No guile seduced, no force could violate;
   And when she took unto herself a mate,
She must espouse the everlasting Sea.

And what if she had seen those glories fade,
   Those titles vanish, and that strength decay,—   10
Yet shall some tribute of regret be paid

   When her long life hath reach'd its final day:
Men are we, and must grieve when even the shade
   Of that which once was great is pass'd away.

                                        W. Wordsworth

212

LONDON, MDCCCII

O Friend! I know not which way I must look
   For comfort, being, as I am, opprest
   To think that now our life is only drest
For show; mean handiwork of craftsman, cook,

Or groom!—We must run glittering like a brook   5
   In the open sunshine, or we are unblest;
   The wealthiest man among us is the best:
No grandeur now in Nature or in book

Delights us.   Rapine, avarice, expense,
   This is idolatry; and these we adore: 10
   Plain living and high thinking are no more:

     The homely beauty of the good old cause
Is gone; our peace, our fearful innocence,
   And pure religion breathing household laws.
W. Wordsworth

213

THE SAME

Milton! thou shouldst be living at this hour:
   England hath need of thee: she is a fen
   Of stagnant waters: altar, sword, and pen,
Fireside, the heroic wealth of hall and bower,

Have forfeited their ancient English dower   5
   Of inward happiness.   We are selfish men:
   O! raise us up, return to us again;
And give us manners, virtue, freedom, power.

Thy soul was like a Star, and dwelt apart:
   Thou hadst a voice whose sound was like the sea,
   Pure as the naked heavens, majestic, free;   11

     So didst thou travel on life's common way
In cheerful godliness; and yet thy heart
   The lowliest duties on herself did lay.
W. Wordsworth

214

When I have borne in memory what has tamed
   Great nations; how ennobling thoughts depart
   When men change swords for ledgers, and desert
The student's bower for gold,—some fears unnamed

I had, my Country!—am I to be blamed?   5
  Now, when I think of thee, and what thou art,
  Verily, in the bottom of my heart
Of those unfilial fears I am ashamed.

For dearly must we prize thee; we who find
  In thee a bulwark for the cause of men;   10
  And I by my affection was beguiled:

What wonder if a Poet now and then,
Among the many movements of his mind,
  Felt for thee as a lover or a child!
W. Wordsworth

215

HOHENLINDEN

On Linden, when the sun was low,
All bloodless lay the untrodden snow;
And dark as winter was the flow
    Of Iser, rolling rapidly.

But Linden saw another sight,   5
When the drum beat at dead of night,
Commanding fires of death to light
    The darkness of her scenery.

By torch and trumpet fast array'd
Each horseman drew his battle blade   10
And furious every charger neigh'd
    To join the dreadful revelry.

Then shook the hills with thunder riven,
Then rush'd the steed, to battle driven,
And louder than the bolts of Heaven   15
    Far flash'd the red artillery.

But redder yet that light shall glow
On Linden's hills of stainéd snow;
And bloodier yet the torrent flow
    Of Iser, rolling rapidly.   20

'Tis morn; but scarce yon level sun
Can pierce the war-clouds, rolling dun,
Where furious Frank and fiery Hun
    Shout in their sulphurous canopy.

The combat deepens.   On, ye brave   25
Who rush to glory, or the grave!
Wave, Munich, all thy banners wave,
    And charge with all thy chivalry!

Few, few shall part, where many meet!
The snow shall be their winding-sheet,   30
And every turf beneath their feet
    Shall be a soldier's sepulchre.

                                    T. Campbell

216

AFTER BLENHEIM

It was a summer evening,
    Old Kaspar's work was done,
And he before his cottage door
    Was sitting in the sun;
And by him sported on the green   5
His little grandchild Wilhelmine.

She saw her brother Peterkin
    Roll something large and round
Which he beside the rivulet
    In playing there had found;   10
He came to ask what he had found
That was so large and smooth and round.

Old Kaspar took it from the boy
    Who stood expectant by;
And then the old man shook his head,   15
    And with a natural sigh
' 'Tis some poor fellow's skull,' said he,
'Who fell in the great victory.

'I find them in the garden,
   For there 's many here about;   20
And often when I go to plough
   The ploughshare turns them out.
For many thousand men,' said he,
'Were slain in that great victory.'

'Now tell us what 'twas all about,'   25
   Young Peterkin he cries;
And little Wilhelmine looks up
   With wonder-waiting eyes;
'Now tell us all about the war,
And what they fought each other for.'   30

'It was the English,' Kaspar cried,
   'Who put the French to rout;
But what they fought each other for
   I could not well make out.
But everybody said,' quoth he,   35
'That 'twas a famous victory.

'My father lived at Blenheim then,
   Yon little stream hard by;
They burnt his dwelling to the ground,
   And he was forced to fly: 40
So with his wife and child he fled,
Nor had he where to rest his head.

'With fire and sword the country round
   Was wasted far and wide,
And many a childing mother then   45
   And new-born baby died:
But things like that, you know, must be
At every famous victory.

'They say it was a shocking sight
   After the field was won;   50
For many thousand bodies here
   Lay rotting in the sun:
But things like that, you know, must be
After a famous victory.

'Great praise the Duke of Marlbro' won   55
    And our good Prince Eugene';
'Why, 'twas a very wicked thing!'
    Said little Wilhelmine;
'Nay . . nay . . my little girl,' quoth he,
'It was famous victory.   60

'And everybody praised the Duke
    Who this great fight did win.'
'But what good came of it at last?'
    Quoth little Peterkin:—
'Why, that I cannot tell,' said he,   65
'But 'twas a famous victory.'

                                    R. Southey

217

PRO PATRIA MORI

When he who adores thee has left but the name
    Of his fault and his sorrows behind,
O! say wilt thou weep, when they darken the fame
    Of a life that for thee was resign'd?
Yes, weep, and however my foes may condemn,   5
    Thy tears shall efface their decree;
For, Heaven can witness, though guilty to them,
    I have been but too faithful to thee.

With thee were the dreams of my earliest love,
    Every thought of my reason was thine: 10
In my last humble prayer to the Spirit above
    Thy name shall be mingled with mine!
O! blest are the lovers and friends who shall live
    The days of thy glory to see;
But the next dearest blessing that Heaven can give
    Is the pride of thus dying for thee.   16
                                    T. Moore

218

THE BURIAL OF SIR JOHN MOORE
AT CORUNNA

Not a drum was heard, not a funeral note,
  As his corse to the rampart we hurried;
Not a soldier discharged his farewell shot
  O'er the grave where our Hero we buried.

We buried him darkly at dead of night,   5
  The sods with our bayonets turning;
By the struggling moonbeam's misty light
  And the lantern dimly burning.

No useless coffin enclosed his breast,
  Not in sheet or in shroud we wound him;   10
But he lay like a Warrior taking his rest
  With his martial cloak around him.

Few and short were the prayers we said,
  And we spoke not a word of sorrow;
But we steadfastly gaz'd on the face that was dead, 15
  And we bitterly thought of the morrow.

We thought, as we hollow'd his narrow bed
  And smooth'd down his lonely pillow,
That the Foe and the Stranger would tread o'er his head,
  And we far away on the billow!   20

Lightly they'll talk of the Spirit that's gone
  And o'er his cold ashes upbraid him,—
But little he'll reck, if they let him sleep on
  In the grave where a Briton has laid him.

But half of our heavy task was done   25
  When the clock struck the hour for retiring:
And we heard the distant and random gun
  That the foe was sullenly firing.

Slowly and sadly we laid him down,
　　From the field of his fame fresh and gory;　　30
We carved not a line, and we raised not a stone—
　　But we left him alone with his glory.

　　　　　　　　　　　　　　　　　　C. Wolfe

219

SIMON LEE THE OLD HUNTSMAN

In the sweet shire of Cardigan,
　　Not far from pleasant Ivor Hall,
An old man dwells, a little man,—
　　'Tis said he once was tall.
Full five-and-thirty years he lived　　　　5
　　A running huntsman merry;
And still the centre of his cheek
　　Is red as a ripe cherry.

No man like him the horn could sound,
　　And hill and valley rang with glee　　　10
When Echo bandied round and round
　　The halloo of Simon Lee.
In those proud days he little cared
　　For husbandry or tillage;
To blither tasks did Simon rouse　　　　15
　　The sleepers of the village.

He all the country could outrun,
　　Could leave both man and horse behind;
And often, ere the chase was done,
　　He reeled and was stone-blind.　　　　20
And still there 's something in the world
　　At which his heart rejoices;
For when the chiming hounds are out,
　　He dearly loves their voices!

But O the heavy change!—bereft　　　　25
　　Of health, strength, friends, and kindred, see!
Old Simon to the world is left
　　In liveried poverty:

　　　　　　　　　　　　　　　　　　　　H*

His master's dead, and no one now
   Dwells in the Hall of Ivor;   30
Men, dogs, and horses, all are dead;
   He is the sole survivor.

And he is lean and he is sick;
   His body, dwindled and awry,
Rests upon ankles swoln and thick;   35
   His legs are thin and dry.
One prop he has, and only one,
   His wife, an aged woman,
Lives with him, near the waterfall,
   Upon the village common.   40

Beside their moss-grown hut of clay,
   Not twenty paces from the door,
A scrap of land they have, but they
   Are poorest of the poor.
This scrap of land he from the heath   45
   Enclosed when he was stronger;
But what to them avails the land
   Which he can till no longer?

Oft, working by her husband's side,
   Ruth does what Simon cannot do;   50
For she, with scanty cause for pride,
   Is stouter of the two.
And, though you with your utmost skill
   From labour could not wean them,
'Tis little, very little, all   55
   That they can do between them.

Few months of life has he in store
   As he to you will tell,
For still, the more he works, the more
   Do his weak ankles swell.   60
My gentle reader, I perceive
   How patiently you've waited,
And now I fear that you expect
   Some tale will be related.

O reader! had you in your mind   65
   Such stores as silent thought can bring,
O gentle reader! you would find
   A tale in every thing.
What more I have to say is short,
   And you must kindly take it: 70
It is no tale; but, should you think,
   Perhaps a tale you'll make it.

One summer-day I chanced to see
   This old man doing all he could
To unearth the root of an old tree,   75
   A stump of rotten wood.
The mattock totter'd in his hand;
   So vain was his endeavour
That at the root of the old tree
   He might have work'd for ever.   80

'You're overtask'd, good Simon Lee,
   Give me your tool,' to him I said;
And at the word right gladly he
   Received my proffer'd aid.
I struck, and with a single blow   85
   The tangled root I sever'd,
At which the poor old man so long
   And vainly had endeavour'd.

The tears into his eyes were brought,
   And thanks and praises seem'd to run   90
So fast out of his heart, I thought
   They never would have done.
—I've heard of hearts unkind, kind deeds
   With coldness still returning;
Alas! the gratitude of men   95
   Hath oftener left me mourning.

                        W. Wordsworth

220

THE OLD FAMILIAR FACES

I have had playmates, I have had companions
In my days of childhood, in my joyful school-days;
   All, all are gone, the old familiar faces.

I have been laughing, I have been carousing,
Drinking late, sitting late, with my bosom cronies;   5
   All, all are gone, the old familiar faces.

I loved a love once, fairest among women:
Closed are her doors on me, I must not see her—
   All, all are gone, the old familiar faces.

I have a friend, a kinder friend has no man: 10
Like an ingrate, I left my friend abruptly;
   Left him, to muse on the old familiar faces.

Ghost-like I paced round the haunts of my childhood;
Earth seem'd a desert I was bound to traverse,
   Seeking to find the old familiar faces.   15

Friend of my bosom, thou more than a brother,
Why wert not thou born in my father's dwelling?
   So might we talk of the old familiar faces,

How some they have died, and some they have left me,
And some are taken from me; all are departed;   20
   All, all are gone, the old familiar faces.
                               C. Lamb

221

THE JOURNEY ONWARDS

As slow our ship her foamy track
   Against the wind was cleaving,
Her trembling pennant still look'd back
   To that dear isle 'twas leaving.
So loth we part from all we love,   5
   From all the links that bind us;
So turn our hearts, as on we rove,
   To those we've left behind us!

When, round the bowl, of vanish'd years
  We talk with joyous seeming—   10
With smiles that might as well be tears,
  So faint, so sad their beaming;
While memory brings us back again
  Each early tie that twined us,
O, sweet's the cup that circles then   15
  To those we've left behind us!

And when in other climes we meet
  Some isle or vale enchanting,
Where all looks flowery, wild, and sweet,
  And nought but love is wanting;   20
We think how great had been our bliss
  If Heaven had but assign'd us
To live and die in scenes like this,
  With some we've left behind us!

As travellers oft look back at eve   25
  When eastward darkly going,
To gaze upon that light they leave
  Still faint behind them glowing,—
So, when the close of pleasure's day
  To gloom hath near consign'd us,   30
We turn to catch one fading ray
  Of joy that's left behind us.

T. Moore

YOUTH AND AGE

There's not a joy the world can give like that it takes
    away,
When the glow of early thought declines in feeling's dull
    decay;
'Tis not on youth's smooth cheek the blush alone which
    fades so fast,
But the tender bloom of heart is gone, ere youth itself
    be past.

Then the few whose spirits float above the wreck of
    happiness   5
Are driven o'er the shoals of guilt or ocean of excess:
The magnet of their course is gone, or only points in vain
The shore to which their shiver'd sail shall never stretch
    again.

Then the mortal coldness of the soul like death itself
    comes down;
It cannot feel for others' woes, it dare not dream its
    own;   10
That heavy chill has frozen o'er the fountain of our tears,
And though the eye may sparkle still, 'tis where the ice
    appears.

Though wit may flash from fluent lips, and mirth distract
    the breast,
Through midnight hours that yield no more their former
    hope of rest;
'Tis but as ivy-leaves around the ruin'd turret wreathe, 15
All green and wildly fresh without, but worn and grey
    beneath.

O could I feel as I have felt, or be what I have been,
Or weep as I could once have wept o'er many a vanish'd
    scene,—
As springs in deserts found seem sweet, all brackish
    though they be,
So midst the wither'd waste of life, those tears would
    flow to me!   20
                                                 Lord Byron

223

A LESSON

There is a flower, the Lesser Celandine,
    That shrinks like many more from cold and rain,
And, the first moment that the sun may shine,
    Bright as the sun himself, 'tis out again!

When hailstones have been falling, swarm on swarm,
   Or blasts the green field and the trees distrest,   6
Oft have I seen it muffled up from harm
   In close self-shelter, like a thing at rest.

But lately, one rough day, this flower I past,
   And recognized it, though an alter'd form,   10
Now standing forth an offering to the blast,
   And buffeted at will by rain and storm.

I stopp'd and said, with inly-mutter'd voice,
   'It doth not love the shower, nor seek the cold;
This neither is its courage nor its choice,   15
   But its necessity in being old.

'The sunshine may not cheer it, nor the dew;
   It cannot help itself in its decay;
Stiff in its members, wither'd, changed of hue,'
   And, in my spleen, I smiled that it was grey.   20

To be a prodigal's favourite—then, worse truth,
   A miser's pensioner—behold our lot!
O Man! that from thy fair and shining youth
   Age might but take the things Youth needed not!

                             W. Wordsworth

224

PAST AND PRESENT

    I remember, I remember
      The house where I was born,
    The little window where the sun
      Came peeping in at morn;
    He never came a wink too soon   5
      Nor brought too long a day;
    But now, I often wish the night
      Had borne my breath away.

    I remember, I remember
      The roses, red and white,   10
    The violets, and the lily-cups—
      Those flowers made of light!

The lilacs where the robin built,
   And where my brother set
The laburnum on his birth-day,—   15
   The tree is living yet!

I remember, I remember
   Where I was used to swing,
And thought the air must rush as fresh
   To swallows on the wing;   20
My spirit flew in feathers then
   That is so heavy now,
And summer pools could hardly cool
   The fever on my brow.

I remember, I remember   25
   The fir trees dark and high;
I used to think their slender tops
   Were close against the sky:
It was a childish ignorance,
   But now 'tis little joy   30
To know I'm farther off from Heaven
   Than when I was a boy.

T. Hood

225

THE LIGHT OF OTHER DAYS

Oft in the stilly night,
   Ere slumber's chain has bound me,
Fond Memory brings the light
   Of other days around me:
     The smiles, the tears   5
     Of boyhood's years,
   The words of love then spoken;
     The eyes that shone,
     Now dimm'd and gone,
   The cheerful hearts now broken!   10
Thus in the stilly night,
   Ere slumber's chain has bound me,
Sad Memory brings the light
   Of other days around me.

When I remember all 15
    The friends so link'd together
I've seen around me fall
    Like leaves in wintry weather,
      I feel like one
      Who treads alone 20
Some banquet-hall deserted,
      Whose lights are fled,
      Whose garlands dead,
    And all but he departed!
Thus in the stilly night, 25
    Ere slumber's chain has bound me,
Sad Memory brings the light
    Of other days around me.

T. Moore

226

INVOCATION

Rarely, rarely, comest thou,
    Spirit of Delight!
Wherefore hast thou left me now
    Many a day and night?
Many a weary night and day 5
'Tis since thou art fled away.

How shall ever one like me
    Win thee back again?
With the joyous and the free
    Thou wilt scoff at pain. 10
Spirit false! thou hast forgot
All but those who need thee not.

As a lizard with the shade
    Of a trembling leaf,
Thou with sorrow art dismay'd; 15
    Even the sighs of grief
Reproach thee, that thou art not near,
And reproach thou wilt not hear.

Let me set my mournful ditty
  To a merry measure;   20
Thou wilt never come for pity,
  Thou wilt come for pleasure;
Pity then will cut away
Those cruel wings, and thou wilt stay.

I love all that thou lovest,   25
  Spirit of Delight!
The fresh Earth in new leaves drest
  And the starry night;
Autumn evening, and the morn
When the golden mists are born.   30

I love snow and all the forms
  Of the radiant frost;
I love waves, and winds, and storms,
  Everything almost
Which is Nature's, and may be   35
Untainted by man's misery.

I love tranquil solitude,
  And such society
As is quiet, wise, and good;
  Between thee and me   40
What diff'rence?   but thou dost possess
The things I seek, not love them less.

I love Love—though he has wings,
  And like light can flee,
But above all other things,   45
  Spirit, I love thee—
Thou art love and life!   O come!
Make once more my heart thy home!
                                        P. B. Shelley

227

STANZAS WRITTEN IN DEJECTION NEAR NAPLES

The sun is warm, the sky is clear,
  The waves are dancing fast and bright,
Blue isles and snowy mountains wear
  The purple noon's transparent might:
  The breath of the moist earth is light   5
Around its unexpanded buds;
  Like many a voice of one delight—
The winds, the birds, the ocean-floods—
The City's voice itself is soft like Solitude's.

I see the Deep's untrampled floor   10
  With green and purple seaweeds strown;
I see the waves upon the shore,
  Like light dissolved in star-showers, thrown:
  I sit upon the sands alone;
The lightning of the noontide ocean   15
  Is flashing round me, and a tone
Arises from its measured motion—
How sweet! did any heart now share in my emotion.

Alas! I have nor hope nor health,
  Nor peace within nor calm around,   20
Nor that content, surpassing wealth,
  The sage in meditation found,
  And walked with inward glory crowned—
Nor fame, nor power, nor love, nor leisure;
  Others I see whom these surround—   25
Smiling they live, and call life pleasure;
To me that cup has been dealt in another measure.

Yet now despair itself is mild
  Even as the winds and waters are;
I could lie down like a tired child,   30
  And weep away the life of care

Which I have borne, and yet must bear,
Till death like sleep might steal on me,
    And I might feel in the warm air
My cheek grow cold, and hear the sea   35
Breathe o'er my dying brain its last monotony.

P. B. Shelley

228

THE SCHOLAR

My days among the Dead are past;
    Around me I behold,
Where'er these casual eyes are cast,
    The mighty minds of old:
My never-failing friends are they,   5
With whom I converse day by day.

With them I take delight in weal
    And seek relief in woe;
And while I understand and feel
    How much to them I owe,   10
My cheeks have often been bedew'd
With tears of thoughtful gratitude.

My thoughts are with the Dead; with them
    I live in long-past years,
Their virtues love, their faults condemn,   15
    Partake their hopes and fears,
And from their lessons seek and find
Instruction with an humble mind.

My hopes are with the Dead; anon
    My place with them will be,   20
And I with them shall travel on
    Through all Futurity;
Yet leaving here a name, I trust,
That will not perish in the dust.

R. Southey

229

THE MERMAID TAVERN

Souls of Poets dead and gone,
What Elysium have ye known,
Happy field or mossy cavern,
Choicer than the Mermaid Tavern?
Have ye tippled drink more fine   5
Than mine host's Canary wine?
Or are fruits of Paradise
Sweeter than those dainty pies
Of venison?   O generous food!
Drest as though bold Robin Hood   10
Would, with his Maid Marian,
Sup and bowse from horn and can.

I have heard that on a day
Mine host's signboard flew away
Nobody knew whither, till   15
An astrologer's old quill
To a sheepskin gave the story—
Said he saw you in your glory
Underneath a new-old Sign
Sipping beverage divine,   20
And pledging with contented smack
The Mermaid in the Zodiac.

Souls of Poets dead and gone,
What Elysium have ye known—
Happy field or mossy cavern—   25
Choicer than the Mermaid Tavern?

J. Keats

230

THE PRIDE OF YOUTH

Proud Maisie is in the wood,
    Walking so early;
Sweet Robin sits on the bush
    Singing so rarely.

'Tell me, thou bonny bird,   5
  When shall I marry me?'
—'When six braw gentlemen
  Kirkward shall carry ye.'

'Who makes the bridal bed,
  Birdie, say truly?'   10
—'The grey-headed sexton
  That delves the grave duly.

'The glow-worm o'er grave and stone
  Shall light thee steady;
The owl from the steeple sing   15
  Welcome, proud lady.'
                                    Sir W. Scott

                        231

            THE BRIDGE OF SIGHS

        One more Unfortunate
          Weary of breath,
        Rashly importunate,
          Gone to her death!

        Take her up tenderly,   5
          Lift her with care;
        Fashion'd so slenderly,
          Young, and so fair!

        Look at her garments
          Clinging like cerements,   10
        Whilst the wave constantly
          Drips from her clothing;
        Take her up instantly.
          Loving, not loathing.

        Touch her not scornfully;   15
        Think of her mournfully,
          Gently and humanly;
        Not of the stains of her—
        All that remains of her
          Now is pure womanly.   20

Make no deep scrutiny
Into her mutiny
  Rash and undutiful:
Past all dishonour,
Death has left on her   25
  Only the beautiful.

Still, for all slips of hers,
  One of Eve's family—
Wipe those poor lips of hers
  Oozing so clammily.   30

Loop up her tresses
  Escaped from the comb,
Her fair auburn tresses;
Whilst wonderment guesses
  Where was her home?   35

Who was her father?
  Who was her mother?
Had she a sister?
  Had she a brother?
Or was there a dearer one   40
Still, and a nearer one
  Yet, than all other?

Alas! for the rarity
Of Christian charity
  Under the sun!   45
O! it was pitiful!
Near a whole city full,
  Home she had none.

Sisterly, brotherly,
Fatherly, motherly   50
  Feelings had changed:
Love, by harsh evidence,
Thrown from its eminence,
Even God's providence
  Seeming estranged.   55

Where the lamps quiver
So far in the river,
  With many a light
From window and casement,
From garret to basement,   60
She stood, with amazement,
  Houseless by night.

The bleak wind of March
  Made her tremble and shiver;
But not the dark arch,   65
  Or the black flowing river:
Mad from life's history,
Glad to death's mystery
  Swift to be hurl'd—
Any where, any where   70
  Out of the world!

In she plunged boldly,
No matter how coldly
  The rough river ran,
Over the brink of it,—   75
Picture it, think of it,
  Dissolute Man!
Lave in it, drink of it
  Then, if you can!

Take her up tenderly,   80
  Lift her with care;
Fashion'd so slenderly,
  Young, and so fair!

Ere her limbs frigidly
Stiffen too rigidly,   85
  Decently, kindly,
Smooth and compose them;
And her eyes, close them,
  Staring so blindly!

Dreadfully staring   90
  Thro' muddy impurity,
As when with the daring

Last look of despairing
　　Fix'd on futurity
Perishing gloomily,   95
Spurr'd by contumely,
Cold inhumanity,
Burning insanity,
　　Into her rest.
—Cross her hands humbly,   100
As if praying dumbly,
　　Over her breast!

Owning her weakness,
　　Her evil behaviour,
And leaving, with meekness,   105
　　Her sins to her Saviour!

　　　　　　　　　　　　　　　　　　　　T. Hood

232

ELEGY

O snatch'd away in beauty's bloom!
On thee shall press no ponderous tomb;
　　But on thy turf shall roses rear
　　Their leaves, the earliest of the year,
And the wild cypress wave in tender gloom: 5

And oft by yon blue gushing stream
　　Shall Sorrow lean her drooping head,
And feed deep thought with many a dream,
　　And lingering pause and lightly tread;
Fond wretch! as if her step disturb'd the dead!   10

Away! we know that tears are vain,
　　That Death nor heeds nor hears distress:
Will this unteach us to complain?
　　Or make one mourner weep the less?
And thou, who tell'st me to forget,   15
Thy looks are wan, thine eyes are wet.

　　　　　　　　　　　　　　　　　　　Lord Byron

233

HESTER

When maidens such as Hester die,
Their place ye may not well supply,
Though ye among a thousand try
      With vain endeavour.
A month or more hath she been dead,   5
Yet cannot I by force be led
To think upon the wormy bed
      And her together.

A springy motion in her gait,
A rising step, did indicate   10
Of pride and joy no common rate
      That flush'd her spirit:
I know not by what name beside
I shall it call: if 'twas not pride,
It was a joy to that allied   15
      She did inherit.

Her parents held the Quaker rule,
Which doth the human feeling cool;
But she was train'd in Nature's school,
      Nature had blest her.   20
A waking eye, a prying mind,
A heart that stirs, is hard to bind;
A hawk's keen sight ye cannot blind,
      Ye could not Hester.

My sprightly neighbour! gone before   25
To that unknown and silent shore,
Shall we not meet, as heretofore
      Some summer morning—
When from thy cheerful eyes a ray
Hath struck a bliss upon the day,   30
A bliss that would not go away,
      A sweet fore-warning?

C. Lamb

234

CORONACH

He is gone on the mountain,
  He is lost to the forest,
Like a summer-dried fountain,
  When our need was the sorest.
The font reappearing   5
  From the raindrops shall borrow,
But to us comes no cheering,
  To Duncan no morrow!

The hand of the reaper
  Takes the ears that are hoary,   10
But the voice of the weeper
  Wails manhood in glory.
The autumn winds rushing
  Waft the leaves that are serest,
But our flower was in flushing   15
  When blighting was nearest.

Fleet foot on the correi,
  Sage counsel in cumber,
Red hand in the foray,
  How sound is thy slumber!   20
Like the dew on the mountain,
  Like the foam on the river,
Like the bubble on the fountain,
  Thou art gone, and for ever!

Sir W. Scott

235

THE DEATH-BED

We watch'd her breathing thro' the night,
  Her breathing soft and low,
As in her breast the wave of life
  Kept heaving to and fro.

But when the morn came dim and sad   5
    And chill with early showers,
Her quiet eyelids closed—she had
    Another morn than ours.

T. Hood

236

ROSABELLE

O listen, listen, ladies gay!
    No haughty feat of arms I tell;
Soft is the note, and sad the lay
    That mourns the lovely Rosabelle.

Moor, moor the barge, ye gallant crew!   5
    And, gentle ladye, deign to stay!
Rest thee in Castle Ravensheuch,
    Nor tempt the stormy firth to-day.

'The blackening wave is edged with white;
    To inch and rock the sea-mews fly;   10
The fishers have heard the Water-Sprite,
    Whose screams forebode that wreck is nigh.

'Last night the gifted Seer did view
    A wet shroud swathed round ladye gay;
Then stay thee, Fair, in Ravensheuch;   15
    Why cross the gloomy firth to-day?'

' 'Tis not because Lord Lindesay's heir
    To-night at Roslin leads the ball,
But that my ladye-mother there
    Sits lonely in her castle-hall.   20

' 'Tis not because the ring they ride,
    And Lindesay at the ring rides well,
But that my sire the wine will chide
    If 'tis not fill'd by Rosabelle.'

—O'er Roslin all that dreary night   25
    A wondrous blaze was seen to gleam;
'Twas broader than the watch-fire's light,
    And redder than the bright moonbeam.

It glared on Roslin's castled rock,
　　It ruddied all the copse-wood glen;   30
'Twas seen from Dryden's groves of oak,
　　And seen from cavern'd Hawthornden.

Seem'd all on fire that chapel proud,
　　Where Roslin's chiefs uncoffin'd lie,
Each Baron, for a sable shroud,   35
　　Sheath'd in his iron panoply.

Seem'd all on fire within, around,
　　Deep sacristy and altar's pale;
Shone every pillar foliage-bound,
　　And glimmer'd all the dead men's mail.   40

Blazed battlement and pinnet high,
　　Blazed every rose-carved buttress fair—
So still they blaze, when fate is nigh
　　The lordly line of high St. Clair.

There are twenty of Roslin's barons bold   45
　　Lie buried within that proud chapelle;
Each one the holy vault doth hold,
　　But the sea holds lovely Rosabelle!

And each St. Clair was buried there
　　With candle, with book, and with knell;   50
But the sea-caves rung, and the wild winds sung
　　The dirge of lovely Rosabelle.

Sir W. Scott

237

ON AN INFANT DYING AS SOON AS BORN

　　I saw where in the shroud did lurk
　　A curious frame of Nature's work;
　　A flow'ret crushéd in the bud,
　　A nameless piece of Babyhood,
　　Was in her cradle-coffin lying;   5
　　Extinct, with scarce the sense of dying:
　　So soon to exchange the imprisoning womb
　　For darker closets of the tomb!

She did but ope an eye, and put
A clear beam forth, then straight up shut   10
For the long dark : ne'er more to see
Through glasses of mortality.
Riddle of destiny, who can show
What thy short visit meant, or know
What thy errand here below?   15
Shall we say, that Nature blind
Check'd her hand, and changed her mind,
Just when she had exactly wrought
A finish'd pattern without fault?
Could she flag, or could she tire,   20
Or lack'd she the Promethean fire
(With her nine moons' long workings sicken'd)
That should thy little limbs have quicken'd?
Limbs so firm, they seem'd to assure
Life of health, and days mature;   25
Woman's self in miniature!
Limbs so fair, they might supply
(Themselves now but cold imagery)
The sculptor to make Beauty by.
Or did the stern-eyed Fate descry   30
That babe or mother, one must die;
So in mercy left the stock
And cut the branch; to save the shock
Of young years widow'd, and the pain
When Single State comes back again   35
To the lone man who, 'reft of wife,
Thenceforward drags a maiméd life?
The economy of Heaven is dark,
And wisest clerks have miss'd the mark,
Why human buds, like this, should fall   40
More brief than fly ephemeral
That has his day; while shrivell'd crones
Stiffen with age to stocks and stones;
And crabbéd use the conscience sears
In sinners of an hundred years.   45
—Mother's prattle, mother's kiss,
Baby fond, thou ne'er wilt miss:
Rites, which custom does impose,
Silver bells, and baby clothes;

Coral redder than those lips   50
Which pale death did late eclipse;
Music framed for infants' glee,
Whistle never tuned for thee;
Though thou want'st not, thou shalt have them,
Loving hearts were they which gave them.   55
Let not one be missing; nurse,
See them laid upon the hearse
Of infant slain by doom perverse.
Why should kings and nobles have
Pictured trophies to their grave,   60
And we, churls, to thee deny
Thy pretty toys with thee to lie—
A more harmless vanity?

                                                    C. Lamb

238

THE AFFLICTION OF MARGARET

Where art thou, my beloved Son,
    Where art thou, worse to me than dead?
O find me, prosperous or undone!
    Or, if the grave be now thy bed,
Why am I ignorant of the same   5
That I may rest; and neither blame
Nor sorrow may attend thy name?

Seven years, alas! to have received
    No tidings of an only child;
To have despaired, have hoped, believed,   10
    And been for evermore beguiled,—
Sometimes with thoughts of very bliss!
I catch at them, and then I miss;
Was ever darkness like to this?

He was among the prime in worth,   15
    An object beauteous to behold;
Well born, well bred; I sent him forth
    Ingenuous, innocent, and bold:

If things ensued that wanted grace,
As hath been said, they were not base;   20
And never blush was on my face.

Ah! little doth the young one dream,
    When full of play and childish cares,
What power is in his wildest scream
    Heard by his mother unawares!   25
He knows it not, he cannot guess:
Years to a mother bring distress;
But do not make her love the less.

Neglect me! no, I suffered long
    From that ill thought; and being blind   30
Said, 'Pride shall help me in my wrong:
    Kind mother have I been, as kind
As ever breathed': and that is true;
I've wet my path with tears like dew,
Weeping for him when no one knew.   35

My Son, if thou be humbled, poor,
    Hopeless of honour and of gain,
O! do not dread thy mother's door;
    Think not of me with grief and pain:
I now can see with better eyes;   40
And worldly grandeur I despise,
And fortune with her gifts and lies.

Alas! the fowls of heaven have wings,
    And blasts of heaven will aid their flight;
They mount—how short a voyage brings   45
    The wanderers back to their delight!
Chains tie us down by land and sea;
And wishes, vain as mine, may be
All that is left to comfort thee.

Perhaps some dungeon hears thee groan,   50
    Maim'd, mangled by inhuman men;
Or thou upon a desert thrown
    Inheritest the lion's den;
Or hast been summon'd to the deep,
Thou, thou, and all thy mates, to keep   55
An incommunicable sleep.

I look for ghosts; but none will force
   Their way to me: 'tis falsely said
That there was ever intercourse
   Between the living and the dead;   60
For surely then I should have sight
Of him I wait for day and night
With love and longings infinite.

My apprehensions come in crowds;
   I dread the rustling of the grass;   65
The very shadows of the clouds
   Have power to shake me as they pass:
I question things, and do not find
One that will answer to my mind;
And all the world appears unkind.   70

Beyond participation lie
   My troubles, and beyond relief:
If any chance to heave a sigh,
   They pity me, and not my grief.
Then come to me, my Son, or send   75
Some tidings, that my woes may end;
I have no other earthly friend.

                          W. Wordsworth

239

HUNTING SONG

Waken, lords and ladies gay!
On the mountain dawns the day;
All the jolly chase is here
With hawk and horse and hunting-spear;
Hounds are in their couples yelling,   5
Hawks are whistling, horns are knelling,
Merrily merrily mingle they,
'Waken, lords and ladies gay!'

Waken, lords and ladies gay!
The mist has left the mountain grey,   10
Springlets in the dawn are steaming,
Diamonds on the brake are gleaming;

I

And foresters have busy been
To track the buck in thicket green;
Now we come to chant our lay,   15
'Waken, lords and ladies gay!'

Waken, lords and ladies gay!
To the greenwood haste away;
We can show you where he lies,
Fleet of foot and tall of size;   20
We can show the marks he made
When 'gainst the oak his antlers fray'd;
You shall see him brought to bay;
'Waken, lords and ladies gay!'

Louder, louder chant the lay,   25
Waken, lords and ladies gay!
Tell them youth and mirth and glee
Run a course as well as we;
Time, stern huntsman! who can balk,
Stanch as hound and fleet as hawk;   30
Think of this, and rise with day,
Gentle lords and ladies gay!

Sir W. Scott

240

TO THE SKYLARK

Ethereal minstrel! pilgrim of the sky!
  Dost thou despise the earth where cares abound?
Or, while the wings aspire, are heart and eye
  Both with thy nest upon the dewy-ground?
Thy nest which thou canst drop into at will,   5
Those quivering wings composed, that music still!

To the last point of vision, and beyond,
  Mount, daring warbler!—that love-prompted strain
('Twixt thee and thine a never-failing bond),
  Thrills not the less the bosom of the plain: 10
Yet might'st thou seem, proud privilege! to sing
All independent of the leafy spring.

Leave to the nightingale her shady wood;
  A privacy of glorious light is thine,
Whence thou dost pour upon the world a flood   15
  Of harmony, with instinct more divine;
Type of the wise, who soar, but never roam—
True to the kindred points of Heaven and Home!

                 W. Wordsworth

241

TO A SKYLARK

Hail to thee, blithe Spirit!
  Bird thou never wert,
That from heaven, or near it,
  Pourest thy full heart
In profuse strains of unpremeditated art.   5

Higher still and higher
  From the earth thou springest
Like a cloud of fire;
  The blue deep thou wingest,   9
And singing still dost soar, and soaring ever singest.

In the golden lightning
  Of the sunken sun,
O'er which clouds are brightening,
  Thou dost float and run,
Like an unbodied joy whose race is just begun.   15

The pale purple even
  Melts around thy flight;
Like a star of heaven
  In the broad daylight   19
Thou art unseen, but yet I hear thy shrill delight:

Keen as are the arrows
  Of that silver sphere,
Whose intense lamp narrows
  In the white dawn clear
Until we hardly see, we feel that it is there.   25

All the earth and air
  With thy voice is loud,
As, when night is bare,
  From one lonely cloud
The moon rains out her beams, and heaven is over-
        flow'd.   30

What thou art we know not;
  What is most like thee?
From rainbow clouds there flow not
  Drops so bright to see
As from thy presence showers a rain of melody.   35

Like a poet hidden
  In the light of thought,
Singing hymns unbidden,
  Till the world is wrought
To sympathy with hopes and fears it heeded not: 40

Like a high-born maiden
  In a palace tower,
Soothing her love-laden
  Soul in secret hour   44
With music sweet as love, which overflows her bower:

Like a glow-worm golden
  In a dell of dew,
Scattering unbeholden
  Its aerial hue
Among the flowers and grass, which screen it from the
        view: 50

Like a rose embower'd
  In its own green leaves,
By warm winds deflower'd,
  Till the scent it gives
Makes faint with too much sweet these heavy-wingèd
        thieves.   55

Sound of vernal showers
  On the twinkling grass,
Rain-awaken'd flowers,
  All that ever was   59
Joyous, and clear, and fresh, thy music doth surpass.

Teach us, sprite or bird,
   What sweet thoughts are thine:
I have never heard
   Praise of love or wine
That panted forth a flood of rapture so divine.   65

Chorus hymeneal,
   Or triumphal chant,
Match'd with thine would be all
   But an empty vaunt—
A thing wherein we feel there is some hidden want.   70

What objects are the fountains
   Of thy happy strain?
What fields, or waves, or mountains?
   What shapes of sky or plain?
What love of thine own kind? what ignorance of pain? 75

With thy clear keen joyance
   Languor cannot be:
Shadow of annoyance
   Never came near thee:
Thou lovest; but ne'er knew love's sad satiety.   80

Waking or asleep
   Thou of death must deem
Things more true and deep
   Than we mortals dream,
Or how could thy notes flow in such a crystal stream? 85

We look before and after,
   And pine for what is not:
Our sincerest laughter
   With some pain is fraught;   89
Our sweetest songs are those that tell of saddest thought.

Yet if we could scorn
   Hate, and pride, and fear;
If we were things born
   Not to shed a tear,
I know not how thy joy we ever should come near.   95

Better than all measures
    Of delightful sound,
Better than all treasures
    That in books are found,   99
Thy skill to poet were, thou scorner of the ground!

Teach me half the gladness
    That thy brain must know,
Such harmonious madness
    From my lips would flow   104
The world should listen then, as I am listening now!
                                            P. B. Shelley

242

THE GREEN LINNET

Beneath these fruit-tree boughs that shed
Their snow-white blossoms on my head,
With brightest sunshine round me spread
    Of spring's unclouded weather,
In this sequestered nook how sweet   5
To sit upon my orchard-seat!
And birds and flowers once more to greet,
    My last year's friends together.

One have I marked, the happiest guest
In all this covert of the blest: 10
Hail to Thee, far above the rest
    In joy of voice and pinion!
Thou, Linnet! in thy green array,
Presiding Spirit here to-day,
Dost lead the revels of the May,   15
    And this is thy dominion.

While birds, and butterflies, and flowers,
Make all one band of paramours,
Thou, ranging up and down the bowers,
    Art sole in thy employment;   20
A Life, a Presence like the Air,
Scattering thy gladness without care,
Too blest with any one to pair,
    Thyself thy own enjoyment.

Amid yon tuft of hazel trees,   25
That twinkle to the gusty breeze,
Behold him perch'd in ecstasies,
    Yet seeming still to hover;
There! where the flutter of his wings
Upon his back and body flings   30
Shadows and sunny glimmerings,
    That cover him all over.

My dazzled sight he oft deceives—
A Brother of the dancing leaves;
Then flits, and from the cottage-eaves   35
    Pours forth his song in gushes;
As if by that exulting strain
He mocked and treated with disdain
The voiceless Form he chose tc feign,
    While fluttering in the bushes.   40

                              W. Wordsworth

243

TO THE CUCKOO

O blithe new-comer! I have heard,
    I hear thee and rejoice:
O Cuckoo! shall I call thee Bird,
    Or but a wandering Voice?

While I am lying on the grass   5
    Thy twofold shout I hear;
From hill to hill it seems to pass,
    At once far off and near.

Though babbling only to the vale
    Of sunshine and of flowers,   10
Thou bringest unto me a tale
    Of visionary hours.

Thrice welcome, darling of the Spring!
    Even yet thou art to me
No bird, but an invisible thing,   15
    A voice, a mystery;

The same whom in my school-boy days
   I listen'd to; that Cry
Which made me look a thousand ways
   In bush, and tree, and sky.   20

To seek thee did I often rove
   Through woods and on the green;
And thou wert still a hope, a love;
   Still longed for, never seen.

And I can listen to thee yet;   25
   Can lie upon the plain
And listen, till I do beget
   That golden time again.

O blesséd Bird! the earth we pace
   Again appears to be   30
An unsubstantial, fairy place,
   That is fit home for Thee!

W. Wordsworth

244

ODE TO A NIGHTINGALE

My heart aches, and a drowsy numbness pains
   My sense, as though of hemlock I had drunk,
Or emptied some dull opiate to the drains
   One minute past, and Lethe-wards had sunk:
'Tis not through envy of thy happy lot,   5
   But being too happy in thine happiness,—
      That thou, light-wingéd Dryad of the trees,
         In some melodious plot
Of beechen green, and shadows numberless,
   Singest of summer in full-throated ease.   10

O for a draught of vintage! that hath been
   Cool'd a long age in the deep-delvéd earth,
Tasting of Flora and the country green,
   Dance, and Provençal song, and sunburnt mirth!
O for a beaker full of the warm South,   15
   Full of the true, the blushful Hippocrene,

With beaded bubbles winking at the brim,
  And purple-stainéd mouth;
That I might drink, and leave the world unseen,
  And with thee fade away into the forest dim: 20

Fade far away, dissolve, and quite forget
  What thou among the leaves hast never known,
The weariness, the fever, and the fret
  Here, where men sit and hear each other groan;
Where palsy shakes a few, sad, last grey hairs, 25
  Where youth grows pale, and spectre-thin, and dies;
    Where but to think is to be full of sorrow
      And leaden-eyed despairs;
  Where Beauty cannot keep her lustrous eyes,
    Or new Love pine at them beyond to-morrow. 30

Away! away! for I will fly to thee,
  Not charioted by Bacchus and his pards,
But on the viewless wings of Poesy,
  Though the dull brain perplexes and retards:
Already with thee! tender is the night, 35
  And haply the Queen-Moon is on her throne,
    Cluster'd around by all her starry Fays;
      But here there is no light,
  Save what from heaven is with the breezes blown
    Through verdurous glooms and winding mossy
      ways. 40

I cannot see what flowers are at my feet,
  Nor what soft incense hangs upon the boughs,
But, in embalméd darkness, guess each sweet
  Wherewith the seasonable month endows
The grass, the thicket, and the fruit-tree wild; 45
  White hawthorn, and the pastoral eglantine;
    Fast-fading violets cover'd up in leaves;
      And mid-May's eldest child
  The coming musk-rose, full of dewy wine,
    The murmurous haunt of flies on summer eves. 50

Darkling I listen; and, for many a time
  I have been half in love with easeful Death,
Call'd him soft names in many a muséd rhyme,
  To take into the air my quiet breath;

1*

Now more than ever seems it rich to die,   55
　　To cease upon the midnight with no pain,
　　　　While thou art pouring forth thy soul abroad
　　　　　　In such an ecstasy!
　　Still wouldst thou sing, and I have ears in vain—
　　　　To thy high requiem become a sod.   60

Thou wast not born for death, immortal Bird!
　　No hungry generations tread thee down;
The voice I hear this passing night was heard
　　In ancient days by emperor and clown:
Perhaps the self-same song that found a path   65
　　Through the sad heart of Ruth, when, sick for home,
　　　　She stood in tears amid the alien corn;
　　　　　　The same that oft-times hath
　　Charm'd magic casements, opening on the foam
　　Of perilous seas, in faery lands forlorn.   70

Forlorn! the very word is like a bell
　　To toll me back from thee to my sole self!
Adieu! the fancy cannot cheat so well
　　As she is famed to do, deceiving elf.
Adieu! adieu! thy plaintive anthem fades   75
　　Past the near meadows, over the still stream,
　　　　Up the hill-side; and now 'tis buried deep
　　　　　　In the next valley-glades:
　　Was it a vision, or a waking dream?
　　Fled is that music:—do I wake or sleep?   80

J. Keats

245

UPON WESTMINSTER BRIDGE

Sept. 3, 1802

Earth has not anything to show more fair:
　　Dull would he be of soul who could pass by
　　A sight so touching in its majesty:
This City now doth like a garment wear

The beauty of the morning: silent, bare,   5
    Ships, towers, domes, theatres, and temples lie
    Open unto the fields, and to the sky,
All bright and glittering in the smokeless air.

Never did sun more beautifully steep
    In his first splendour valley, rock, or hill;   10
Ne'er saw I, never felt, a calm so deep!

The river glideth at his own sweet will:
Dear God! the very houses seem asleep;
    And all that mighty heart is lying still!
                                        W. Wordsworth

246

OZYMANDIAS OF EGYPT

I met a traveller from an antique land
    Who said: Two vast and trunkless legs of stone
Stand in the desert.   Near them on the sand,
    Half sunk, a shatter'd visage lies, whose frown

And wrinkled lip and sneer of cold command   5
    Tell that its sculptor well those passions read
Which yet survive, stamp'd on these lifeless things,
    The hand that mock'd them and the heart that fed;

And on the pedestal these words appear:
'My name is Ozymandias, king of kings: 10
    Look on my works, ye Mighty, and despair!'

Nothing beside remains.   Round the decay
    Of that colossal wreck, boundless and bare,
The lone and level sands stretch far away.
                                        P. B. Shelley

247

COMPOSED AT NEIDPATH CASTLE, THE PROPERTY OF LORD QUEENSBERRY, 1803

Degenerate Douglas! O the unworthy lord!
  Whom mere despite of heart could so far please
  And love of havoc, (for with such disease
Fame taxes him,) that he could send forth word

To level with the dust a noble horde,   5
  A brotherhood of venerable trees,
  Leaving an ancient dome, and towers like these,
Beggar'd and outraged!—Many hearts deplored

The fate of those old trees; and oft with pain
  The traveller at this day will stop and gaze   10
    On wrongs, which Nature scarcely seems to heed:

  For sheltered places, bosoms, nooks, and bays,
    And the pure mountains, and the gentle Tweed,
And the green silent pastures, yet remain.

                                        W. Wordsworth

248

ADMONITION TO A TRAVELLER

Yes, there is holy pleasure in thine eye!
  The lovely cottage in the guardian nook
  Hath stirr'd thee deeply; with its own dear brook,
Its own small pasture, almost its own sky!

But covet not the abode; forbear to sigh   5
  As many do, repining while they look;
  Intruders who would tear from Nature's book
This precious leaf with harsh impiety:

Think what the home must be if it were thine,
  Even thine, though few thy wants!—Roof, window,
      door,   10
  The very flowers are sacred to the Poor,

The roses to the porch which they entwine:
  Yea, all that now enchants thee, from the day
  On which it should be touch'd, would melt away!
W. Wordsworth

249

TO THE HIGHLAND GIRL OF INVERSNEYDE

    Sweet Highland Girl, a very shower
    Of beauty is thy earthly dower!
    Twice seven consenting years have shed
    Their utmost bounty on thy head:
    And these grey rocks; that household lawn;   5
    Those trees—a veil just half withdrawn;
    This fall of water that doth make
    A murmur near the silent lake;
    This little bay; a quiet road
    That holds in shelter thy abode;   10
    In truth together do ye seem
    Like something fashion'd in a dream;
    Such forms as from their covert peep
    When earthly cares are laid asleep!
    But O fair Creature! in the light   15
    Of common day, so heavenly bright,
    I bless Thee, Vision as thou art,
    I bless thee with a human heart:
    God shield thee to thy latest years!
    Thee, neither know I, nor thy peers;   20
    And yet my eyes are fill'd with tears.

    With earnest feeling I shall pray
    For thee when I am far away;
    For never saw I mien or face
    In which more plainly I could trace   25
    Benignity and home-bred sense
    Ripening in perfect innocence.
    Here scattered like a random seed,
    Remote from men, Thou dost not need
    The embarrassed look of shy distress,   30
    And maidenly shamefacedness:

Thou wear'st upon thy forehead clear
The freedom of a mountaineer:
A face with gladness overspread;
Soft smiles, by human kindness bred;   35
And seemliness complete, that sways
Thy courtesies, about thee plays;
With no restraint, but such as springs
From quick and eager visitings
Of thoughts that lie beyond the reach   40
Of thy few words of English speech:
A bondage sweetly brook'd, a strife
That gives thy gestures grace and life!
So have I, not unmoved in mind,
Seen birds of tempest-loving kind   45
Thus beating up against the wind.

What hand but would a garland cull
For thee who art so beautiful?
O happy pleasure! here to dwell
Beside thee in some heathy dell;   50
Adopt your homely ways and dress,
A shepherd, thou a shepherdess!
But I could frame a wish for thee
More like a grave reality:
Thou art to me but as a wave   55
Of the wild sea: and I would have
Some claim upon thee, if I could,
Though but of common neighbourhood,
What joy to hear thee, and to see!
Thy elder brother I would be,   60
Thy father—anything to thee!

Now thanks to Heaven! that of its grace
Had led me to this lonely place.
Joy have I had; and going hence
I bear away my recompense.   65
In spots like these it is we prize
Our memory, feel that she hath eyes:
Then why should I be loth to stir?
I feel this place was made for her;

To give new pleasure like the past,   70
Continued long as life shall last.
Nor am I loth, though pleased at heart,
Sweet Highland Girl! from thee to part;
For I, methinks, till I grow old,
As fair before me shall behold   75
As I do now, the cabin small,
The lake, the bay, the waterfall;
And Thee, the Spirit of them all!

W. Wordsworth

250

THE REAPER

Behold her, single in the field,
   Yon solitary Highland Lass!
Reaping and singing by herself;
   Stop here, or gently pass!
Alone she cuts and binds the grain,   5
And sings a melancholy strain;
O listen! for the vale profound
Is overflowing with the sound.

No nightingale did ever chant
   More welcome notes to weary bands   10
Of travellers in some shady haunt,
   Among Arabian sands:
A voice so thrilling ne'er was heard
In spring-time from the cuckoo-bird,
Breaking the silence of the seas   15
Among the farthest Hebrides.

Will no one tell me what she sings?
   Perhaps the plaintive numbers flow
For old, unhappy, far-off things,
   And battles long ago: 20
Or is it some more humble lay,
Familiar matter of to-day?
Some natural sorrow, loss, or pain,
That has been, and may be again?

Whate'er the theme, the maiden sang   25
    As if her song could have no ending;
I saw her singing at her work,
    And o'er the sickle bending;
I listen'd, motionless and still;
And, as I mounted up the hill,   30
The music in my heart I bore,
Long after it was heard no more.

                                    W. Wordsworth

                        251

THE REVERIE OF POOR SUSAN

At the corner of Wood Street, when daylight appears,
Hangs a Thrush that sings loud, it has sung for three
        years:
Poor Susan has pass'd by the spot, and has heard
In the silence of morning the song of the bird.

'Tis a note of enchantment; what ails her? She sees   5
A mountain ascending, a vision of trees;
Bright volumes of vapour through Lothbury glide,
And a river flows on through the vale of Cheapside.

Green pastures she views in the midst of the dale,
Down which she so often has tripp'd with her pail;   10
And a single small cottage, a nest like a dove's,
The one only dwelling on earth that she loves.

She looks, and her heart is in heaven: but they fade,
The mist and the river, the hill and the shade;
The stream will not flow, and the hill will not rise,   15
And the colours have all pass'd away from her eyes!

                                    W. Wordsworth

252

TO A LADY, WITH A GUITAR

Ariel to Miranda:—Take
This slave of Music, for the sake
Of him who is the slave of thee;
And teach it all the harmony
In which thou canst, and only thou,   5
Make the delighted spirit glow,
Till joy denies itself again
And, too intense, is turn'd to pain.
For by permission and command
Of thine own Prince Ferdinand,   10
Poor Ariel sends this silent token
Of more than ever can be spoken;
Your guardian spirit, Ariel, who
From life to life must still pursue
Your happiness; for thus alone   15
Can Ariel ever find his own.
From Prospero's enchanted cell,
As the mighty verses tell,
To the throne of Naples he
Lit you o'er the trackless sea,   20
Flitting on, your prow before,
Like a living meteor.
When you die, the silent Moon
In her interlunar swoon
Is not sadder in her cell   25
Than deserted Ariel.
When you live again on earth,
Like an unseen star of birth
Ariel guides you o'er the sea
Of life from your nativity.   30
Many changes have been run
Since Ferdinand and you begun
Your course of love, and Ariel still
Has tracked your steps and served your will.
Now in humbler, happier lot,   35
This is all remember'd not;

And now, alas! the poor sprite is
Imprisoned for some fault of his
In a body like a grave;—
From you he only dares to crave,   40
For his service and his sorrow,
A smile to-day, a song to-morrow.

The artist who this idol wrought
To echo all harmonious thought,
Felled a tree, while on the steep   45
The woods were in their winter sleep,
Rocked in that repose divine
On the wind-swept Apennine;
And dreaming, some of Autumn past,
And some of Spring approaching fast,   50
And some of April buds and showers,
And some of songs in July bowers,
And all of love; and so this tree,—
O that such our death may be!—
Died in sleep, and felt no pain,   55
To live in happier form again:
From which, beneath Heaven's fairest star,
The artist wrought this loved Guitar;
And taught it justly to reply
To all who question skilfully   60
In language gentle as thine own;
Whispering in enamoured tone
Sweet oracles of woods and dells,
And summer winds in sylvan cells;
—For it had learnt all harmonies   65
Of the plains and of the skies,
Of the forests and the mountains,
And the many-voicéd fountains;
The clearest echoes of the hills,
The softest notes of falling rills,   70
The melodies of birds and bees,
The murmuring of summer seas,
And pattering rain, and breathing dew,
And airs of evening; and it knew
That seldom-heard mysterious sound   75
Which, driven on its diurnal round,

As it floats through boundless day,
Our world enkindles on its way:
—All this it knows, but will not tell
To those who cannot question well   80
The Spirit that inhabits it;
It talks according to the wit
Of its companions; and no more
Is heard than has been felt before
By those who tempt it to betray   85
These secrets of an elder day.
But, sweetly as its answers will
Flatter hands of perfect skill,
It keeps its highest holiest tone
For our belovéd friend alone.   90

                                        P. B. Shelley

253

THE DAFFODILS

I wandered lonely as a cloud
    That floats on high o'er vales and hills,
When all at once I saw a crowd,
    A host, of golden daffodils,
Beside the lake, beneath the trees,   5
Fluttering and dancing in the breeze.

Continuous as the stars that shine
    And twinkle on the milky way,
They stretched in never-ending line
    Along the margin of a bay: 10
Ten thousand saw I at a glance
Tossing their heads in sprightly dance.

The waves beside them danced, but they
    Out-did the sparkling waves in glee:
A Poet could not but be gay   15
    In such a jocund company!
I gazed—and gazed—but little thought
What wealth the show to me had brought:

For oft, when on my couch I lie
   In vacant or in pensive mood,   20
They flash upon that inward eye
   Which is the bliss of solitude;
And then my heart with pleasure fills,
And dances with the daffodils.

                  W. Wordsworth

254

TO THE DAISY

With little here to do or see
Of things that in the great world be,
Daisy! again I talk to thee,
   For thou art worthy,
Thou unassuming Commonplace   5
Of Nature, with that homely face,
And yet with something of a grace
   Which love makes for thee!

Oft on the dappled turf at ease
I sit and play with similes,   10
Loose types of things through all degrees,
   Thoughts of thy raising;
And many a fond and idle name
I give to thee, for praise or blame,
As is the humour of the game,   15
   While I am gazing.

A nun demure, of lowly port;
Or sprightly maiden, of Love's court,
In thy simplicity the sport
   Of all temptations;   20
A queen in crown of rubies drest;
A starveling in a scanty vest;
Are all, as seems to suit thee best,
   Thy appellations.

A little Cyclops, with one eye   25
Staring to threaten and defy,
That thought comes next—and instantly
   The freak is over.

The shape will vanish, and behold!
A silver shield with boss of gold   30
That spreads itself, some fairy bold
    In fight to cover.

I see thee glittering from afar—
And then thou art a pretty star,
Not quite so fair as many are   35
    In heaven above thee!
Yet like a star, with glittering crest,
Self-poised in air thou seem'st to rest;—
May peace come never to his nest
    Who shall reprove thee!   40

Sweet Flower! for by that name at last
When all my reveries are past
I call thee, and to that cleave fast,
    Sweet silent creature!
That breath'st with me in sun and air,   45
Do thou, as thou art wont, repair
My heart with gladness, and a share
    Of thy meek nature!
              W. Wordsworth

255

ODE TO AUTUMN

Season of mists and mellow fruitfulness,
  Close bosom-friend of the maturing sun;
Conspiring with him how to load and bless
  With fruit the vines that round the thatch-eaves run;
To bend with apples the moss'd cottage-trees,   5
  And fill all fruit with ripeness to the core;
    To swell the gourd, and plump the hazel shells
  With a sweet kernel; to set budding more,
And still more, later flowers for the bees,
Until they think warm days will never cease;   10
  For Summer has o'erbrimm'd their clammy cells.

Who hath not seen thee oft amid thy store?
  Sometimes whoever seeks abroad may find
Thee sitting careless on a granary floor,
  Thy hair soft-lifted by the winnowing wind;   15
Or on a half-reap'd furrow sound asleep,
  Drows'd with the fume of poppies, while thy hook
    Spares the next swath and all its twinéd flowers;
And sometimes like a gleaner thou dost keep
  Steady thy laden head across a brook;   20
  Or by a cider-press, with patient look,
    Thou watchest the last oozings, hours by hours.

Where are the songs of Spring?   Aye, where are they?
  Think not of them,—thou hast thy music too,
While barréd clouds bloom the soft-dying day   25
  And touch the stubble-plains with rosy hue;
Then in a wailful choir the small gnats mourn
  Among the river sallows, borne aloft
    Or sinking as the light wind lives or dies;
And full-grown lambs loud bleat from hilly bourn;   30
  Hedge-crickets sing, and now with treble soft
  The redbreast whistles from a garden-croft,
    And gathering swallows twitter in the skies.
                                                        J. Keats

256

ODE TO WINTER

Germany, December 1800

When first the fiery-mantled Sun
His heavenly race began to run,
Round the earth and ocean blue
His children four the Seasons flew:—
    First, in green apparel dancing,   5
The young Spring smiled with angel-grace;
    Rosy Summer, next advancing,
Rush'd into her sire's embrace—
Her bright-hair'd sire, who bade her keep
For ever nearest to his smiles.   10

On Calpe's olive-shaded steep
    Or India's citron-cover'd isles.
More remote, and buxom-brown,
    The Queen of vintage bow'd before his throne;
A rich pomegranate gemm'd her crown,   15
    A ripe sheaf bound her zone.

But howling Winter fled afar
To hills that prop the polar star;
And loves on deer-borne car to ride
With barren darkness at his side,   20
Round the shore where loud Lofoden
    Whirls to death the roaring whale,
Round the hall where Runic Odin
    Howls his war-song to the gale—
Save when adown the ravaged globe   25
    He travels on his native storm,
Deflowering Nature's grassy robe
    And trampling on her faded form;
Till light's returning lord assume
    The shaft that drives him to his polar field,   30
Of power to pierce his raven plume
    And crystal-cover'd shield.

O sire of storms! whose savage ear
The Lapland drum delights to hear,
When Frenzy with her bloodshot eye   35
Implores thy dreadful deity—
Archangel! power of desolation!
    Fast descending as thou art,
Say, hath mortal invocation
    Spells to touch thy stony heart?   40
Then, sullen Winter! hear my prayer
And gently rule the ruin'd year;
Nor chill the wanderer's bosom bare,
Nor freeze the wretch's falling tear:
To shuddering Want's unmantled bed   45
    Thy horror-breathing agues cease to lend,
And gently on the orphan head
    Of innocence descend.

But chiefly spare, O king of clouds!
The sailor on his airy shrouds,   50
When wrecks and beacons strew the steep
And spectres walk along the deep.
Milder yet thy snowy breezes
    Pour on yonder tented shores,
Where the Rhine's broad billow freezes,   55
    Or the dark-brown Danube roars.
O winds of Winter! list ye there
    To many a deep and dying groan?
Or start, ye demons of the midnight air,
    At shrieks and thunders louder than your own?   60
Alas! e'en your unhallow'd breath
    May spare the victim fallen low;
But man will ask no truce to death,
    No bounds to human woe.

T. Campbell

257

YARROW UNVISITED

1803

From Stirling Castle we had seen
    The mazy Forth unravell'd,
Had trod the banks of Clyde and Tay,
    And with the Tweed had travell'd;
And when we came to Clovenford,   5
    Then said my 'winsome Marrow,'
'Whate'er betide, we'll turn aside,
    And see the Braes of Yarrow.'

'Let Yarrow folk, frae Selkirk town,
    Who have been buying, selling,   10
Go back to Yarrow, 'tis their own,
    Each maiden to her dwelling!
On Yarrow's banks let herons feed,
    Hares couch, and rabbits burrow,
But we will downward with the Tweed,   15
    Nor turn aside to Yarrow.

'There 's Galla Water, Leader Haughs,
   Both lying right before us;
And Dryburgh, where with chiming Tweed
   The lintwhites sing in chorus;   20
There 's pleasant Tiviot-dale, a land
   Made blithe with plough and harrow:
Why throw away a needful day
   To go in search of Yarrow?

'What 's Yarrow but a river bare   25
   That glides the dark hills under?
There are a thousand such elsewhere
   As worthy of your wonder.'
—Strange words they seem'd of slight and scorn;
   My True-love sigh'd for sorrow,   30
And look'd me in the face, to think
   I thus could speak of Yarrow!

'O green,' said I, 'are Yarrow's holms,
   And sweet is Yarrow flowing!
Fair hangs the apple frae the rock,   35
   But we will leave it growing.
O'er hilly path and open Strath
   We'll wander Scotland thorough;
But, though so near, we will not turn
   Into the dale of Yarrow.   40

'Let beeves and home-bred kine partake
   The sweets of Burn-mill meadow;
The swan on still St. Mary's Lake
   Float double, swan and shadow!
We will not see them; will not go   45
   To-day, nor yet to-morrow;
Enough if in our hearts we know
   There 's such a place as Yarrow.

'Be Yarrow stream unseen, unknown!
   It must, or we shall rue it: 50
We have a vision of our own,
   Ah! why should we undo it?

The treasured dreams of times long past,
  We'll keep them, winsome Marrow!
For when we're there, although 'tis fair,   55
  'Twill be another Yarrow!

'If Care with freezing years should come,
  And wandering seem but folly,—
Should we be loth to stir from home,
  And yet be melancholy;   60
Should life be dull, and spirits low,
  'Twill soothe us in our sorrow
That earth has something yet to show,
  The bonny holms of Yarrow!'

                                              W. Wordsworth

258

YARROW VISITED

September 1814

And is this—Yarrow?—*This* the Stream
  Of which my fancy cherish'd
So faithfully, a waking dream,
  An image that hath perish'd?
O that some Minstrel's harp were near   5
  To utter notes of gladness
And chase this silence from the air,
  That fills my heart with sadness!

Yet why?—a silvery current flows
  With uncontroll'd meanderings;   10
Nor have these eyes by greener hills
  Been soothed, in all my wanderings.
And, through her depths, St. Mary's Lake
  Is visibly delighted;
For not a feature of those hills   15
  Is in the mirror slighted.

A blue sky bends o'er Yarrow Vale,
  Save where that pearly whiteness
Is round the rising sun diffused,
  A tender hazy brightness;   20

Mild dawn of promise! that excludes
   All profitless dejection;
Though not unwilling here to admit
   A pensive recollection.

Where was it that the famous Flower   25
   Of Yarrow Vale lay bleeding?
His bed perchance was yon smooth mound
   On which the herd is feeding:
And haply from this crystal pool,
   Now peaceful as the morning,   30
The Water-wraith ascended thrice,
   And gave his doleful warning.

Delicious is the Lay that sings
   The haunts of happy lovers,
The path that leads them to the grove,   35
   The leafy grove that covers:
And pity sanctifies the verse
   That paints, by strength of sorrow,
The unconquerable strength of love;
   Bear witness, rueful Yarrow!   40

But thou, that didst appear so fair
   To fond imagination,
Dost rival in the light of day
   Her delicate creation:
Meek loveliness is round thee spread,   45
   A softness still and holy:
The grace of forest charms decay'd,
   And pastoral melancholy.

That region left, the vale unfolds
   Rich groves of lofty stature,   50
With Yarrow winding through the pomp
   Of cultivated nature;
And, rising from those lofty groves,
   Behold a ruin hoary,
The shatter'd front of Newark's Towers,   55
   Renown'd in Border story.

Fair scenes for childhood's opening bloom,
  For sportive youth to stray in,
For manhood to enjoy his strength,
  And age to wear away in!   60
Yon cottage seems a bower of bliss,
  A covert for protection
Of tender thoughts, that nestle there—
  The brood of chaste affection.

How sweet on this autumnal day   65
  The wild-wood fruits to gather,
And on my True-love's forehead plant
  A crest of blooming heather!
And what if I enwreathed my own?
  'Twere no offence to reason;   70
The sober hills thus deck their brows
  To meet the wintry season.

I see—but not by sight alone,
  Loved Yarrow, have I won thee;
A ray of Fancy still survives—   75
  Her sunshine plays upon thee!
Thy ever-youthful waters keep
  A course of lively pleasure;
And gladsome notes my lips can breathe
  Accordant to the measure.   80

The vapours linger round the heights,
  They melt, and soon must vanish;
One hour is theirs, nor more is mine—
  Sad thought! which I would banish,
But that I know, where'er I go,   85
  Thy genuine image, Yarrow!
Will dwell with me—to heighten joy,
  And cheer my mind in sorrow.

                                        W. Wordsworth

259

THE INVITATION

Best and brightest, come away,
Fairer far than this fair Day,
Which, like thee to those in sorrow,
Comes to bid a sweet good-morrow
To the rough Year just awake   5
In its cradle on the brake.
The brightest hour of unborn Spring
Through the winter wandering,
Found, it seems, the halcyon Morn
To hoar February born;   10
Bending from Heaven, in azure mirth,
It kiss'd the forehead of the Earth,
And smiled upon the silent sea,
And bade the frozen streams be free,
And waked to music all their fountains,   15
And breathed upon the frozen mountains,
And like a prophetess of May
Strew'd flowers upon the barren way,
Making the wintry world appear
Like one on whom thou smilest, dear.   20

Away, away, from men and towns,
To the wild wood and the downs—
To the silent wilderness
Where the soul need not repress
Its music, lest it should not find   25
An echo in another's mind,
While the touch of Nature's art
Harmonizes heart to heart.

Radiant Sister of the Day
Awake! arise! and come away!   30
To the wild woods and the plains,
And the pools where winter rains
Image all their roof of leaves,
Where the pine its garland weaves

Of sapless green and ivy dun   35
Round stems that never kiss the sun;
Where the lawns and pastures be
And the sandhills of the sea;
Where the melting hoar-frost wets
The daisy-star that never sets,   40
And wind-flowers and violets,
Which yet join not scent to hue,
Crown the pale year weak and new;
When the night is left behind
In the deep east, dun and blind,   45
And the blue noon is over us,
And the multitudinous
Billows murmur at our feet,
Where the earth and ocean meet,
And all things seem only one   50
In the universal sun.

P. B. Shelley

260

THE RECOLLECTION

Now the last day of many days,
 All beautiful and bright as thou,
  The loveliest and the last, is dead,
Rise, Memory, and write its praise!
Up,—to thy wonted work! come, trace   5
  The epitaph of glory fled,
For now the Earth has changed its face,
 A frown is on the Heaven's brow.

We wander'd to the Pine Forest
 That skirts the Ocean's foam;   10
The lightest wind was in its nest,
 The tempest in its home,
The whispering waves were half asleep,
 The clouds were gone to play,
And on the bosom of the deep   15
 The smile of Heaven lay;

It seem'd as if the hour were one
　　Sent from beyond the skies
Which scatter'd from above the sun
　　A light of Paradise.   20

We paused amid the pines that stood
　　The giants of the waste,
Tortured by storms to shapes as rude
　　As serpents interlaced,
And soothed by every azure breath   25
　　That under Heaven is blown
To harmonies and hues beneath,
　　As tender as its own:
Now all the tree-tops lay asleep
　　Like green waves on the sea,   30
As still as in the silent deep
　　The ocean woods may be.

How calm it was!—the silence there
　　By such a chain was bound,
That even the busy woodpecker   35
　　Made stiller by her sound
The inviolable quietness;
　　The breath of peace we drew
With its soft motion made not less
　　The calm that round us grew.   40
There seem'd from the remotest seat
　　Of the white mountain waste,
To the soft flower beneath our feet
　　A magic circle traced,—
A spirit interfused around,   45
　　A thrilling silent life;
To momentary peace it bound
　　Our mortal nature's strife;—
And still I felt the centre of
　　The magic circle there   50
Was one fair form that fill'd with love
　　The lifeless atmosphere.

We paused beside the pools that lie
   Under the forest bough;
Each seem'd as 'twere a little sky   55
   Gulf'd in a world below;
A firmament of purple light
   Which in the dark earth lay,
More boundless than the depth of night,
   And purer than the day—   60
In which the lovely forests grew
   As in the upper air,
More perfect both in shape and hue
   Than any spreading there.
There lay the glade and neighbouring lawn,   65
   And through the dark green wood
The white sun twinkling like the dawn
   Out of a speckled cloud.
Sweet views which in our world above
   Can never well be seen   70
Were imaged by the water's love
   Of that fair forest green:
And all was interfused beneath
   With an Elysian glow,
An atmosphere without a breath,   75
   A softer day below.
Like one beloved, the scene had lent
   To the dark water's breast
Its every leaf and lineament
   With more than truth exprest;   80
Until an envious wind crept by,
   Like an unwelcome thought
Which from the mind's too faithful eye
   Blots one dear image out.
Though thou art ever fair and kind,   85
   The forests ever green,
Less oft is peace in Shelley's mind
   Than calm in waters seen.

                              P. B. Shelley

261

BY THE SEA

It is a beauteous evening, calm and free;
  The holy time is quiet as a Nun
  Breathless with adoration; the broad sun
Is sinking down in its tranquillity;

The gentleness of heaven broods o'er the Sea: 5
  Listen! the mighty Being is awake,
  And doth with his eternal motion make
A sound like thunder—everlastingly.

Dear child! dear girl! that walkest with me here,
  If thou appear untouch'd by solemn thought   10
    Thy nature is not therefore less divine:

Thou liest in Abraham's bosom all the year,
  And worshipp'st at the Temple's inner shrine,
  God being with thee when we know it not.

                                        W. Wordsworth

262

TO THE EVENING STAR

Star that bringest home the bee,
And sett'st the weary labourer free!
  If any star shed peace, 'tis thou,
    That send'st it from above,
    Appearing when Heaven's breath and brow   5
  Are sweet as hers we love.

Come to the luxuriant skies,
Whilst the landscape's odours rise,
  Whilst far-off lowing herds are heard,
    And songs when toil is done,   10
  From cottages whose smoke unstirr'd
    Curls yellow in the sun.

Star of love's soft interviews,
Parted lovers on thee muse;
   Their remembrancer in Heaven   15
     Of thrilling vows thou art,
   Too delicious to be riven
     By absence from the heart.
                     T. Campbell

263

DATUR HORA QUIETI

The sun upon the lake is low,
   The wild birds hush their song,
The hills have evening's deepest glow,
   Yet Leonard tarries long.
Now all whom varied toil and care   5
   From home and love divide,
In the calm sunset may repair
   Each to the loved one's side.

The noble dame on turret high,
   Who waits her gallant knight,   10
Looks to the western beam to spy
   The flash of armour bright.
The village maid, with hand on brow
   The level ray to shade,
Upon the footpath watches now   15
   For Colin's darkening plaid.

Now to their mates the wild swans row,
   By day they swam apart,
And to the thicket wanders slow
   The hind beside the hart.   20
The woodlark at his partner's side
   Twitters his closing song—
All meet whom day and care divide,
   But Leonard tarries long!
                     Sir W. Scott

264

TO THE MOON

Art thou pale for weariness
Of climbing heaven, and gazing on the earth,
   Wandering companionless
Among the stars that have a different birth,—
And ever-changing, like a joyless eye   5
That finds no object worth its constancy?

P. B. Shelley

265

A widow bird sate mourning for her love
   Upon a wintry bough;
The frozen wind crept on above,
   The freezing stream below.

There was no leaf upon the forest bare,   5
   No flower upon the ground,
And little motion in the air
   Except the mill-wheel's sound.

P. B. Shelley

266

TO SLEEP

A flock of sheep that leisurely pass by,
   One after one; the sound of rain, and bees
   Murmuring; the fall of rivers, winds and seas,
Smooth fields, white sheets of water, and pure sky;

I have thought of all by turns, and yet do lie   5
   Sleepless; and soon the small birds' melodies
   Must hear, first uttered from my orchard trees,
And the first cuckoo's melancholy cry.

Even thus last night, and two nights more, I lay,
   And could not win thee, Sleep! by any stealth: 10
So do not let me wear to-night away:

Without Thee what is all the morning's wealth?
Come, blessèd barrier between day and day,
  Dear mother of fresh thoughts and joyous health!
                                        W. Wordsworth

267

THE SOLDIER'S DREAM

Our bugles sang truce, for the night-cloud had lower'd,
  And the sentinel stars set their watch in the sky;
And thousands had sunk on the ground overpower'd,
  The weary to sleep, and the wounded to die.

When reposing that night on my pallet of straw   5
  By the wolf-scaring faggot that guarded the slain,
At the dead of the night a sweet vision I saw;
  And thrice ere the morning I dreamt it again.

Methought from the battle-field's dreadful array
  Far, far I had roam'd on a desolate track: 10
'Twas autumn,—and sunshine arose on the way
  To the home of my fathers, that welcomed me back.

I flew to the pleasant fields traversed so oft
  In life's morning march, when my bosom was young;
I heard my own mountain-goats bleating aloft,   15
  And knew the sweet strain that the corn-reapers sung.

Then pledged we the wine-cup, and fondly I swore
  From my home and my weeping friends never to
    part;
My little ones kiss'd me a thousand times o'er,
  And my wife sobb'd aloud in her fullness of heart.   20

'Stay—stay with us!—rest!—thou art weary and
    worn!'—
  And fain was their war-broken soldier to stay;—
But sorrow return'd with the dawning of morn,
  And the voice in my dreaming ear melted away.
                                        T. Campbell

268

A DREAM OF THE UNKNOWN

I dream'd that as I wander'd by the way
   Bare Winter suddenly was changed to Spring,
And gentle odours led my steps astray,
   Mix'd with a sound of waters murmuring
Along a shelving bank of turf, which lay   5
   Under a copse, and hardly dared to fling
Its green arms round the bosom of the stream,
But kiss'd it and then fled, as thou mightest in dream.

There grew pied wind-flowers and violets,
   Daisies, those pearl'd Arcturi of the earth,   10
The constellated flower that never sets;
   Faint oxlips; tender blue-bells, at whose birth
The sod scarce heaved; and that tall flower that wets—
   Like a child, half in tenderness and mirth—
Its mother's face with heaven's collected tears,   15
When the low wind, its playmate's voice, it hears.

And in the warm hedge grew lush eglantine,
   Green cow-bind and the moonlight-colour'd may,
And cherry-blossoms, and white cups, whose wine
   Was the bright dew yet drain'd not by the day;   20
And wild roses, and ivy serpentine
   With its dark buds and leaves, wandering astray;
And flowers azure, black, and streak'd with gold,
Fairer than any waken'd eyes behold.

And nearer to the river's trembling edge   25
   There grew broad flag-flowers, purple prank with
     white,
And starry river buds among the sedge,
   And floating water-lilies, broad and bright,
Which lit the oak that overhung the hedge
   With moonlight beams of their own watery light;   30
And bulrushes, and reeds of such deep green
As soothed the dazzled eye with sober sheen.

Methought that of these visionary flowers
  I made a nosegay, bound in such a way
That the same hues, which in their natural bowers
  Were mingled or opposed, the like array   36
Kept these imprison'd children of the Hours
  Within my hand,—and then, elate and gay,
I hasten'd to the spot whence I had come,
That I might there present it—O! to Whom?   40
                          P. B. Shelley

269

THE INNER VISION

Most sweet it is with unuplifted eyes
  To pace the ground, if path be there or none,
While a fair region round the traveller lies
  Which he forbears again to look upon;

Pleased rather with some soft ideal scene,   5
  The work of Fancy, or some happy tone
Of meditation, slipping in between
  The beauty coming and the beauty gone.

If Thought and Love desert us, from that day
  Let us break off all commerce with the Muse: 10
With Thought and Love companions of our way—

  Whate'er the senses take or may refuse,—
  The Mind's internal heaven shall shed her dews
Of inspiration on the humblest lay.
                          W. Wordsworth

270

THE REALM OF FANCY

    Ever let the Fancy roam!
    Pleasure never is at home:
    At a touch sweet Pleasure melteth,
    Like to bubbles when rain pelteth;

Then let wingéd Fancy wander   5
Through the thought still spread beyond her:
Open wide the mind's cage-door,
She'll dart forth, and cloudward soar.
O sweet Fancy! let her loose;
Summer's joys are spoilt by use,   10
And the enjoying of the Spring
Fades as does its blossoming:
Autumn's red-lipp'd fruitage too,
Blushing through the mist and dew,
Cloys with tasting: What do then?   15
Sit thee by the ingle, when
The sear faggot blazes bright,
Spirit of a winter's night;
When the soundless earth is muffled,
And the cakéd snow is shuffled   20
From the ploughboy's heavy shoon;
When the Night doth meet the Noon
In a dark conspiracy
To banish Even from her sky.
—Sit thee there, and send abroad,   25
With a mind self-overawed,
Fancy, high-commission'd:—send her!
She has vassals to attend her;
She will bring, in spite of frost,
Beauties that the earth hath lost;   30
She will bring thee, all together,
All delights of summer weather;
All the buds and bells of May
From dewy sward or thorny spray;
All the heapéd Autumn's wealth,   35
With a still, mysterious stealth;
She will mix these pleasures up
Like three fit wines in a cup,
And thou shalt quaff it;—thou shalt hear
Distant harvest-carols clear;   40
Rustle of the reapéd corn;
Sweet birds antheming the morn:
And in the same moment—hark!
'Tis the early April lark,

Or the rooks, with busy caw,   45
Foraging for sticks and straw.
Thou shalt, at one glance, behold
The daisy and the marigold;
White-plumed lilies, and the first
Hedge-grown primrose that hath burst;   50
Shaded hyacinth, alway
Sapphire queen of the mid-May;
And every leaf, and every flower
Pearléd with the self-same shower.
Thou shalt see the field-mouse peep   55
Meagre from its celléd sleep;
And the snake all winter-thin
Cast on sunny bank its skin;
Freckled nest-eggs thou shalt see
Hatching in the hawthorn-tree,   60
When the hen-bird's wing doth rest
Quiet on her mossy nest;
Then the hurry and alarm
When the bee-hive casts its swarm;
Acorns ripe down-pattering   65
While the autumn breezes sing.

    O sweet Fancy! let her loose;
Everything is spoilt by use:
Where 's the cheek that doth not fade,
Too much gazed at?   Where 's the maid   70
Whose lip mature is ever new?
Where 's the eye, however blue,
Doth not weary?   Where 's the face
One would meet in every place?
Where 's the voice, however soft,   75
One would hear so very oft?
At a touch sweet Pleasure melteth
Like to bubbles when rain pelteth.
Let then wingéd Fancy find
Thee a mistress to thy mind: 80
Dulcet-eyed as Ceres' daughter,
Ere the God of Torment taught her
How to frown and how to chide;
With a waist and with a side

White as Hebe's, when her zone   85
  Slipt its golden clasp, and down
Fell her kirtle to her feet,
While she held the goblet sweet,
And Jove grew languid.—Break the mesh
  Of the Fancy's silken leash;   90
Quickly break her prison-string,
And such joys as these she'll bring.
—Let the wingéd Fancy roam!
Pleasure never is at home.

                                          J. Keats

                    271

HYMN TO THE SPIRIT OF NATURE

Life of Life! thy lips enkindle
  With their love the breath between them;
And thy smiles before they dwindle
  Make the cold air fire; then screen them
In those looks, where whoso gazes   5
Faints, entangled in their mazes.

Child of Light! thy limbs are burning
  Through the vest which seems to hide them,
As the radiant lines of morning
  Through the clouds, ere they divide them;   10
And this atmosphere divinest
Shrouds thee wheresoe'er thou shinest.

Fair are others: none beholds thee;
  But thy voice sounds low and tender
Like the fairest, for it folds thee   15
  From the sight, that liquid splendour;
And all feel, yet see thee never,—
As I feel now, lost for ever!

Lamp of Earth! where'er thou movest
  Its dim shapes are clad with brightness.   20

                                          K*

And the souls of whom thou lovest
   Walk upon the winds with lightness
Till they fail, as I am failing,
   Dizzy, lost, yet unbewailing!

P. B. Shelley

272

WRITTEN IN EARLY SPRING

I heard a thousand blended notes
   While in a grove I sat reclined,
In that sweet mood when pleasant thoughts
   Bring sad thoughts to the mind.

To her fair works did Nature link   5
   The human soul that through me ran;
And much it grieved my heart to think
   What man has made of man.

Through primrose tufts, in that green bower,
   The periwinkle trail'd its wreaths;   10
And 'tis my faith that every flower
   Enjoys the air it breathes.

The birds around me hopp'd and play'd,
   Their thoughts I cannot measure—
But the least motion which they made   15
   It seem'd a thrill of pleasure.

The budding twigs spread out their fan
   To catch the breezy air;
And I must think, do all I can,
   That there was pleasure there.   20

If this belief from heaven be sent,
   If such be Nature's holy plan,
Have I not reason to lament
   What man has made of man?

W. Wordsworth

273

RUTH: OR THE INFLUENCES OF NATURE

When Ruth was left half desolate
Her father took another mate;
   And Ruth, not seven years old,
A slighted child, at her own will
Went wandering over dale and hill,   5
   In thoughtless freedom, bold.

And she had made a pipe of straw,
And music from that pipe could draw
   Like sounds of winds and floods;
Had built a bower upon the green,   10
As if she from her birth had been
   An infant of the woods.

Beneath her father's roof, alone
She seem'd to live; her thoughts her own;
   Herself her own delight: 15
Pleased with herself, nor sad nor gay.
And, passing thus the live-long day,
   She grew to woman's height.

There came a youth from Georgia's shore—
A military casque he wore   20
   With splendid feathers drest;
He brought them from the Cherokees;
The feathers nodded in the breeze
   And made a gallant crest.

From Indian blood you deem him sprung: 25
But no! he spake the English tongue
   And bore a soldier's name;
And, when America was free
From battle and from jeopardy,
   He 'cross the ocean came.   30

With hues of genius on his cheek,
In finest tones the youth could speak:
   —While he was yet a boy
The moon, the glory of the sun,
And streams that murmur as they run,   35
   Had been his dearest joy.

He was a lovely youth! I guess
The panther in the wilderness
   Was not so fair as he;
And when he chose to sport and play,   40
No dolphin ever was so gay
   Upon the tropic sea.

Among the Indians he had fought;
And with him many tales he brought
   Of pleasure and of fear;   45
Such tales as, told to any maid
By such a youth, in the green shade,
   Were perilous to hear.

He told of girls, a happy rout!
Who quit their fold with dance and shout,   50
   Their pleasant Indian town,
To gather strawberries all day long;
Returning with a choral song
   When daylight is gone down.

He spake of plants that hourly change   55
Their blossoms, through a boundless range
   Of intermingling hues;
With budding, fading, faded flowers,
They stand the wonder of the bowers
   From morn to evening dews.   60

He told of the magnolia, spread
High as a cloud, high over head!
   The cypress and her spire;
—Of flowers that with one scarlet gleam
Cover a hundred leagues, and seem   65
   To set the hills on fire.

The youth of green savannahs spake,
And many an endless, endless lake
  With all its fairy crowds
Of islands, that together lie   70
As quietly as spots of sky
  Among the evening clouds.

'How pleasant,' then he said, 'it were
A fisher or a hunter there,
  In sunshine or in shade   75
To wander with an easy mind,
And build a household fire, and find
  A home in every glade!

'What days and what bright years!   Ah me!
Our life were life indeed, with thee   80
  So pass'd in quiet bliss;
And all the while,' said he, 'to know
That we were in a world of woe,
  On such an earth as this!'

And then he sometimes interwove   85
Fond thoughts about a father's love,
  'For there,' said he, 'are spun
Around the heart such tender ties,
That our own children to our eyes
  Are dearer than the sun.   90

'Sweet Ruth! and could you go with me
My helpmate in the woods to be,
  Our shed at night to rear;
Or run, my own adopted bride,
A sylvan huntress at my side,   95
  And drive the flying deer!

'Beloved Ruth!'—No more he said.
The wakeful Ruth at midnight shed
  A solitary tear:
She thought again—and did agree   100
With him to sail across the sea,
  And drive the flying deer.

'And now, as fitting is and right,
We in the church our faith will plight,
    A husband and a wife.'   105
Even so they did; and I may say
That to sweet Ruth that happy day
    Was more than human life.

Through dream and vision did she sink,
Delighted all the while to think   110
    That, on those lonesome floods
And green savannahs, she should share
His board with lawful joy, and bear
    His name in the wild woods.

But, as you have before been told,   115
This Stripling, sportive, gay, and bold,
    And with his dancing crest
So beautiful, through savage lands
Had roam'd about, with vagrant bands
    Of Indians in the West.   120

The wind, the tempest roaring high,
The tumult of a tropic sky
    Might well be dangerous food
For him, a youth to whom was given
So much of earth—so much of heaven,   125
    And such impetuous blood.

Whatever in those climes he found
Irregular in sight or sound
    Did to his mind impart
A kindred impulse, seem'd allied   130
To his own powers, and justified
    The workings of his heart.

Nor less, to feed voluptuous thought,
The beauteous forms of Nature wrought,—
    Fair trees and gorgeous flowers;   135
The breezes their own languor lent;
The stars had feelings, which they sent
    Into those favour'd bowers.

Yet, in his worst pursuits, I ween
That sometimes there did intervene   140
   Pure hopes of high intent:
For passions, link'd to forms so fair
And stately, needs must have their share
   Of noble sentiment.

But ill he lived, much evil saw,   145
With men to whom no better law
   Nor better life was known;
Deliberately and undeceived
Those wild men's vices he received,
   And gave them back his own.   150

His genius and his moral frame
Were thus impair'd, and he became
   The slave of low desires:
A man who without self-control
Would seek what the degraded soul   155
   Unworthily admires.

And yet he with no feign'd delight
Had woo'd the maiden, day and night
   Had loved her, night and morn:
What could he less than love a maid   160
Whose heart with so much nature play'd—
   So kind and so forlorn?

Sometimes most earnestly he said,
'O Ruth! I have been worse than dead;
   False thoughts, thoughts bold and vain   165
Encompass'd me on every side
When I, in confidence and pride,
   Had cross'd the Atlantic main.

'Before me shone a glorious world
Fresh as a banner bright, unfurl'd   170
   To music suddenly:
I look'd upon those hills and plains,
And seem'd as if let loose from chains
   To live at liberty.

'No more of this—for now, by thee,   175
Dear Ruth! more happily set free,
    With nobler zeal I burn;
My soul from darkness is released
Like the whole sky when to the east
    The morning doth return.'   180

Full soon that better mind was gone;
No hope, no wish remain'd, not one,—
    They stirr'd him now no more;
New objects did new pleasure give,
And once again he wish'd to live   185
    As lawless as before.

Meanwhile, as thus with him it fared,
They for the voyage were prepared,
    And went to the sea-shore:
But, when they thither came, the youth   190
Deserted his poor bride, and Ruth
    Could never find him more.

God help thee, Ruth!—Such pains she had,
That she in half a year was mad,
    And in a prison housed;   195
And there, with many a doleful song
Made of wild words, her cup of wrong
    She fearfully caroused.

Yet sometimes milder hours she knew,
Nor wanted sun, nor rain, nor dew,   200
    Nor pastimes of the May,
—They all were with her in her cell;
And a clear brook with cheerful knell
    Did o'er the pebbles play.

When Ruth three seasons thus had lain,   205
There came a respite to her pain;
    She from her prison fled;
But of the Vagrant none took thought;
And where it liked her best she sought
    Her shelter and her bread.   210

Among the fields she breathed again
The master-current of her brain
    Ran permanent and free;
And, coming to the banks of Tone,
There did she rest; and dwell alone   215
    Under the greenwood tree.

The engines of her pain, the tools
That shaped her sorrow, rocks and pools,
    And airs that gently stir
The vernal leaves—she loved them still,   220
Nor ever tax'd them with the ill
    Which had been done to her.

A barn her winter bed supplies;
But, till the warmth of summer skies
    And summer days is gone,   225
(And all do in this tale agree)
She sleeps beneath the greenwood tree,
    And other home hath none.

An innocent life, yet far astray!
And Ruth will, long before her day,   230
    Be broken down and old.
Sore aches she needs must have! but less
Of mind, than body's wretchedness,
    From damp, and rain, and cold.

If she is prest by want of food   235
She from her dwelling in the wood
    Repairs to a road-side;
And there she begs at one steep place,
Where up and down with easy pace
    The horsemen-travellers ride.   240

That oaten pipe of hers is mute
Or thrown away: but with a flute
    Her loneliness she cheers;
This flute, made of a hemlock stalk,
At evening in his homeward walk   245
    The Quantock woodman hears.

I, too, have pass'd her on the hills
Setting her little water-mills
   By spouts and fountains wild—
Such small machinery as she turn'd   250
Ere she had wept, ere she had mourn'd,
   A young and happy child!

Farewell! and when thy days are told,
Ill-fated Ruth! in hallow'd mould
   Thy corpse shall buried be;   255
For thee a funeral bell shall ring,
And all the congregation sing
   A Christian psalm for thee.

                                   W. Wordsworth

                         274

        WRITTEN IN THE EUGANEAN HILLS,
                  NORTH ITALY

      Many a green isle needs must be
      In the deep wide sea of misery,
      Or the mariner, worn and wan,
      Never thus could voyage on
      Day and night, and night and day,   5
      Drifting on his dreary way,
      With the solid darkness black
      Closing round his vessel's track;
      Whilst above, the sunless sky,
      Big with clouds, hangs heavily,   10
      And behind, the tempest fleet
      Hurries on with lightning feet,
      Riving sail, and cord, and plank,
      Till the ship has almost drank
      Death from the o'er-brimming deep;   15
      And sinks down, down, like that sleep
      When the dreamer seems to be
      Weltering through eternity;
      And the dim low line before
      Of a dark and distant shore   20

Still recedes, as ever still
Longing with divided will,
But no power to seek or shun,
He is ever drifted on
O'er the unreposing wave,   25
To the haven of the grave.

Aye, many flowering islands lie
In the waters of wide Agony:
To such a one this morn was led
My bark, by soft winds piloted.   30
—'Mid the mountains Euganean
I stood listening to the paean
With which the legion'd rooks did hail
The sun's uprise majestical:
Gathering round with wings all hoar,   35
Through the dewy mist they soar
Like gray shades, till the eastern heaven
Bursts, and then,—as clouds of even,
Fleck'd with fire and azure, lie
In the unfathomable sky,—   40
So their plumes of purple grain
Starr'd with drops of golden rain
Gleam above the sunlight woods,
As in silent multitudes
On the morning's fitful gale   45
Through the broken mist they sail;
And the vapours cloven and gleaming
Follow down the dark steep streaming,
Till all is bright, and clear, and still
Round the solitary hill.   50

Beneath is spread like a green sea
The waveless plain of Lombardy,
Bounded by the vaporous air,
Islanded by cities fair;
Underneath Day's azure eyes,   55
Ocean's nursling, Venice lies,—
A peopled labyrinth of walls,
Amphitrite's destined halls,
Which her hoary sire now paves
With his blue and beaming waves.   60

Lo! the sun upsprings behind,
Broad, red, radiant, half-reclined
On the level quivering line
Of the waters crystalline;
And before that chasm of light,   65
As within a furnace bright,
Column, tower, and dome, and spire,
Shine like obelisks of fire,
Pointing with inconstant motion
From the altar of dark ocean   70
To the sapphire-tinted skies;
As the flames of sacrifice
From the marble shrines did rise,
As to pierce the dome of gold
Where Apollo spoke of old.   75

Sun-girt City! thou hast been
Ocean's child, and then his queen;
Now is come a darker day,
And thou soon must be his prey,
If the power that raised thee here   80
Hallow so thy watery bier.
A less drear ruin then than now,
With thy conquest-branded brow
Stooping to the slave of slaves
From thy throne, among the waves   85
Wilt thou be,—when the sea-mew
Flies, as once before it flew,
O'er thine isles depopulate,
And all is in its ancient state,
Save where many a palace gate,   90
With green sea-flowers overgrown
Like a rock of ocean's own,
Topples o'er the abandon'd sea
As the tides change sullenly.
The fisher on his watery way   95
Wandering at the close of day,
Will spread his sail and seize his oar
Till he pass the gloomy shore,
Lest thy dead should, from their sleep
Bursting o'er the starlight deep,   100

Lead a rapid masque of death
O'er the waters of his path.

Noon descends around me now:
'Tis the noon of autumn's glow,
When a soft and purple mist   105
Like a vaporous amethyst,
Or an air-dissolvéd star
Mingling light and fragrance, far
From the curved horizon's bound
To the point of Heaven's profound,   110
Fills the overflowing sky;
And the plains that silent lie
Underneath; the leaves unsodden
Where the infant Frost has trodden
With his morning-wingéd feet   115
Whose bright print is gleaming yet;
And the red and golden vines
Piercing with their trellised lines
The rough, dark-skirted wilderness;
The dun and bladed grass no less,   120
Pointing from his hoary tower
In the windless air; the flower
Glimmering at my feet; the line
Of the olive-sandall'd Apennine
In the south dimly islanded;   125
And the Alps, whose snows are spread
High between the clouds and sun;
And of living things each one;
And my spirit, which so long
Darken'd this swift stream of song,—   130
Interpenetrated lie
By the glory of the sky;
Be it love, light, harmony,
Odour, or the soul of all
Which from Heaven like dew doth fall,   135
Or the mind which feeds this verse
Peopling the lone universe.

Noon descends, and after noon
Autumn's evening meets me soon.

Leading the infantine moon   140
And that one star, which to her
Almost seems to minister
Half the crimson light she brings
From the sunset's radiant springs:
And the soft dreams of the morn   145
(Which like wingéd winds had borne
To that silent isle, which lies
'Mid remember'd agonies,
The frail bark of this lone being),
Pass, to other sufferers fleeing,   150
And its ancient pilot, Pain,
Sits beside the helm again.

Other flowering isles must be
In the sea of Life and Agony:
Other spirits float and flee   155
O'er that gulf: even now, perhaps,
On some rock the wild wave wraps,
With folding wings they waiting sit
For my bark, to pilot it
To some calm and blooming cove,   160
Where for me, and those I love,
May a windless bower be built,
Far from passion, pain, and guilt,
In a dell 'mid lawny hills
Which the wild sea-murmur fills,   165
And soft sunshine, and the sound
Of old forests echoing round,
And the light and smell divine,
Of all flowers that breathe and shine.
—We may live so happy there,   170
That the Spirits of the Air
Envying us, may even entice
To our healing Paradise
The polluting multitude;
But their rage would be subdued   175
By that clime divine and calm,
And the winds whose wings rain balm
On the uplifted soul, and leaves
Under which the bright sea heaves;

While each breathless interval   180
In their whisperings musical
The inspired soul supplies
With its own deep melodies;
And the love which heals all strife
Circling, like the breath of life,   185
All things in that sweet abode
With its own mild brotherhood.
They, not it, would change; and soon
Every sprite beneath the moon
Would repent its envy vain,   190
And the earth grow young again.

P. B. Shelley

275

ODE TO THE WEST WIND

(1)

O wild West Wind, thou breath of Autumn's being,
   Thou, from whose unseen presence the leaves dead
Are driven, like ghosts from an enchanter fleeing,

Yellow, and black, and pale, and hectic red,
   Pestilence-stricken multitudes: O thou   5
Who chariotest to their dark wintry bed

The wingéd seeds, where they lie cold and low,
   Each like a corpse within its grave, until
Thine azure sister of the Spring shall blow

Her clarion o'er the dreaming earth, and fill   10
   (Driving sweet buds like flocks to feed in air)
With living hues and odours plain and hill:

Wild Spirit, which art moving everywhere;
Destroyer and Preserver; hear, oh, hear!

(2)

Thou on whose stream, mid the steep sky's commotion, 15
   Loose clouds like earth's decaying leaves are shed,
Shook from the tangled boughs of Heaven and Ocean,

Angels of rain and lightning: there are spread
   On the blue surface of thine airy surge,
Like the bright hair uplifted from the head   20

Of some fierce Maenad, even from the dim verge
   Of the horizon to the zenith's height,
The locks of the approaching storm.   Thou dirge

Of the dying year, to which this closing night
   Will be the dome of a vast sepulchre,   25
Vaulted with all thy congregated might

Of vapours, from whose solid atmosphere
Black rain, and fire, and hail, will burst: oh, hear!

(3)

Thou who didst waken from his summer dreams
   The blue Mediterranean, where he lay,   30
Lull'd by the coil of his crystalline streams,

Beside a pumice isle in Baiae's bay,
   And saw in sleep old palaces and towers
Quivering within the wave's intenser day,

All overgrown with azure moss and flowers   35
   So sweet, the sense faints picturing them!   Thou
For whose path the Atlantic's level powers

Cleave themselves into chasms, while far below
   The sea-blooms and the oozy woods which wear
The sapless foliage of the ocean, know   40

Thy voice, and suddenly grow grey with fear,
And tremble and despoil themselves: oh, hear!

(4)

If I were a dead leaf thou mightest bear;
  If I were a swift cloud to fly with thee;
A wave to pant beneath thy power, and share   45

The impulse of thy strength, only less free
  Than thou, O uncontrollable! If even
I were as in my boyhood, and could be

The comrade of thy wanderings over Heaven,
  As then, when to outstrip thy skyey speed   50
Scarce seemed a vision, I would ne'er have striven

As thus with thee in prayer in my sore need.
  Oh, lift me as a wave, a leaf, a cloud!
I fall upon the thorns of life! I bleed!

A heavy weight of hours has chained and bowed 55
One too like thee: tameless, and swift, and proud.

(5)

Make me thy lyre, even as the forest is:
  What if my leaves are falling like its own!
The tumult of thy mighty harmonies

Will take from both a deep, autumnal tone,   60
  Sweet though in sadness. Be thou, Spirit fierce,
My spirit! Be thou me, impetuous one!

Drive my dead thoughts over the universe
  Like withered leaves to quicken a new birth!
And, by the incantation of this verse,   65

Scatter, as from an unextinguished hearth
  Ashes and sparks, my words among mankind!
Be through my lips to unawakened earth

The trumpet of a prophecy! O Wind,
If Winter comes, can Spring be far behind?   70
                              P. B. Shelley

276

NATURE AND THE POET

*Suggested by a Picture of Peele Castle in a Storm, painted
by Sir George Beaumont*

I was thy neighbour once, thou rugged Pile!
　　Four summer weeks I dwelt in sight of thee:
I saw thee every day; and all the while
　　Thy Form was sleeping on a glassy sea.

So pure the sky, so quiet was the air!   5
　　So like, so very like, was day to day!
Whene'er I look'd, thy image still was there;
　　It trembled, but it never pass'd away.

How perfect was the calm!　It seem'd no sleep,
　　No mood, which season takes away, or brings: 10
I could have fancied that the mighty Deep
　　Was even the gentlest of all gentle things.

Ah! then if mine had been the Painter's hand
　　To express what then I saw; and add the gleam,
The light that never was on sea or land,   15
　　The consecration, and the Poet's dream,—

I would have planted thee, thou hoary Pile,
　　Amid a world how different from this!
Beside a sea that could not cease to smile;
　　On tranquil land, beneath a sky of bliss.   20

A picture had it been of lasting ease,
　　Elysian quiet, without toil or strife;
No motion but the moving tide, a breeze,
　　Or merely silent Nature's breathing life.

Such, in the fond illusion of my heart,   25
　　Such picture would I at that time have made;
And seen the soul of truth in every part,
　　A steadfast peace that might not be betray'd.

So once it would have been,—'tis so no more;
    I have submitted to a new control: 30
A power is gone, which nothing can restore;
    A deep distress hath humanized my soul.

Not for a moment could I now behold
    A smiling sea, and be what I have been
The feeling of my loss will ne'er be old;   35
    This, which I know, I speak with mind serene.

Then, Beaumont, Friend! who would have been the
        Friend
    If he had lived, of him whom I deplore,
This work of thine I blame not, but commend;
    This sea in anger, and that dismal shore.   40

O 'tis a passionate work!—yet wise and well,
    Well chosen is the spirit that is here;
That hulk which labours in the deadly swell,
    This rueful sky, this pageantry of fear!

And this huge Castle, standing here sublime,   45
    I love to see the look with which it braves,
—Cased in the unfeeling armour of old time—
    The lightning, the fierce wind, and trampling waves.

Farewell, farewell the heart that lives alone,
    Housed in a dream, at distance from the Kind!   50
Such happiness, wherever it be known,
    Is to be pitied; for 'tis surely blind.

But welcome fortitude, and patient cheer,
    And frequent sights of what is to be borne!
Such sights, or worse, as are before me here:—   55
    Not without hope we suffer and we mourn.

                               W. Wordsworth

277

THE POET'S DREAM

On a poet's lips I slept
Dreaming like a love-adept
In the sound his breathing kept;
Nor seeks nor finds he mortal blisses,
But feeds on the aerial kisses   5
Of shapes that haunt thought's wildernesses.
He will watch from dawn to gloom
The lake-reflected sun illume
The yellow bees in the ivy-bloom,
    Nor heed nor see what things they be;   10
But from these create he can
Forms more real than living man,
    Nurslings of immortality!

P. B. Shelley

278

The world is too much with us; late and soon,
  Getting and spending, we lay waste our powers
  Little we see in Nature that is ours;
We have given our hearts away, a sordid boon!

This Sea that bares her bosom to the moon,   5
  The winds that will be howling at all hours
  And are up-gather'd now like sleeping flowers,
For this, for everything, we are out of tune;

It moves us not.—Great God! I'd rather be
  A Pagan suckled in a creed outworn,   10
So might I, standing on this pleasant lea,

  Have glimpses that would make me less forlorn;
Have sight of Proteus rising from the sea;
  Or hear old Triton blow his wreathéd horn.

W. Wordsworth

279

WITHIN KING'S COLLEGE CHAPEL, CAMBRIDGE

Tax not the royal Saint with vain expense,
 With ill-match'd aims the Architect who plann'd
  (Albeit labouring for a scanty band
 Of white-robed Scholars only) this immense

And glorious work of fine intelligence!   5
 Give all thou canst; high Heaven rejects the lore
 Of nicely-calculated less or more:
So deem'd the man who fashion'd for the sense

These lofty pillars, spread that branching roof
 Self-poised, and scoop'd into ten thousand cells, 10
 Where light and shade repose, where music dwells

 Lingering—and wandering on as loth to die;
Like thoughts whose very sweetness yieldeth proof
 That they were born for immortality.
          W. Wordsworth

280

YOUTH AND AGE

 Verse, a breeze 'mid blossoms straying,
  Where Hope clung feeding, like a bee—
 Both were mine!   Life went a-maying
   With Nature, Hope, and Poesy,
    When I was young!   5

 When I was young?—Ah, woeful When!
  Ah! for the change 'twixt Now and Then!
 This breathing house not built with hands,
  This body that does me grievous wrong,
 O'er aery cliffs and glittering sands   10
  How lightly then it flash'd along:
 Like those trim skiffs, unknown of yore,
  On winding lakes and rivers wide,

That ask no aid of sail or oar,
   That fear no spite of wind or tide!   15
Nought cared this body for wind or weather
When Youth and I lived in't together.

Flowers are lovely; Love is flower-like;
   Friendship is a sheltering tree;
O! the joys, that came down shower-like,   20
   Of Friendship, Love, and Liberty,
         Ere I was old!

Ere I was old? Ah woeful Ere,
Which tells me, Youth 's no longer here!
O Youth! for years so many and sweet   25
'Tis known that Thou and I were one,
I'll think it but a fond conceit—
   It cannot be that thou art gone!
Thy vesper bell hath not yet toll'd:—
And thou wert ay a masker bold!   30
What strange disguise hast now put on
To make believe that thou art gone?
I see these locks in silvery slips,
   This drooping gait, this alter'd size:
But Springtide blossoms on thy lips,   35
   And tears take sunshine from thine eyes!
Life is but thought: so think I will
That Youth and I are housemates still.

Dew-drops are the gems of morning,
   But the tears of mournful eve!   40
Where no hope is, life 's a warning
   That only serves to make us grieve,
         When we are old:

—That only serves to make us grieve
With oft and tedious taking-leave,   45
Like some poor nigh-related guest
That may not rudely be dismist,
Yet hath outstay'd his welcome while,
And tells the jest without the smile.
                   S. T. Coleridge

THE TWO APRIL MORNINGS

We walk'd along, while bright and red
   Uprose the morning sun;
And Matthew stopp'd, he look'd, and said,
   'The will of God be done!'

A village schoolmaster was he,   5
   With hair of glittering grey;
As blithe a man as you could see
   On a spring holiday.

And on that morning, through the grass
   And by the steaming rills   10
We travell'd merrily, to pass
   A day among the hills.

'Our work,' said I, 'was well begun;
   Then, from thy breast what thought,
Beneath so beautiful a sun,   15
   So sad a sigh has brought?'

A second time did Matthew stop;
   And fixing still his eye
Upon the eastern mountain-top,
   To me he made reply: 20

'Yon cloud with that long purple cleft
   Brings fresh into my mind
A day like this, which I have left
   Full thirty years behind.

'And just above yon slope of corn   25
   Such colours, and no other,
Were in the sky, that April morn,
   Of this the very brother.

'With rod and line I sued the sport
   Which that sweet season gave,   30
And, to the churchyard come, stopp'd short
   Beside my daughter's grave.

'Nine summers had she scarcely seen,
  The pride of all the vale;
And then she sang;—she would have been   35
  A very nightingale.

'Six feet in earth my Emma lay;
  And yet I loved her more—
For so it seem'd,—than till that day
  I e'er had loved before.   40

'And turning from her grave, I met
  Beside the churchyard yew
A blooming Girl, whose hair was wet
  With points of morning dew.

'A basket on her head she bare;   45
  He brow was smooth and white:
To see a child so very fair,
  It was a pure delight!

'No fountain from its rocky cave
  E'er tripp'd with foot so free;   50
She seem'd as happy as a wave
  That dances on the sea.

'There came from me a sigh of pain
  Which I could ill confine;
I looked at her, and looked again: 55
  And did not wish her mine!'

—Matthew is in his grave, yet now
  Methinks I see him stand
As at that moment, with a bough
  Of wilding in his hand.   60

                              W. Wordsworth

                    282

              THE FOUNTAIN

              A Conversation

We talk'd with open heart, and tongue
  Affectionate and true,
A pair of friends, though I was young,
  And Matthew seventy-two.

We lay beneath a spreading oak,   5
  Beside a mossy seat;
And from the turf a fountain broke
  And gurgled at our feet.

'Now, Matthew!' said I, 'let us match
  This water's pleasant tune   10
With some old border-song, or catch
  That suits a summer's noon;

'Or of the church-clock and the chimes
  Sing here beneath the shade
That half-mad thing of witty rhymes   15
  Which you last April made!'

In silence Matthew lay, and eyed
  The spring beneath the tree:
And thus the dear old man replied,
  The grey-hair'd man of glee: 20

'No check, no stay, this Streamlet fears,
  How merrily it goes!
'Twill murmur on a thousand years
  And flow as now it flows.

'And here, on this delightful day,   25
  I cannot choose but think
How oft, a vigorous man, I lay
  Beside this fountain's brink.

'My eyes are dim with childish tears,
  My heart is idly stirr'd,   30
For the same sound is in my ears
  Which in those days I heard.

'Thus fares it still in our decay:
  And yet the wiser mind
Mourns less for what age takes away,   35
  Than what it leaves behind.

'The blackbird amid leafy trees,
  The lark above the hill,
Let loose their carols when they please,
  Are quiet when they will.   40

'With Nature never do they wage
   A foolish strife; they see
A happy youth, and their old age
   Is beautiful and free:

'But we are press'd by heavy laws;   45
   And often, glad no more,
We wear a face of joy, because
   We have been glad of yore.

'If there be one who need bemoan
   His kindred laid in earth,   50
The household hearts that were his own,—
   It is the man of mirth.

'My days, my friend, are almost gone,
   My life has been approved,
And many love me; but by none   55
   Am I enough beloved.'

'Now both himself and me he wrongs,
   The man who thus complains!
I live and sing my idle songs
   Upon these happy plains: 60

'And, Matthew, for thy children dead
   I'll be a son to thee!'
At this he grasp'd my hand and said,
   'Alas! that cannot be.'

We rose up from the fountain-side;   65
   And down the smooth descent
Of the green sheep-track did we glide;
   And through the wood we went;

And, ere we came to Leonard's rock,
   He sang those witty rhymes   70
About the crazy old church-clock
   And the bewilder'd chimes.
                                    W. Wordsworth

283

THE RIVER OF LIFE

The more we live, more brief appear
  Our life's succeeding stages:
A day to childhood seems a year,
  And years like passing ages.

The gladsome current of our youth,   5
  Ere passion yet disorders,
Steals lingering like a river smooth
  Along its grassy borders.

But as the careworn cheek grows wan,
  And sorrow's shafts fly thicker,   10
Ye stars, that measure life to man,
  Why seem your courses quicker?

When joys have lost their bloom and breath,
  And life itself is vapid,
Why, as we reach the Falls of death,   15
  Feel we its tide more rapid?

It may be strange—yet who would change
  Time's course to slower speeding,
When one by one our friends have gone
  And left our bosoms bleeding?   20

Heaven gives our years of fading strength
  Indemnifying fleetness;
And those of youth, a seeming length,
  Proportion'd to their sweetness.
                                T. Campbell

284

THE HUMAN SEASONS

Four seasons fill the measure of the year;
  There are four seasons in the mind of man:
He has his lusty Spring, when fancy clear
  Takes in all beauty with an easy span:

He has his Summer, when luxuriously   5
    Spring's honey'd cud of youthful thought he loves
To ruminate, and by such dreaming nigh
    His nearest unto heaven: quiet coves

His soul has in its Autumn, when his wings
    He furleth close; contented so to look   10
On mists in idleness—to let fair things
    Pass by unheeded as a threshold brook:

He has his Winter too of pale misfeature,
Or else he would forgo his mortal nature.

                                        J. Keats

285

A LAMENT

O World! O Life! O Time!
On whose last steps I climb,
    Trembling at that where I had stood before;
When will return the glory of your prime?
    No more—Oh, never more!   5

Out of the day and night
A joy has taken flight:
    Fresh spring, and summer, and winter hoar
Move my faint heart with grief, but with delight
    No more—Oh, never more!   10

                                    P. B. Shelley

286

My heart leaps up when I behold
    A rainbow in the sky:
So was it when my life began,
So is it now I am a man,
So be it when I shall grow old,   5
    Or let me die!
The Child is father of the Man:
And I could wish my days to be
Bound each to each by natural piety.

                                    W. Wordsworth

287

ODE ON INTIMATIONS OF
IMMORTALITY FROM RECOLLECTIONS
OF EARLY CHILDHOOD

There was a time when meadow, grove, and stream,
    The earth, and every common sight,
        To me did seem
      Apparell'd in celestial light,
The glory and the freshness of a dream,   5
It is not now as it hath been of yore;—
      Turn wheresoe'er I may,
        By night or day,
The things which I have seen I now can see no more.

      The rainbow comes and goes,   10
      And lovely is the rose;
      The moon doth with delight
Look round her when the heavens are bare;
      Waters on a starry night
        Are beautiful and fair;   15
    The sunshine is a glorious birth;
    But yet I know, where'er I go,
That there hath pass'd away a glory from the earth.

Now, while the birds thus sing a joyous song,
      And while the young lambs bound   20
      As to the tabor's sound,
To me alone there came a thought of grief:
A timely utterance gave that thought relief,
      And I again am strong.   24
The cataracts blow their trumpets from the steep,—
   No more shall grief of mine the season wrong:
   I hear the echoes through the mountains throng,
The winds come to me from the fields of sleep,
      And all the earth is gay;
        Land and sea   30
    Give themselves up to jollity,

And with the heart of May
Doth every beast keep holiday;—
Thou child of joy,
Shout round me, let me hear thy shouts, thou happy
Shepherd-boy!   35

Ye blesséd Creatures, I have heard the call
Ye to each other make; I see
The heavens laugh with you in your jubilee;
My heart is at your festival,
My head hath its coronal,   40
The fulness of your bliss, I feel—I feel it all.
O evil day! if I were sullen
While Earth herself is adorning
This sweet May-morning;
And the children are culling   45
On every side
In a thousand valleys far and wide
Fresh flowers; while the sun shines warm,
And the babe leaps up on his mother's arm:—
I hear, I hear, with joy I hear!   50
—But there 's a tree, of many, one,
A single field which I have look'd upon,
Both of them speak of something that is gone:
The pansy at my feet
Doth the same tale repeat: 55
Whither is fled the visionary gleam?
Where is it now, the glory and the dream?

Our birth is but a sleep and a forgetting;
The Soul that rises with us, our life's Star,
Hath had elsewhere its setting,   60
And cometh from afar;
Not in entire forgetfulness,
And not in utter nakedness,
But trailing clouds of glory do we come
From God, who is our home: 65
Heaven lies about us in our infancy!
Shades of the prison-house begin to close
Upon the growing Boy,

But he beholds the light, and whence it flows,
    He sees it in his joy;   70
The Youth, who daily farther from the east
  Must travel, still is Nature's priest,
    And by the vision splendid
    Is on his way attended;
At length the Man perceives it die away,   75
And fade into the light of common day.

Earth fills her lap with pleasures of her own;
Yearnings she hath in her own natural kind,
And, even with something of a mother's mind
    And no unworthy aim,   80
  The homely nurse doth all she can
To make her foster-child, her inmate, Man,
  Forget the glories he hath known,
And that imperial palace whence he came.

Behold the Child among his new-born blisses, 85
 A six years' darling of a pigmy size!
 See, where 'mid work of his own hand he lies,
Fretted by sallies of his mother's kisses,
 With light upon him from his father's eyes!
See, at his feet, some little plan or chart, 90
Some fragment from his dream of human life,
Shaped by himself with newly-learnéd art;
   A wedding or a festival,
   A mourning or a funeral;
    And this hath now his heart, 95
   And unto this he frames his song:
    Then will he fit his tongue
To dialogues of business, love, or strife;
   But it will not be long
   Ere this be thrown aside,   100
   And with new joy and pride
The little actor cons another part;
Filling from time to time his 'humorous stage'
With all the Persons, down to palsied Age,
That life brings with her in her equipage; 105
   As if his whole vocation
   Were endless imitation.

Thou, whose exterior semblance doth belie
      Thy soul's immensity;
Thou best Philosopher, who yet dost keep   110
Thy heritage, thou Eye among the blind,
That, deaf and silent, read'st the eternal deep,
Haunted for ever by the eternal Mind,—
      Mighty Prophet! Seer blest!
      On whom those truths do rest   115
Which we are toiling all our lives to find,
In darkness lost, the darkness of the grave;
Thou, over whom thy Immortality
Broods like the Day, a Master o'er a Slave,
A Presence which is not to be put by;   120
Thou little Child, yet glorious in the might
Of heaven-born freedom on thy being's height,
Why with such earnest pains dost thou provoke
The years to bring the inevitable yoke,
Thus blindly with thy blessedness at strife?   125
Full soon thy Soul shall have her earthly freight,
And custom lie upon thee with a weight
Heavy as frost, and deep almost as life!

      O joy! that in our embers
      Is something that doth live,   130
      That Nature yet remembers
      What was so fugitive!
The thought of our past years in me doth breed
Perpetual benediction: not indeed
For that which is most worthy to be blest,   135
Delight and liberty, the simple creed
Of Childhood, whether busy or at rest,
With new-fledged hope still fluttering in his breast:
      —Not for these I raise
      The song of thanks and praise;   140
   But for those obstinate questionings
   Of sense and outward things,
   Fallings from us, vanishings,
   Blank misgivings of a creature
Moving about in worlds not realized,   145
High instincts, before which our mortal nature
Did tremble like a guilty thing surprised:

But for those first affections,
Those shadowy recollections,
          Which, be they what they may,   150
Are yet the fountain-light of all our day,
Are yet a master-light of all our seeing;
          Uphold us, cherish, and have power to make
Our noisy years seem moments in the being
          Of the eternal silence: truths that wake,   155
                    To perish never;
Which neither listlessness, nor mad endeavour,
                    Nor man nor boy
Nor all that is at enmity with joy,
Can utterly abolish or destroy!   160
     Hence in a season of calm weather
          Though inland far we be,
Our souls have sight of that immortal sea
          Which brought us hither;
          Can in a moment travel thither—   165
And see the children sport upon the shore,
And hear the mighty waters rolling evermore.

Then, sing ye birds, sing, sing a joyous song!
          And let the young lambs bound
          As to the tabor's sound!   170
     We, in thought, will join your throng
          Ye that pipe and ye that play,
          Ye that through your hearts to-day
          Feel the gladness of the May!
What though the radiance which was once so bright
Be now for ever taken from my sight,   176
          Though nothing can bring back the hour
Of splendour in the grass, of glory in the flower;
          We will grieve not, rather find
          Strength in what remains behind;   180
          In the primal sympathy
          Which having been must ever be;
          In the soothing thoughts that spring
          Out of human suffering;
          In the faith that looks through death,   185
     In years that bring the philosophic mind.

                                        L*

And O, ye Fountains, Meadows, Hills, and Groves,
Forbode not any severing of our loves!
Yet in my heart of hearts I feel your might;
I only have relinquish'd one delight   190
To live beneath your more habitual sway;
I love the brooks which down their channels fret,
Even more than when I tripp'd lightly as they;
The innocent brightness of a new-born day
              Is lovely yet;   195
The clouds that gather round the setting sun
Do take a sober colouring from an eye
That hath kept watch o'er man's mortality;
Another race hath been, and other palms are won.
Thanks to the human heart by which we live,   200
Thanks to its tenderness, its joys, and fears,
To me the meanest flower that blows can give
Thoughts that do often lie too deep for tears.

W. Wordsworth

288

    Music, when soft voices die,
    Vibrates in the memory—
    Odours, when sweet violets sicken,
    Live within the sense they quicken.

    Rose leaves, when the rose is dead,   5
    Are heaped for the beloved's bed;
    And so thy thoughts, when thou art gone,
    Love itself shall slumber on.

P. B. Shelley

NOTES TO
THE GOLDEN TREASURY

BY FRANCIS TURNER PALGRAVE

SUMMARY OF BOOK FIRST

THE Elizabethan Poetry, as it is rather vaguely termed, forms the substance of this Book, which contains pieces from Wyatt under Henry VIII to Shakespeare midway through the reign of James I, and Drummond who carried on the early manner to a still later period. There is here a wide range of style; —from simplicity expressed in a language hardly yet broken into verse,—through the pastoral fancies and Italian conceits of the strictly Elizabethan time,—to the passionate reality of Shakespeare: yet a general uniformity of tone prevails. Few readers can fail to observe the natural sweetness of the verse, the single-hearted straightforwardness of the thoughts:—nor less, the limitation of subject to the many phases of one passion which then characterized our lyrical poetry,— unless when, as with Drummond and Shakespeare, the 'purple light of Love' is tempered by a spirit of sterner reflection.

It should be observed that this and the following Summaries apply in the main to the Collection here presented, in which (besides its restriction to Lyrical Poetry) a strictly representative or historical Anthology has not been aimed at. Great excellence, in human art as in human character, has from the beginning of things been even more uniform than Mediocrity, by virtue of the closeness of its approach to Nature:—and so far as the standard of Excellence kept in view has been attained in this volume, a comparative absence of extreme or temporary phases in style, a similarity of tone and manner, will be found throughout:—something neither modern nor ancient, but true in all ages, and, like the works of Creation, perfect as on the first day.

PAGE NO.

13   2   1. 4. *Rouse Memnon's mother*: Awaken the Dawn from the dark Earth and the clouds where she is resting. Aurora in the old mythology is mother of Memnon (the East), and wife of Tithonus (the appearances of Earth and Sky during the last hours of Night). She leaves him every morning in renewed youth, to prepare the way for Phoebus (the Sun), whilst Tithonus remains in perpetual old age and greyness.

327

PAGE NO.
14   2   l. 27. *by Peneüs' streams*: Phoebus loved the Nymph
             Daphne whom he met by the river Peneüs in the vale of
             Tempe. This legend expressed the attachment of the
             Laurel (Daphne) to the Sun, under whose heat the tree
             both fades and flourishes.
                 It has been thought worth while to explain these
             allusions, because they illustrate the character of the
             Grecian Mythology which arose in the Personification
             of natural phenomena, and was totally free from those
             debasing and ludicrous ideas with which, through
             Roman and later misunderstanding or perversion, it
             has been associated.

—   —   l. 31. *Amphion's lyre*: He was said to have built the
             walls of Thebes to the sound of his music.

—   —   l. 39. *Night like a drunkard reels*: Compare *Romeo and
             Juliet*, Act II, Scene 3: 'The grey-eyed morn smiles,'etc.

15   4   l. 10. *Time's chest*: in which he is figuratively sup-
             posed to lay up past treasures. So in *Troilus*, Act III,
             Scene 3, 'Time hath a wallet at his back,' etc.

16   5   A fine example of the highwrought and conventional
             Elizabethan Pastoralism, which it would be ludicrous to
             criticize on the ground of the unshepherdlike or unreal
             character of some images suggested. Stanza 6 was
             probably inserted by Izaak Walton.

18   9   This Poem, with 25 and 94, is taken from Davison's
             Rhapsody, first published in 1602. One stanza has been
             here omitted, in accordance with the principle noticed in
             the Preface. Similar omissions occur in 45, 87, 100, 128,
             160, 165, 227, 235. The more serious abbreviation by
             which it has been attempted to bring Crashaw's 'Wishes'
             and Shelley's 'Euganean Hills' within the limits of lyrical
             unity is commended with much diffidence to the judge-
             ment of readers acquainted with the original pieces.

22   15   This charming little poem, truly 'old and plain, and
             dallying with the innocence of love' like that spoken
             of in *Twelfth Night*, is taken, with 5, 17, 20, 34, and 40,
             from the most characteristic collection of Elizabeth's
             reign, *England's Helicon*, first published in 1600.

—   16   Readers who have visited Italy will be reminded of
             more than one picture by this gorgeous Vision of Beauty,
             equally sublime and pure in its Paradisaical naturalness.
             Lodge wrote it on a voyage to 'the Islands of Terceras
             and the Canaries'; and he seems to have caught, in those
             southern seas, no small portion of the qualities which
             marked the almost contemporary Art of Venice,—the
             glory and the glow of Veronese, or Titian, or Tintoret
             when he most resembles Titian, and all but surpasses him.

—   —   l. 1. *The clear* is the crystalline or outermost heaven
             of the old cosmography. For *resembling* (l. 7) other
             copies give *refining*: the correct reading is perhaps
             revealing.

PAGE   NO.

23   16   l. 43. *for a fair there's fairer none*: If you desire a Beauty, there is none more beautiful than Rosalynde.

25   18   l. 10. *that fair thou owest*: that beauty thou ownest.

27   22   l. 9. *my . . . thy* is here conjecturally printed for 'thy . . . my.' A very few similar corrections of (it is presumed) misprints have been made: as *men* for *me*, 41. l. 3; *dome* for *doom*, 275. l. 25; with two or three more less important.

—   23   ll. 7, 8. *the star . . . Whose worth's unknown, although his height be taken*: apparently, Whose stellar influence is uncalculated although his angular altitude from the plane of the astrolabe or artificial horizon used by astrologers has been determined.

29   27   l. 9. *keel*: skim.

31   29   l. 8. *expense*: waste.

—   30   l. 5. *Nativity, once in the main of light*: when a star has risen and entered on the full stream of light;—another of the astrological phrases no longer familiar.

—   —   l. 7. *Crooked* eclipses: as coming athwart the Sun's apparent course.

                 Wordsworth, thinking probably of the *Venus* and the *Lucrece*, said finely of Shakespeare: 'Shakespeare *could* not have written an Epic; he would have died of plethora of thought.' This prodigality of nature is exemplified equally in his Sonnets. The copious selection here given (which, from the wealth of the material, required greater consideration than any other portion of the Editor's task) contains many that will not be fully felt and understood without some earnestness of thought on the reader's part. But he is not likely to regret the labour.

32   31   l. 11. *upon misprision growing*: either, granted in error, or, on the growth of contempt.

—   32   With the tone of this Sonnet compare Hamlet's 'Give me that man That is not passion's slave,' etc. Shakespeare's writings show the deepest sensitiveness to passion:—hence the attraction he felt in the contrasting effects of apathy.

33   33   l. 4. *grame*: sorrow. It was long before English Poetry returned to the charming simplicity of this and a few other poems by Wyatt.

34   34   l. 23. Pandion in the ancient fable was father to Philomela.

36   38   l. 4. *ramage*: confused noise.

—   39   l. 4. *censures*: judges.

37   40   By its style this beautiful example of old simplicity and feeling may be referred to the early years of Elizabeth.

—   —   l. 3. *late*: lately.

38   41   l. 9. *haggards*: the least tameable hawks.

39   44   l. 2. *cypres* or cyprus,—used by the old writers for *crape*; whether from the French *crespe* or from the Island whence it was imported. Its accidental similarity in

		spelling to *cypress* has, here and in Milton's *Penseroso*, probably confused readers.
41	46-47	'I never saw anything like this funeral dirge,' says Charles Lamb, 'except the ditty which reminds Ferdinand of his drowned father in *The Tempest*. As that is of the water, watery; so this is of the earth, earthy. Both have that intenseness of feeling, which seems to resolve itself into the element which it contemplates.'
43	51	l. 8. *crystal*: fairness.
44	53	This 'Spousal Verse' was written in honour of the Ladies Elizabeth and Katherine Somerset. Although beautiful, it is inferior to the *Epithalamion* on Spenser's own marriage,—omitted with great reluctance as not in harmony with modern manners.
45	—	l. 27. *feateously*: elegantly.
47	—	l. 121. *shend*: put out.
48	—	l. 145. *a noble peer*: Robert Devereux, second Lord Essex, then at the height of his brief triumph after taking Cadiz: hence the allusion following to the Pillars of Hercules, placed near Gades by ancient legend.
—	—	l. 157. *Eliza*: Elizabeth.
—	—	l. 173. *twins of Jove*: the stars Castor and Pollux.
—	—	l. 174. *baldric*, belt; the zodiac.
51	57	A fine example of a peculiar class of Poetry;—that written by thoughtful men who practised this Art but little. Wotton's, 72, is another. Jeremy Taylor, Bishop Berkeley, Dr. Johnson, Lord Macaulay, have left similar specimens.

SUMMARY OF BOOK SECOND

THIS division, embracing the latter eighty years of the seventeenth century, contains the close of our Early poetical style and the commencement of the Modern. In Dryden we see the first master of the new: in Milton, whose genius dominates here as Shakespeare's in the former book,—the crown and consummation of the early period. Their splendid Odes are far in advance of any prior attempts, Spenser's excepted: they exhibit the wider and grander range which years and experience and the struggles of the time conferred on Poetry. Our Muses now give expression to political feeling, to religious thought, to a high philosophic statesmanship in writers such as Marvell, Herbert, and Wotton; whilst in Marvell and Milton, again, we find the first noble attempts at pure description of nature, destined in our own ages to be continued and equalled. Meanwhile the poetry of simple passion, although before 1660 often deformed by verbal fancies and conceits of thought, and afterward by levity and an artificial tone, produced in Herrick and Waller some charming pieces of more finished art than the Elizabethan: until in the courtly compliments of Sedley it seems to exhaust itself, and lie almost dormant for the hundred years between the days of Wither and Suckling and the days of Burns and Cowper.—That the change from our early style to the modern brought with it at first a loss of nature and simplicity is undeniable: yet the far bolder and wider scope which Poetry took between 1620 and 1700, and the successful efforts then made to gain greater clearness in expression, in their results have been no slight compensation.

PAGE   NO.

56   62   l. 64. *whist*: hushed.

—   —   l. 89. *Pan*: used here for the Lord of all.

59   —   l. 191. *Lars and Lemures*: household gods and spirits of relations dead.

—   —   l. 194. *Flamens*: Roman priests.

—   —   l. 199. *that twice-batter'd god*: Dagon.

60   —   l. 213. *Osiris*, the Egyptian god of Agriculture (here, perhaps by confusion with Apis, figured as a Bull), was torn to pieces by Typho and embalmed after death in a sacred chest. This myth, reproduced in Syria and Greece in the legends of Thammuz, Adonis, and perhaps Absyrtus, represents the annual death of the Sun or the Year under the influences of the winter darkness. Horus, the son of Osiris, as the New Year, in his turn overcomes Typho.—It suited the genius of Milton's time to regard this primeval poetry and philosophy of the seasons, which has a further reference to the contest of Good and Evil in Creation, as a malignant idolatry. Shelley's Chorus in *Hellas*, 'Worlds on worlds,' treats the subject in a larger and sweeter spirit.

—   —   l. 215. *unshower'd*: as watered by the Nile only.

63   64   *The Late Massacre*: the Vaudois persecution, carried on in 1655 by the Duke of Savoy. This 'collect in verse,' as it has been justly named, is the most mighty Sonnet in any language known to the Editor. Readers should observe that, unlike our sonnets of the sixteenth century, it is constructed on the original Italian or Provençal model,—unquestionably far superior to the imperfect form employed by Shakespeare and Drummond.

—   65   Cromwell returned from Ireland in 1650. Hence the prophecies, not strictly fulfilled, of his deference to the Parliament, in ll. 81-96.

                This Ode, beyond doubt one of the finest in our language, and more in Milton's style than has been reached by any other poet, is occasionally obscure from imitation of the condensed Latin syntax. The meaning of st. 5 is 'rivalry or hostility are the same to a lofty spirit, and limitation more hateful than opposition.' The allusion in st. 11 is to the old physical doctrines of the non-existence of a vacuum and the impenetrability of matter: —in st. 18 to the omen traditionally connected with the foundation of the Capitol at Rome. The ancient belief that certain years in life complete natural periods and are hence peculiarly exposed to death, is introduced in st. 26 by the word *climacteric*.

67   66   *Lycidas.* The person lamented is Milton's college friend Edward King, drowned in 1637 whilst crossing from Chester to Ireland.

Strict Pastoral Poetry was first written or perfected by the Dorian Greeks settled in Sicily: but the conventional use of it, exhibited more magnificently in *Lycidas* than in any other pastoral, is apparently of Roman origin. Milton, employing the noble freedom of a great artist, has here united ancient mythology with what may be called the modern mythology of Camus and Saint Peter, —to direct Christian images.—The metrical structure of this glorious poem is partly derived from Italian models.

—   —   l. 15. *Sisters of the sacred well*: the Muses, said to frequent the fountain Helicon on Mount Parnassus.

68   —   l. 54. *Mona*: Anglesea, called by the Welsh Inis Dowil or the Dark Island, from its dense forests.

—   —   l. 55. *Deva*: the Dee, a river which probably derived its magical character from Celtic traditions: it was long the boundary of Briton and Saxon.—These places are introduced, as being near the scene of the shipwreck.

—   —   l. 58. *Orpheus* was torn to pieces by Thracian women.

69   —   ll. 68, 69. *Amaryllis* and *Neaera*: names used here for the love-idols of poets: as *Damoetas* previously for a shepherd.

—   —   l. 75. *the blind Fury*: Atropos, fabled to cut the thread of life.

—   —   ll. 85, 86. *Arethuse* and *Mincius*: Sicilian and Italian waters here alluded to as synonymous with the pastoral poetry of Theocritus and Virgil.

—   —   l. 88. *oat*: pipe, used here like Collins' *oaten stop*, No. 146, l. 1, for *Song.*

—   —   l. 96. *Hippotades*: Aeolus, god of the Winds.

—   —   l. 99. *Panope*: a Nereid. The names of local deities in the Hellenic mythology express generally some feature in the natural landscape, which the Greeks studied and analysed with their usual unequalled insight and feeling. *Panope* represents the boundlessness of the ocean-horizon when seen from a height, as compared with the limited horizon of the land in hilly countries such as Greece or Asia Minor.

—   —   l. 103. *Camus*: the Cam; put for King's University.

—   —   l. 106. *that sanguine flower*: the Hyacinth of the ancients; probably our Iris.

70   —   l. 109. *The pilot*: Saint Peter, figuratively introduced as the head of the Church on earth, to foretell 'the ruin of our corrupted clergy, then in their heighth' under Laud's primacy.

—   —   l. 128. *the wolf*: Popery.

—   —   l. 132. *Alpheus*: a stream in Southern Greece, supposed to flow underseas to join the Arethuse.

—   —   l. 138. *swart star*: the Dogstar, called swarthy because

PAGE   NO.

its heliacal rising in ancient times occurred soon after midsummer.

71   66   l. 159. *moist vows*: either tearful prayers, or prayers for one at sea.

—   —   l. 160. *Bellerus*: a giant, apparently created here by Milton to personify Belerium, the ancient title of the Land's End.

—   —   l. 161. *the great Vision*: the story was that the Archangel Michael had appeared on the rock by Marazion in Mount's Bay which bears his name. Milton calls on him to turn his eyes from the south homeward, and to pity Lycidas, if his body has drifted into the troubled waters off the Land's End. Finisterre being the land due south of Marazion, two places in that district (then by our trade with Corunna probably less unfamiliar to English ears) are named,—*Namancos* now Mujio in Galicia, *Bayona* north of the Minho, or perhaps a fortified rock (one of the *Cies* Islands) not unlike Saint Michael's Mount, at the entrance of Vigo Bay.

—   —   l. 170. *ore*: rays of golden light.

72   —   l. 189. *Doric*: Sicilian, pastoral.

74   70   *The assault* was an attack on London expected in 1642, when the troops of Charles I reached Brentford. 'Written on his door' was in the original title of this sonnet. Milton was then living in Aldersgate Street.

—   —   l. 10. *The Emathian conqueror*: When Thebes was destroyed (B.C. 335) and the citizens massacred by thousands, Alexander ordered the house of Pindar to be spared. He was as incapable of appreciating the Poet as Lewis XIV of appreciating Racine; but even the narrow and barbarian mind of Alexander could understand the advantage of a showy act of homage to Poetry.

—   —   ll. 12, 13. *the repeated air Of sad Electra's poet*: Amongst Plutarch's vague stories, he says that when the Spartan confederacy in 404 B.C. took Athens, a proposal to demolish it was rejected through the effect produced on the commanders by hearing part of a chorus from the Electra of Euripides sung at a feast. There is, however, no apparent congruity between the lines quoted (167-8, ed. Dindorf) and the result ascribed to them.

76   73   This high-toned and lovely Madrigal is quite in the style, and worthy of, the 'pure Simonides.'

77   75   Vaughan's beautiful though quaint verses should be compared with Wordsworth's great Ode, No. 287.

78   76   l. 6. *Favonius*: the spring wind.

79   77   l. 2. *Themis*: the goddess of justice. Skinner was grandson by his mother to Sir E. Coke:—hence, as pointed out by Mr. Keightley, Milton's allusion to the *bench*.

—   —   l. 8. Sweden was then at war with Poland, and France with the Spanish Netherlands.

PAGE NO.
81   79   l. 28. *Sidneian showers*: either in allusion to the
                conversations in the *Arcadia*, or to Sidney himself as a
                model of 'gentleness' in spirit and demeanour.

85   84   *Elizabeth of Bohemia*: daughter to James I, and
                ancestor to Sophia of Hanover. These lines are a fine
                specimen of gallant and courtly compliment.

86   85   Lady M. Ley was daughter to Sir J. Ley, afterwards
                Earl of Marlborough, who died March, 1628-9, coin-
                cidently with the dissolution of the third Parliament of
                Charles's reign. Hence Milton poetically compares his
                death to that of the Orator Isocrates of Athens, after
                Philip's victory in 328 B.C.

90-91 92-93   These are quite a Painter's poems.

94   99   *From Prison*: to which his active support of Charles I
                twice brought the high-spirited writer.

99   105   Inserted in Book II as written in the character of a
                Soldier of Fortune in the seventeenth century.

100   106   *waly waly*: an exclamation of sorrow, the root and the
                pronunciation of which are preserved in the word
                caterwaul. *Brae*, hillside: *burn*, brook: *busk*, adorn.
                Saint Anton's Well: at the foot of Arthur's Seat by
                Edinburgh. *Cramasie*, crimson.

101   107   l. 7. *burd*, maiden.

102   108   *corbies*, crows: *fail*, turf: *hause*, neck: *theek*, thatch.—
                If not in their origin, in their present form this and the
                two preceding poems appear due to the seventeenth
                century, and have therefore been placed in Book II.

104   111   The remark quoted in the note to No. 47 applies
                equally to these truly wonderful verses, which, like
                Lycidas, may be regarded as a test of any reader's insight
                into the most poetical aspects of Poetry. The general
                differences between them are vast: but in imaginative
                intensity Marvell and Shelley are closely related.—This
                poem is printed as a translation in Marvell's works:
                but the original Latin is obviously his own. The most
                striking verses in it, here quoted as the book is rare,
                answer more or less to stanzas 2 and 6:—

                     Alma Quies, teneo te! et te, Germana Quietis
                     Simplicitas! vos ergo diu per Templa, per urbes,
                     Quaesivi, Regum perque alta Palatia frustra.
                     Sed vos Hortorum per opaca silentia longe
                     Celarant Plantae virides, et concolor Umbra.

106   112   *L'Allegro* and *Il Penseroso*. It is a striking proof of
110   113   Milton's astonishing power that these, the earliest pure
                Descriptive Lyrics in our language, should still remain
                the best in a style which so many great poets have since
                attempted. The Bright and the Thoughtful aspects of
                Nature are their subjects: but each is preceded by a
                mythological introduction in a mixed Classical and

PAGE NO.

Italian manner. The meaning of the first is that
Gaiety is the child of Nature; of the second, that
Pensiveness is the daughter of Sorrow and Genius.

106 112   l. 2. Perverse ingenuity has conjectured that for
Cerberus we should read *Erebus*, who in the Mythology is
brother at once and husband of Night. But the issue of
that union is not Sadness, but Day and Aether:—com-
pleting the circle of primary Creation, as the parents are
both children of Chaos, the first-begotten of all things.
(Hesiod.)

107 —   l. 36. *the mountain nymph*; compare Wordsworth's
Sonnet, No. 210.

108 —   l. 62. is in *apposition* to the preceding, by a gramma-
tical license not uncommon with Milton.

— —   l. 67. *tells his tale*: counts his flock.

— —   l. 80. *Cynosure*: the Pole Star.

— —   ll. 83 *sqq. Corydon, Thyrsis*, etc.: shepherd names
from the old Idylls.

109 —   l. 132. *Jonson's learned sock*: the gaiety of our age
would find little pleasure in his elaborate comedies.

110 —   l. 136. *Lydian airs*: a light and festive style of ancient
music.

110 113   l. 3. *bestead*: avail.

111 —   l. 19. *starr'd Ethiop queen*: Cassiopeia, the legendary
Queen of Ethiopia, and thence translated amongst the
constellations.

112 —   l. 59. *Cynthia*: the Moon: her chariot is drawn by
dragons in ancient representations.

— —   l. 88. *Hermes*, called Trismegistus, a mystical writer
of the Neo-Platonist school.

113 —   l. 99. *Thebes*, etc. : subjects of Athenian Tragedy.

— —   l. 102. *buskin'd*: tragic.

— —   l. 104. *Musaeus*: a poet in Mythology.

— —   l. 109. *him that left half-told*: Chaucer, in his incom-
plete 'Squire's Tale.'

— —   l. 116. *great bards*: Ariosto, Tasso, and Spenser are here
intended.

— —   l. 123. *frounced*: curled.

— —   l. 124, *the Attic Boy*: Cephalus.

115 114   Emigrants supposed to be driven towards America by
the Government of Charles I.

— —   ll. 23-4. *But apples*, etc. A fine example of Marvell's
imaginative hyperbole.

116 115   l. 6. *concent*: harmony.

SUMMARY OF BOOK THIRD

IT is more difficult to characterize the English Poetry of the eighteenth century than that of any other. For it was an age not only
of spontaneous transition, but of bold experiment: it includes not
only such divergences of thought as distinguish the *Rape of the Lock*

from the *Parish Register*, but such vast contemporaneous differences as lie between Pope and Collins, Burns and Cowper. Yet we may clearly trace three leading moods or tendencies:—the aspects of courtly or educated life represented by Pope and carried to exhaustion by his followers; the poetry of Nature and of Man, viewed through a cultivated, and at the same time an impassioned frame of mind by Collins and Gray:—lastly, the study of vivid and simple narrative, including natural description, begun by Gay and Thomson, pursued by Burns and others in the north, and established in England by Goldsmith, Percy, Crabbe, and Cowper. Great varieties in style accompanied these diversities in aim: poets could not always distinguish the manner suitable for subjects so far apart: and the union of the language of courtly and of common life, exhibited most conspicuously by Burns, has given a tone to the poetry of that century which is better explained by reference to its historical origin than by naming it, in the common criticism of our day, artificial. There is, again, a nobleness of thought, a courageous aim at high and, in a strict sense, manly excellence in many of the writers:— nor can that period be justly termed tame and wanting in originality, which produced poems such as Pope's *Satires*, Gray's *Odes and Elegy*, the ballads of Gay and Carey, the songs of Burns and Cowper. In truth Poetry at this as at all times was a more or less unconscious mirror of the genius of the age: and the brave and admirable spirit of inquiry which made the eighteenth century the turning-time in European civilization is reflected faithfully in its verse. An intelligent reader will find the influence of Newton as markedly in the poems of Pope, as of Elizabeth in the plays of Shakespeare. On this great subject, however, these indications must here be sufficient.

PAGE NO.

127   123   *The Bard.* This Ode is founded on a fable that Edward I, after conquering Wales, put the native Poets to death.—After lamenting his comrades (st. 2, 3) the Bard prophesies the fate of Edward II and the conquests of Edward III (4): his death and that of the Black Prince (5): of Richard II, with the wars of York and Lancaster, the murder of Henry VI (the *meek usurper*), and of Edward V and his brother (6). He turns to the glory and prosperity following the accession of the Tudors (7), through Elizabeth's reign (8): and concludes with a vision of the poetry of Shakespeare and Milton.

—   —   l. 13. *Glo'ster*: Gilbert de Clare, son-in-law to Edward. *Mortimer*, one of the Lords Marchers of Wales.

128   —   l. 35. *Arvon*: the shores of Carnarvonshire opposite Anglesey.

—   —   l. 57. *She-wolf*: Isabel of France, adulterous Queen of Edward II.

129   —   l. 87. *towers of Julius*: the Tower of London, built in part, according to tradition, by Julius Caesar.

—   —   l. 93. *bristled boar*: the badge of Richard III.

—   —   l. 99. *Half of thy heart*: Queen Eleanor died soon after the conquest of Wales.

PAGE NO.

130 123   l. 109.   *Arthur*: Henry VII named his eldest son thus, in deference to British feeling and legend.

131 125   l. 5.   The Highlanders called the battle of Culloden, Drumossie.

132 126   *lilting*, singing blithely: *loaning*, broad lane: *bughts*, pens: *scorning*, rallying: *dowie*, dreary: *daffing* and *gabbing*, joking and chatting: *leglin*, milk-pail: *shearing*, reaping: *bandsters*, sheaf-binders: *runkled*, wrinkled: *lyart*, grizzled: *fleeching*, coaxing: *gloaming*, twilight: *bogle*, ghost: *dool*, sorrow.

134 128   The Editor has found no authoritative text of this poem, in his judgement superior to any other of its class in melody and pathos. Part is probably not later than the seventeenth century: in other stanzas a more modern hand, much resembling Scott's, is traceable. Logan's poem (127) exhibits a knowledge rather of the old legend than of the old verses.—*Hecht*, promised—the obsolete *hight*: *mavis*, thrush: *ilka*, every: *lav'rock*, lark: *haughs*, valley-meadows: *twined*, parted from: *marrow*, mate: *syne*, then.

135 129   The Royal George, of 108 guns, whilst undergoing a partial careening in Portsmouth Harbour, was overset about 10 A.M. Aug. 29, 1782. The total loss was believed to be near 1000 souls.

138 131   A little masterpiece in a very difficult style: Catullus himself could hardly have bettered it. In grace, tenderness, simplicity, and humour it is worthy of the Ancients; and even more so, from the completeness and unity of the picture presented.

142 136   Perhaps no writer who has given such strong proofs of the poetic nature has left less satisfactory poetry than Thomson. Yet he touched little which he did not beautify: and this song, with ' Rule, Britannia' and a few others, must make us regret that he did not more seriously apply himself to lyrical writing.

144 140   l. 1.   *Aeolian lyre*: the Greeks ascribed the origin of their Lyrical Poetry to the colonies of Aeolis in Asia Minor.

— —   l. 17.   *Thracia's hills*: supposed a favourite resort of Mars.

145 —   l. 21.   *feather'd king*: the Eagle of Jupiter, admirably described by Pindar in a passage here imitated by Gray.

— —   l. 27.   *Idalia* in Cyprus, where *Cytherea* (Venus) was especially worshipped.

— —   l. 53.   *Hyperion*: the Sun. St. 6-8 allude to the Poets of the islands and mainland of Greece, to those of Rome and of England.

147 —   l. 115.   *Theban Eagle*: Pindar.

150 141   l. 75.   *chaste-eyed Queen*: Diana.

151 142   l. 5.   *Attic warbler*: the nightingale.

PAGE NO.
153 144   *sleekit*, sleek : *bickering brattle*, flittering flight : *laith*, loath : *pattle*, ploughstaff : *whiles*, at times : *a daimen-icker*, a corn-ear now and then : *thrave*, shock : *lave*, rest : *foggage*, aftergrass : *snell*, biting : but *hald*, without dwelling-place : *thole*, bear : *cranreuch*, hoarfrost : *thy lane*, alone : *a-gley*, off the right line, awry.

157 147   Perhaps the noblest stanzas in our language.
161 148   *stouré*, dust-storm : *braw*, smart.
162 149   *scaith*, hurt : *ent*, guard : *steer*, molest.
163 151   *drumlie*, muddy : *birk*, birch.
165 152   *greet*, cry : *daurna*, dare not.—There can hardly exist a poem more truly tragic in the highest sense than this : nor, except Sappho, has any Poetess known to the Editor equalled it in excellence.

—   153   *fou*, merry with drink : *coost*, carried : *unco skeigh*, very proud : *gart*, forced : *abeigh*, aside : *Ailsa Craig*, a rock in the Firth of Clyde : *grat his een bleert*, cried till his eyes were bleared : *lowpin*, leaping : *linn*, waterfall : *sair*, sore : *smoor'd*, smothered : *crouse and canty*, blithe and gay.

166 154   Burns justly named this 'one of the most beautiful songs in the Scots or any other language.' One verse, interpolated by Beattie, is here omitted :—it contains two good lines, but is quite out of harmony with the original poem. *Bigonet*, little cap—probably altered from *beguinette* : *thraw*, twist : *caller*, fresh.

168 155   *airts*, quarters : *row*, roll : *shaw*, small wood in a hollow, spinney : *knowes*, knolls.
169 156   *jo*, sweetheart : *brent*, smooth : *pow*, head.
—   157   *leal*, faithful : *fain*, happy.
170 158   Henry VI founded Eton.
176 161   The Editor knows no Sonnet more remarkable than this, which, with 162, records Cowper's gratitude to the lady whose affectionate care for many years gave what sweetness he could enjoy to a life radically wretched. Petrarch's sonnets have a more ethereal grace and a more perfect finish ; Shakespeare's more passion ; Milton's stand supreme in stateliness, Wordsworth's in depth and delicacy. But Cowper's unites with an exquisiteness in the turn of thought which the Ancients would have called Irony, an intensity of pathetic tenderness peculiar to his loving and ingenuous nature.—There is much mannerism, much that is unimportant or of now exhausted interest in his poems : but where he is great, it is with that elementary greatness which rests on the most universal human feelings. Cowper is our highest master in simple pathos.

178 163   l. 19. *fancied green*: cherished garden.
179 164   Little more than his name appears recoverable with regard to the author of this truly noble poem. It should be noted as exhibiting a rare excellence—the climax of simple sublimity.

It is a lesson of high instructiveness to examine the essential qualities which give first-rate poetical rank to lyrics such as 'To-morrow' or 'Sally in our Alley,' when compared with poems written (if the phrase may be allowed) in keys so different as the subtle sweetness of Shelley, the grandeur of Gray and Milton, or the delightful Pastoralism of the Elizabethan verse. Intelligent readers will gain hence a clear understanding of the vast imaginative range of Poetry;—through what wide oscillations the mind and the taste of a nation may pass; —how many are the roads which Truth and Nature open to Excellence.

SUMMARY OF BOOK FOURTH

IT proves sufficiently the lavish wealth of our own age in Poetry, that the pieces which, without conscious departure from the standard of Excellence, render this Book by far the longest, were with very few exceptions composed during the first thirty years of the nineteenth century. Exhaustive reasons can hardly be given for the strangely sudden appearance of individual genius: but none, in the Editor's judgement, can be less adequate than that which assigns the splendid national achievements of our recent poetry to an impulse from the follies and wars that at the time disgraced our foreign neighbours. The first French Revolution was rather, in his opinion, one result, and in itself by no means the most important, of that far wider and greater spirit which through inquiry and doubt, through pain and triumph, sweeps mankind round the circles of its gradual development: and it is to this that we must trace the literature of modern Europe. But, without more detailed discussion on the motive causes of Scott, Wordsworth, Campbell, Keats, and Shelley, we may observe that these Poets, with others, carried to further perfection the later tendencies of the century preceding, in simplicity of narrative, reverence for human Passion and Character in every sphere, and impassioned love of Nature:—that, whilst maintaining on the whole the advances in art made since the Restoration, they renewed the half-forgotten melody and depth of tone which marked the best Elizabethan writers:—that, lastly, to what was thus inherited they added a richness in language and a variety in metre, a force and fire in narrative, a tenderness and bloom in feeling, an insight into the finer passages of the Soul and the inner meanings of the landscape, a larger and wiser Humanity,—hitherto hardly attained, and perhaps unattainable even by predecessors of not inferior individual genius. In a word, the nation which, after the Greeks in their glory, has been the most gifted of all nations for Poetry, expressed in these men the highest strength and prodigality of its nature. They interpreted the age to itself—hence the many phases of thought and style they present:—to sympathize with each, fervently and impartially, without fear and without fancifulness, is no doubtful step in the higher education of the Soul. For, as with the Affections and the Conscience, Purity in Taste is absolutely proportionate to Strength:— and when once the mind has raised itself to grasp and to delight in Excellence, those who love most will be found to love most wisely.

PAGE NO.
181 166   l. 11. *stout Cortez*: History requires here *Balboa*:
              (A. T.) It may be noticed that to find in Chapman's
              Homer the 'pure serene' of the original, the reader must
              bring with him the imagination of the youthful poet;—
              he must be 'a Greek himself,' as Shelley finely said of
              Keats.

185 169   The most tender and true of Byron's smaller poems.

186 170   This Poem, with 236, exemplifies the peculiar skill with
              which Scott employs proper names:—nor is there a surer
              sign of high poetical genius.

203 191   The Editor in this and in other instances has risked the
              addition (or the change) of a Title, that the aim of the
              verses following may be grasped more clearly and
              immediately.

209 198   l. 4. *nature's Eremite*: like a solitary thing in Nature.—
              This beautiful Sonnet was the last word of a poet deserv-
              ing the title 'marvellous boy' in a much higher sense than
              Chatterton. If the fulfilment may ever safely be pro-
              phesied from the promise, England appears to have lost
              in Keats one whose gifts in Poetry have rarely been
              surpassed. Shakespeare, Milton, and Wordsworth, had
              their lives been closed at twenty-five, would (so far as we
              know) have left poems of less excellence and hope than
              the youth who, from the petty school and the London
              surgery, passed at once to a place with them of 'high
              collateral glory.'

211 201   It is impossible not to regret that Moore has written
              so little in this sweet and genuinely national style.

—   202   A masterly example of Byron's command of strong
              thought and close reasoning in verse:—as the next is
              equally characteristic of Shelley's wayward intensity,
              and 204 of the dramatic power, the vital identification of
              the poet with other times and characters, in which Scott
              is second only to Shakespeare.

221 209   Bonnivard, a Genevese, was imprisoned by the Duke
              of Savoy in Chillon on the lake of Geneva for his courage-
              ous defence of his country against the tyranny with which
              Piedmont threatened it during the first half of the seven-
              teenth century.—This noble Sonnet is worthy to stand
              near Milton's on the Vaudois massacre.

221 210   Switzerland was usurped by the French under
              Napoleon in 1800: Venice in 1797 (211).

224 215   This battle was fought Dec. 2, 1800, between the
              Austrians under Archduke John and the French under
              Moreau, in a forest near Munich. *Hohen Linden* means
              High Limetrees.

228 218   After the capture of Madrid by Napoleon, Sir J. Moore
              retreated before Soult and Ney to Corunna, and was
              killed whilst covering the embarkation of his troops. His
              tomb, built by Ney, bears this inscription—'John Moore,
              leader of the English armies, slain in battle, 1809.'

PAGE NO.
241   229   The Mermaid was the club-house of Shakespeare, Ben Jonson, and other choice spirits of that age.

—   230   *Maisie*: Mary. Scott has given us nothing more complete and lovely than this little Song, which unites simplicity and dramatic power to a wildwood music of the rarest quality. No moral is drawn, far less any conscious analysis of feeling attempted:—the pathetic meaning is left to be suggested by the mere presentment of the situation. Inexperienced critics have often named this, which may be called the Homeric manner, superficial, from its apparent simple facility:—but first-rate excellence in it (as shown here, in 196, 156, and 129) is in truth one of the least common triumphs of Poetry.—This style should be compared with what is not less perfect in its way, the searching out of inner feeling, the expression of hidden meanings, the revelation of the heart of Nature and of the Soul within the Soul,—the Analytical method, in short,—most completely represented by Wordsworth and by Shelley.

247   234   *correi*: covert on a hillside; *cumber*: trouble.

—   235   Two intermediate stanzas have been here omitted. They are very ingenious, but, of all poetical qualities, ingenuity is least in accordance with pathos.

259   243   This Poem has an exaltation and a glory, joined with an exquisiteness of expression, which place it in the highest rank amongst the many masterpieces of its illustrious Author.

269   252   l. 24. *interlunar swoon*: interval of the Moon's invisibility.

275   256   l. 11. *Calpe*: Gibraltar.

—   —   l. 21. *Lofoden*: the Maelstrom whirlpool off the N.W. coast of Norway.

276   257   This lovely Poem refers here and there to a ballad by Hamilton on the subject better treated in 127 and 128.

289   268   l. 10. *Arcturi*: seemingly used for *northern stars*.

—   —   l. 21. *And wild roses*, etc. Our language has no line modulated with more subtle sweetness. A good poet *might* have written *And roses wild*,—yet this slight change would disenchant the verse of its peculiar beauty.

292   270   l. 81. *Ceres' daughter*: Proserpine.

—   —   l. 82. *God of Torment*: Pluto.

293   271   This impassioned Address expresses Shelley's most rapt imaginations, and is the direct modern representative of the feeling which led the Greeks to the worship of Nature.

302   274   The leading idea of this beautiful description of a day's landscape in Italy is expressed with an obscurity not unfrequent with its author. It appears to be,—On the voyage of life are many moments of pleasure, given by the sight of Nature, who has power to heal even the worldliness and the uncharity of man.

PAGE	NO.	
303	274	l. 58. Amphitrite was daughter to Ocean.
304	—	l. 76. *Sun-girt* City: It is difficult not to believe that the correct reading is *Sea-girt*. Many of Shelley's poems appear to have been printed in England during his residence abroad: others were printed from his manuscripts after his death. Hence probably the text of no English Poet after 1600 contains so many errors. See the Note on No. 9.
308	275	l. 21. *Maenad*: a frenzied Nymph, attendant on Dionysus in the Greek mythology.
—	—	l. 39. Plants under water sympathize with the seasons of the land, and hence with the winds which affect them.
310	276	Written soon after the death, by shipwreck, of Wordsworth's brother John. This Poem should be compared with Shelley's following it. Each is the most complete expression of the innermost spirit of his art given by these great Poets:—of that Idea which, as in the case of the true Painter (to quote the words of Reynolds), 'subsists only in the mind: The sight never beheld it, nor has the hand expressed it; it is an idea residing in the breast of the artist, which he is always labouring to impart, and which he dies at last without imparting.'
311	—	l. 50. *the Kind*: the human race.
312	278	l. 13. Proteus represented the everlasting changes, united with ever-recurrent sameness, of the Sea.
313	279	l. 1. *the royal Saint*: Henry VI.

INDEX OF WRITERS

WITH DATES OF BIRTH AND DEATH, FIRST LINES
OF THE POEMS, AND TITLES

INDEX OF FIRST LINES

354

THE END